I0110284

Being and Becoming European in Poland

Being and Becoming European in Poland

European Integration and Self-Identity

Marysia H. Galbraith

ANTHEM PRESS
LONDON · NEW YORK · DELHI

Anthem Press
An imprint of Wimbledon Publishing Company
www.anthempress.com

This edition first published in UK and USA 2015
by ANTHEM PRESS
75–76 Blackfriars Road, London SE1 8HA, UK
or PO Box 9779, London SW19 7ZG, UK
and
244 Madison Ave #116, New York, NY 10016, USA

First published in hardback by Anthem Press in 2014

Copyright © 2015 Marysia H. Galbraith

The author asserts the moral right to be identified as the author of this work.

All rights reserved. Without limiting the rights under copyright reserved above,
no part of this publication may be reproduced, stored or introduced into
a retrieval system, or transmitted, in any form or by any means
(electronic, mechanical, photocopying, recording or otherwise),
without the prior written permission of both the copyright
owner and the above publisher of this book.

British Library Cataloguing-in-Publication Data
A catalogue record for this book is available from the British Library.

Library of Congress Cataloging-in-Publication Data
The Library of Congress has cataloged the hardcover edition as follows:
Galbraith Marysia H.
Being and becoming European in Poland : European integration and self-identity /
Marysia H. Galbraith.
pages cm
Includes bibliographical references and index.
ISBN-13: 978-1-78308-230-8 (hardcover : alk. paper)
ISBN-10: 1-78308-230-5 (hardcover : alk. paper)
1. Polish people–Ethnic identity. 2. European Union–Membership–Social aspects–
Poland. 3. National characteristics, Polish. 4. Post-communism–Poland. I. Title.
DK4121.G35 2014
303.48'243804–dc23
2014011577

ISBN-13: 978 1 78308 428 9 (Pbk)
ISBN-10: 1 78308 428 6 (Pbk)

Cover photo courtesy of Paweł Dobosz.

This title is also available as an ebook.

CONTENTS

LIST OF FIGURES AND TABLES

Figures

Tables

ACKNOWLEDGMENTS

The topic of this book has in substantial ways defined my life for more than twenty years. I could not have done it without the support, participation, advice and encouragement of numerous friends and colleagues.

First and foremost, I am indebted to the many participants in Poland who taught me about *polska gościnność* firsthand – with their warmth, generosity and some of the best food I've ever eaten. My personal connections with them are what make Poland such a special place for me. I can't name all participants by name due to the constraints of confidentiality, but I will mention some of my friends: the Błażusiaks, Bożyks, Gałęzas, Podgórskas, Smolarczyks and the late Marta Sienicka. Special thanks to Ewelina and Paweł Dobosz for agreeing to appear on the cover of the book.

I especially appreciate my mother, Maria Renata Bereday Galbraith, who taught me the importance of family, education, perseverance and forgiveness. My earliest person-centered explorations were with her, to try and understand how her experiences of belonging and dislocation shaped the person she became.

I first heard Roy D'Andrade talk when I crashed the American Anthropological Association Annual Meeting in 1986. I did not understand all of his paper on "directive force" but I wanted to, and that's why I applied to study psychological anthropology at the University of California, San Diego. Roy proved to be a gracious and supportive thesis advisor who offered his advice but then let me make and learn from my own mistakes. I'm also grateful to Freddie Bailey, especially for the critical day he invited me over when I was in need of mentoring. With just two questions – What are the three things your project is about? And how are they related? – he got my dissertation writing back on track. In Krakow, my *promotor* Zdzisław Mach gave me an academic home at the Jagiellonian University.

I am thankful to colleagues and friends who have read portions of the book: Andy Brown, Jeremy Butler, Roy D'Andrade, Michael Murphy and Jaro Stacul. Anonymous reviewers and Rob Reddick and Tej Sood at Anthem Press also offered helpful comments. And of course, I have had many enriching conversations with my fantastic colleagues at New College and the Department of Anthropology at the University of Alabama.

I have been fortunate to receive research funding from IIE Fulbright, Institute for Global Conflict and Cooperation, IREX, Fulbright Hays and the University of Alabama, including a Research Advisory Committee Grant and travel funds from New College, the Department of Anthropology, the College of Arts and Sciences, and Capstone International Programs.

I'm also grateful to my research assistant Ian, who has willingly accompanied me anywhere involving a ride in a tram, a visit to a playground, a walk in the woods or a visit to a farm. And, of course, my deepest debt of gratitude goes to Jeremy, who makes my life better and makes me a better person.

Chapter 1

INTRODUCTION:
BEING AND BECOMING EUROPEAN
IN POSTCOMMUNIST POLAND

Poland's membership in the European Union (EU) marked a major crossroad in the country's extraordinary path of reform since the peaceful overthrow of communism in 1989. Drawing on life stories told to me over the course of twenty years, I examine this critical period from the perspective of the generation who came of age in the earliest years of neoliberal and democratic transformation, and established careers and families as Poland negotiated its place within the EU. I also advance an approach to identity that recognizes the primacy of people's experiences and their associated thoughts and feelings. I start with the assumption that the only way to understand why some collective identities resonate while others fall flat is by considering what individual selves think, feel and do in response to historical circumstances. In other words, identity is an inherently psychological phenomenon; it takes shape within people's minds.

This may seem to some readers like an obvious point, but much scholarship in anthropology has started with the premise that there is no way of knowing what goes on in people's heads. Those inclined toward interpretive approaches have instead focused on collective representations, especially symbols, rituals, media reports and other forms of communication *between* people; those taking a materialist approach have tended to focus on objects, institutions and power hierarchies. Correspondingly, rather than talking about "selves" or "individuals," studies have instead discussed "subject positions," "social actors" or "roles and statuses," and thus avoid dealing with the particular people who fill those categories. I argue, by contrast, that unless we take into account the personal experiences, thoughts and feelings of bounded, integrated selves, we diminish what we are able to understand about two fundamental areas of anthropological interest: identity and culture. If we do not pose questions that take into account psychological phenomena, we close ourselves off from ever understanding why people do what they do or believe what they believe.

In 2005, only a year after Poland's historic entrance into the EU, I talked with Poles about their experiences as EU citizens, as well as their thoughts and feelings about EU membership. Their responses were often surprising considering conventional expectations based on socioeconomic and other demographic factors. Consider this small, characteristically varied sample of what they said about their attachment to Europe:[1]

> I don't know how I feel toward Europe. I think that if, for example, my country was, I don't know, in Asia, that wouldn't bother me either. Maybe I'm more attached to my country, to *ojczyzna* [fatherland], you know? And I'm also incredibly attached to this region. Because I'm by nature that kind of person who loves mountains and valleys. [...] And whether I'm attached to Europe? I don't know. Maybe if I look from the perspective of history, of the past ... yes, there is a kind of sentiment to certain things. But I don't have any kind of feeling like we belong to Europe, or that there is some kind of unity or something, or that I will for example fight to protect France. I don't feel that kind of bond with them. (Joasia, a school librarian from a village in Bieszczady)

> I don't think I have [any attachment to Europe] ... I'm not a racist. But it hurts me that in Germany – I can only compare that country because I've been there – we aren't treated well. We are treated as lower, poorer, you could say; fingers are pointed at us. It shouldn't be this way. We're already in the EU and we should be treated the same as French people, as every person in the EU. I treat them the same, so I think they should me. (Agata, a farmer in Bieszczady)

> I haven't thought about it this way before, but I could easily live abroad ... I'm not sure what's changed inside me, maybe it's the EU, maybe it's because everything has opened, borders have opened, and you can cross the German border and they don't even check your passport. Psychologically, these opportunities give you the attitude that you can at any time board [a plane] and go and return, without cutting yourself off from your own country. And you don't have the feeling of that Iron Curtain, as they used to call it, that something big separates us from the rest of the world, some kind of wall. That has all been destroyed, like symbolically that Berlin Wall. It was an amazing experience when it was destroyed. It was as if all of Europe felt relieved; that whole history went into the past; something opened, a new chance, a new society. [...] I feel the same solidarity [to Poland], but suddenly I also feel it toward other people in Europe. As if they have become closer to me. (Ania, an artist from Krakow)

> I'm not the kind of person who identifies with the nation. I don't have any kind of nationalist aspirations, so ... I haven't ever even thought about this. I am a

European and that's it. Poles are in the EU, but also we are European, we have been European, and we will be European, unless, perhaps, geographic divisions change. Maybe if I traveled, I would feel it more. As a resident of the EU, I have that freedom to move around the EU. But besides that, not much [has changed]. (Paweł, a sales manager and resident of Lesko, a small town in Bieszczady)

These responses help to show why many researchers avoid personal accounts. Every answer is different; these are not issues that participants usually think about; and personal idiosyncrasies seem to obscure more general cultural patterns. In a word, these data are messy; they do not provide easy or unambiguous answers to the questions posed. But, at the same time, their complexity is what makes this kind of information compelling. Even in the disparate responses I have quoted, certain significant patterns emerge. First, what it means to be European is almost always considered in relation to national loyalties. Often local loyalties or comparisons with other nationalities are taken into account as well. Second, travel or work abroad is the situation in which European identity and attachment to Europe is most likely to matter. Third, participants talk about their attachment to Europe (or lack thereof) in terms of their sense of the kind of person they are; for them, discrete, enduring selves are not a fiction but rather a starting point for navigating in the world. Finally, I must note that many Poles spend more time thinking and talking about identity issues than they themselves seem to realize; as a long-term observer, I have years of field notes that attest to that fact. From such personal reflections I distill what I call "constellations of debate" – common areas of negotiation and interest around which various positions and responses emerge.

In this book, I examine the personal life stories of Polish citizens I have known since they were high school students in the early 1990s, to reveal ways of thinking about the EU in relation to the nation and the particular region of Poland in which they live. These stories show how the EU is regarded as both an *idea* and an *instrument*. As an idea, it is shaped by and helps to shape the contours of identity and ideology. As an instrument, it is wielded for personal interests, and also for advancing collective interests (both economic and symbolic) at the local and national scales. The study draws on extensive participant observation and interviews and, especially because it has occurred over an extended period of time, reveals both stable and shifting notions of Europe, nation and local region, as individuals navigate everyday experiences and reflect upon their own lives, current events and concepts like identity, integration and freedom. I argue that close attention to particular lives in all their complexity is essential for grasping the impact of the EU in member states, as well as the ways in which the institution itself has been and is likely to be shaped from the bottom up. Ordinary citizens – even those who know little about the process of integration, who are not directly involved in shaping EU policy, and who may not even think much about macro-level institutional processes – make choices in their everyday lives that have an impact on the shape of European identity, and correspondingly, the degree of legitimacy EU institutions can gain from that identity. By linking three bodies of theory – about the EU, national identity and the self – I develop a person-centered approach to the study of group identities as they are reinscribed, revised and reinvented in the face of democratization, market liberalization and supranational integration. Although the study focuses on a discrete number of people from a specific locale (southern Poland), I explore global processes, and as such I hope this case sheds light on similar processes occurring within and beyond the postsocialist world.[2]

Long-Term Fieldwork

Most participants in this study were born between 1972 and 1976. This places them within a bridge generation that came of age during a period of fundamental institutional transformation; they have childhood memories of life under state socialism, but were young enough to adapt to the expectations placed on persons by global capitalism and European integration. When I first met them in 1992, they were high school students in the city of Krakow in south-central Poland, and in the small town of Lesko in southeastern Poland. I chose these two field sites because I wanted to compare urban and rural experiences of postcommunist reforms. Because I was interested in national identity, Krakow was an obvious choice due to its symbolic significance as the "heart of Poland." Krakow is home to Wawel Castle, the seat of the Polish kings until the capitol was moved to Warsaw in 1596. Furthermore, the city was not destroyed during World War II as was Warsaw, and it has long been regarded as an artistic and cultural center, with its many universities, galleries, theaters and cafes. In recent years, Krakow's ongoing links with the past have led some to characterize the city as provincial, with an insular elite out of touch with the more rapid forces of global integration that have transformed Warsaw and the cities in western Poland. Nevertheless, Krakow's cultural life and symbolic significance remains vital, and it is one of Poland's largest cities, with nearly 800,000 residents (figure 1.1).

Choosing a rural field site was more challenging. I wanted to find a small town that nevertheless had the full range of high schools: *licea* (lycea; college-preparatory high schools), technical programs that teach both technical skills and academic subjects, and trade programs that prioritize job training. Although state socialism officially promoted a classless society, functionally and rhetorically, the population was divided into three main occupational groups: farmers, workers and intelligentsia. Because schools were instrumental in reproducing these groups, and associated cultural and socioeconomic differences, it was important that students from a variety of programs were

Figure 1.1. Krakow's Old City is vibrant with street life, art and history

included in the study. With four schools, comprised of one lyceum and three technical/trade schools, Lesko fit the bill. Lesko itself is small – with a population of about 6,000 – but it draws students from villages throughout the Bieszczady mountain region. In the early 1990s, students who lived in villages spent the week in school dormitories and only traveled home on weekends. I lived in one of these dormitories, which made it easy to spend time with students inside and outside of school. Lesko is a center of regional history and culture, though on a much smaller scale than Krakow (figure 1.2). It feels in some ways like a medieval town that never grew larger. Historic buildings include a castle, a Catholic church and a former synagogue. Lesko is also home to regional government offices and a hospital. The town attracts a small number of tourists, most of whom are on their way to Lake Solina and the higher mountains of Bieszczady National Park (figure 1.3).

I do not want to overlook, either, the importance of choosing field sites that resonate with me. From the beginning, I envisioned this as a longitudinal study, and I wanted to find places I would gladly return to again and again. The Bieszczady Mountains are beautiful, and Lesko itself has an attractive historic center and is situated on a hill overlooking the San River. Krakow is a vibrant city full of students and artists. Something is always going on the city

Figure 1.2. A recently renovated fountain at the center of Lesko

Figure 1.3. Village on Lake Solina in the Bieszczady Region

Figure 1.4. Every hour, a trumpeter plays an interrupted tune from the tower of St. Mary's Church in Krakow's Central Square

center, whether a music festival, street theater or maybe a religious procession. Numerous cafes provide a view of the comings and goings on the central market square. Every hour, on the hour, a trumpeter plays an interrupted tune in each of the four directions from the tower of St. Mary's Church (figure 1.4), to commemorate a musician who was shot warning the city of the Tartar invasion in the thirteenth century (hence the sudden break in the melody).

Initially, I was drawn to Poland because my mother is Polish. She raised me on stories about the place in which she grew up and her experiences as a courier and nurse in the Home Army during World War II. I first visited Krakow in 1986 when Poland was still a state-socialist country. This was after the Solidarity movement was suppressed and after martial law was lifted. The Poles I met generally agreed that the state-socialist system was not working – with chronic shortages and ongoing restrictions on liberties – but they had no idea how or when meaningful change would occur. My initial impressions of Krakow, captured in my journal, were rather lukewarm. I wrote about the gray and crumbling architecture, the trucks that billowed black exhaust, and the sullen, disobliging workers in post offices and shops. After several weeks, however, I began to notice the sculptures adorning the exteriors of buildings, subtly carved window frames, and large gateways that led to dilapidated but nevertheless majestic courtyards. I developed acquaintances with Poles who went out of their way to show me less-traveled sites, treated me to home-cooked meals, and helped me navigate the complex and unpredictable Polish bureaucracy. I developed an appreciation for the resilience they showed in the face of institutionalized oppression.

When I became a graduate student, I did not plan to do research in Poland. Rather, I anticipated going to a more typical location (for ethnographic fieldwork, that is) such as New Guinea. However, I continued to think about my time in Poland, and I found myself formulating research questions based on what I was learning in my classes. In the summer of 1989, I decided to do ethnographic research in Poland, just as word was leaking out about the Round Table Agreement in which government officials and members of the outlawed Solidarity union worked out a plan to hold free elections for representatives to the lower house in parliament. Within months, the Berlin Wall fell, and it became clear that state socialism was collapsing. Whereas Eastern Europe had been a relatively closed region, difficult to get into and with restrictions on the kinds of questions that could be asked, after 1989 it became the new frontier for anthropological scholarship. Very little was known about what it had been like (although a few notable ethnographies of Poland during state socialism include Hann 1985; Nagengast 1991; and Wedel 1986), and even less was known about what it was going to become.

I went to Poland again for the summer of 1990, mostly to hone my language skills and to set the groundwork for ethnographic fieldwork on young Poles' national identity after the fall of state socialism. I did my dissertation fieldwork from September 1991 until July 1993 and have been back to Poland numerous times for a total of 41 months. Throughout this time, I have maintained contact with the same participants, many of whom I also consider friends. This long-term engagement not only with the country, but also with particular individuals is a strength of my study. My work fits within the "coming of age" genre first introduced by Margaret Mead ([1928] 1961) in her classic study of Samoan youth,[3] except that rather than speculating about how Polish youth would mature, I have personally witnessed the adults they have become. A life story gives us a view into a person's life; from their words and the way they tell their story, we get a sense of who they are, what is important to them and what motivates them to make the choices they do. The particular challenges individuals face, however, are significantly shaped by the particular cultural and historical context in which they live (what Hallowell [1955] called their behavioral environment). What interests me here is the interaction of the personal and the broader social environment – what people do with the options available to them, and how their thoughts and actions can in turn shape the behavioral environment in which they live. Although I focus on events and reflections from 2005, I view them from the perspective of two trajectories of change over twenty years – across the life course (from youth to adulthood) and through the cultural, political and economic transformations that have taken Poland from state socialism to EU integration.

The methods I employ include participant observation, interviews and analysis of public discourse in the popular press. My initial point of contact with participants was at their high schools. I selected six schools in Krakow representing a variety of profiles – college track, or technical and trade – and all four high schools in Lesko. I obtained permission from each school's administration to conduct semistructured interviews with groups of eight students. I interviewed each group twice in 1992 and once more in 1993. All interviews were taped and, soon afterwards, transcribed. In addition, I wrote notes and reflections about the context of each interview, the qualities of the students and their interactions with each other, and the content of the discussions. Typically, these semistructured interviews were followed with an informal gathering afterschool with those who were interested. I also interviewed principals and teachers, observed lessons, and attended special events such as graduations, assemblies and field trips. Lesko provided more informal opportunities to cross paths with students outside of school. I lived in the dorm of the agricultural high school, which meant students would stop by my room for tea and conversation, and I would visit theirs as they studied, or more often socialized with their roommates and friends. We ate together in the cafeteria, attended sporting events and strolled through town together. I also spent time with dorm staff; for instance, on Fridays, I joined everyone in the kitchen to make *pierogi*. Students and staff invited me to their homes, where I met their families.

In addition to group interviews, in 1993, I conducted individual life story interviews with twenty students (ten each from Bieszczady and Krakow) who attended the whole range of high school programs and came from a variety of backgrounds. With each successive visit to Poland, I asked participants to update me on their life story as well as recent changes in the country. Interview questions also prompted them to reflect on abstract topics that are only rarely addressed in everyday interactions, such as nationalism, patriotism, democracy and capitalism. In successive years, I have added questions about other dimensions of their lives. In 1999, we discussed social networks; in 2005, we talked about European integration; in 2008 we considered family issues and work–life balance; in 2011 I dispensed with taped interviews, and instead caught up with everyone informally. In 2005, I expanded the number of life story interviews to 34 by enlisting more participants from Lesko who had attended the lyceum and agricultural high school classes I had known best. In 2008, I also interviewed some spouses of participants. Nvivo qualitative research software was used to code interview transcripts and field notes. Coding facilitated identifying patterns in responses and grouping references to common themes.

Perhaps because I originally elected to do individual interviews with the most articulate students with interesting things to say about issues related to national identity, most participants in my study continued on to higher education, eventually found good jobs and are doing pretty well. By adding participants in 2005 (all of whom I have known since 1992), I have been able to hear from more of a cross-section of Bieszczady residents, including some who tend to be more concrete thinkers. Each has a story to tell that provides a richer picture of life in Poland since the fall of state socialism.

I deliberated a long time about how best to refer to the people involved in this study. I settled on the term "participants" because it signals their willing engagement in semiformal interviews and informal conversations. Participants were active agents in this study, interacting with me as cultural translators, as friends and sometimes as collaborators (as for instance when Jurek deconstructed the definition of identity implicit in my line of questioning, or Basia suggested that supporters of different political parties also have different orientations toward the past and future). I decided against the term "respondent," even though Levy used it in his seminal person-centered ethnographies, because it highlights the verbal dimension of research, and also is the term commonly used for people who answer questionnaires. The term "interlocutor" is currently in style, but it too emphasizes verbal exchanges. The term favored by early ethnographers, "informant" tended not to refer to individual "selves" so much as to representatives of generalized social statuses with privileged access to information of interest to the ethnographer (see for example Malinowski [1922] 1961). Even more problematically, references to "informants" or "collaborators" are suspect in the postsocialist world because of past associations with espionage and the state-socialist apparatus that relied on informers to squash dissent. During the first ten years I visited Poland, people would sometimes ask me if I was a spy; from their perspective, why else would I spend so much time in a small town like Lesko asking so many questions?

Attention to scale, and the kinds of allegiances participants form at various levels of geopolitical organization (Europe, nation, region), is essential for understanding how ordinary citizens can shape and be shaped by higher-level institutions. Below, I outline important developments in the study of the EU, the nation and the self. I review each of these bodies of theory in turn, and explain how they inform the person-centered approach I develop.

Anthropological Studies of the European Union

The EU is an area of growing interest in anthropology, but it remains understudied. Perhaps not surprisingly, much of the most interesting work has been done by European scholars and/or published in Europe (see especially

Bellier and Wilson 2000a; Herrmann et al. 2004; and on Poland, Mach and Niedźwiedzki 2002). By way of contrast, a search for the keywords "European Union" in Anthrosource, the database of all publications of the American Anthropological Association, yields barely more than a handful of articles.[4] I argue that the EU *should* be at the forefront of anthropological research because it involves a whole new form of social organization, one that challenges the nation-state divisions that have dominated world politics at least since the early twentieth century.

The EU is also a key site for understanding processes of globalization. Whereas economic factors have tended to be emphasized in globalization research, anthropology has helped shift attention toward cultural phenomena, to flows of people, and to the complex ways in which local and global are mutually constitutive. While my research probes individuals' everyday experiences, and argues for the importance of close attention to the thoughts, feelings and actions of discrete selves, it also explores the various ways individuals navigate ever widening (and intertwined) social scales from local, to national, to European and finally to global. This attention to scale reveals that, despite globalizing pressures and the strong federalist, cosmopolitan orientation of European integration, national loyalties remain solid, and are in some cases strengthened within the EU. It is also notable that, even as new forms of social identity are taking shape within an increasingly interconnected world, identities are not infinitely malleable. It would be difficult to explain why this is so – what motivates people to forge attachments to broader social groups, and why certain imagined communities are easier to conceive of and identify with than others – without attention to subjectivity.

Much of the earliest anthropological literature on the EU focuses on the elites and Eurocrats who actively shape public discourse about the EU within a transnational social sphere (Abélès 2000; Bellier 2000; MacDonald 1996; Shore 1995; Shore and Black 1994; see also more recent studies by Feldman 2005; Siapera 2004; Wodak 2004). I am more interested in the way the EU is viewed and molded from the bottom up, by ordinary citizens who are only peripherally engaged with the EU, and only rarely think about it directly. Studies that have taken a bottom-up approach have explored the appropriation of European values (Stacul 2006) or resources (Wilson 2000a) to promote local or national interests, theorized instrumental engagements with the EU (Galbraith and Wilson 2011), examined how the imagined Soviet past and European present are simultaneously invoked in postsocialist consumption practices (Klumbyte 2010), and looked at generational and occupational differences in perceptions of postsocialism and EU integration (Ilieva 2010; Knudsen 2012). They have also looked at conflicts and the production of meaning across national borders (Anderson et al. 2003; Asher 2005, 2011; Meinhof 2004; Wilson 1996).

Although "Europeanization" has become a shorthand way of referring to the complex processes of integration (Borneman and Fowler 1997), I reserve the term for top-down strategies through which power elites shape collective representations. Participants in my study often reject the idea that Poland must Europeanize or that they must "become" European. Instead, they argue "being" European is a fundamental condition of their geographic and national position. Within broader scholarship about the EU, studies based on survey research have been useful for documenting overall support for membership and for distinguishing levels of support among various demographic groups (see Herrmann et al. 2004; Kolarska-Bobińska 2001; Mach 1998; Mucha 1999; Roguska 2005), but they reveal little about the complex cultural, ideological and personal factors that shape opinions.[5] Indeed, "Europeanness may be reinterpreted in the context of everyday life" (Stacul et al. 2006, 7).

Bellier and Wilson's *An Anthropology of the European Union* (2000a) outlines a specifically anthropological approach to the study of the EU. In their introduction, they explore the related processes of building, imagining and experiencing Europe. "Building" refers to the establishment of EU institutions and associated policies, while "imagining" signals the social construction of the idea of "Europe" and European identity via institutional discourse and symbols. The authors point out that building and imagining are "flip sides of the same coin" (Bellier and Wilson 2000b, 9). In other words, the construction of institutions and ideas occur simultaneously, each supporting the other. "Experiencing" shifts the focus to the local level where civil servants and others encounter and engage with EU institutions, policies, symbols and ideas. My book answers Bellier and Wilson's call for more studies that interrogate cultural and identity aspects of the EU, and engage with everyday lived experience. I look closely at belonging and identity for people who are not Eurocrats. Like Wilson (2000b), I explore the ongoing relevance and reassertion of national and local claims, and like Zabusky (2000), I concentrate on the everyday lives of people and local contexts where ideas of Europe and European integration are subjects of explicit engagement.

The interdisciplinary collection, *Transnational Identities: Becoming European in the EU*, edited by Herrmann et al. (2004), offers some important clues for understanding the processes by which "experiencing Europe" can become incorporated into collective identities and personal subjectivities. The volume asks questions similar to my own about the ways in which EU integration is affecting people's sense of belonging to Europe, to their nation and to other social categories, and about the implications of these patterns of identification for the EU. The articles in the collection rely on a variety of data and methods, but remain at the core interested in the social and psychological composition of European identity. They rely on a concept of "social identity" that "incorporates cognitive, evaluative, and affective meaning. Beyond mere recognition of membership in a social group or category, identification implies that the group and its defining characteristics have become integral to the person's self-concept, with associated values, emotions, and extensions of individual self-esteem" (Herrmann and Brewer 2004, 6). The authors also consider the behavioral implications of attachments, loyalties and obligations. They include a number of theoretical and empirical insights that are relevant to my own project. Most notably, they point out that "it is wrong to conceptualize European identity in zero sum terms" (Risse 2004, 248). In other words, growing European identity does not necessarily mean that other social identities weaken. On the contrary, mass survey data suggest that EU citizens are adopting the perspective "country first, but Europe, too" (Citrin and Sides 2004). In other words, even as European identity has grown, national identity has remained stronger.

The essays in *Transnational Identities* also probe the substantive content of European identity. On the one hand, Europe as a category has been characterized as "empty" in that it means different things to different people at different times. This can lead to what Mummendey and Waldzus (2004) call an "in-group projection model," wherein "European" is seen to include the characteristics associated with one's own nation, and which thus can contribute to stronger divisions within Europe if other national and ethnic groups are seen as not measuring up to those standards. This view challenges more simplistic assumptions that "more" European identity should correlate with greater tolerance and acceptance within Europe. An alternative view explores the "entitativity" of European identity (Costano 2004). It examines the ways and places in which Europeanness becomes salient and "real" for people. My study considers similar identity factors, but within one of the Central European nations that became a member after their book was published; I explore how the categories of "Europe" and "European" are understood and deployed in participants' life stories and daily lives.

A number of authors have noted how "Europeanization" is a future-oriented project, especially when considered in terms of EU institutions that are still being formed and ongoing EU expansion to include new members. About the discourse of EU officials, Abélès (2000, 31) remarks, "It does not seem possible to be European without projecting oneself into a world which does not yet exist." Borneman and Fowler (1997, 492) observe, "Europeanization has little to which it can appeal outside of future-oriented narratives of individualism and the market." Europe, as such, functions as a "social *imaginaire*," or "a constructed landscape of collective aspirations [...] mediated through the complex prism of modern media" (Appadurai 2008, 49–50).[6] The social imaginary is useful for understanding how Poles think of themselves in relation to other national groups within and beyond Europe. The past certainly figures in this imaginary, but it is a past mediated by a vision of a united Europe that is peaceful, democratic and prosperous, and in which Poles will (they hope) play a central role. In Appadurai's words, "The imagination has become an organized field of social practices, a form of work (in the sense of both labor and culturally organized practice), and a form of negotiation between sites of agency (individuals) and globally defined fields of possibility" (2008, 50). Although Appadurai notes the role that individuals play in this process, his own work interrogates collective representations. As I develop in Chapters 2 and 3, the shift from a past orientation to a present orientation, and the even more recent movement toward a future orientation, is one of the most striking transformations of self-identity I have witnessed over my twenty-year engagement with Poland. I explore the ways in which this future is imagined, and what is included in it.

Before moving down in scale, and considering theories of national-level identities, it is important to consider other aspects of globalization theory that can be fruitfully applied to the study of the EU. Hannerz (1996, 17) defines globalization as "increasing long-distance interconnectedness" across nations, and ideally continents. The EU is both a product of the intensification of global social interactions, and an engine of further connections and interdependencies. Its origins lay in a post–World War II utopian vision of a future without war. Economic integration was seen as a material basis upon which to build peaceful relations among European nation-states. Eastern Europe plays a particular role in narratives about globalization, too, to the extent that the end of the Cold War is often seen as the pivotal event that ushered in the global era.[7] Nevertheless, the most active debates, even in anthropology, have largely bypassed Eastern Europe – the formerly communist second world – when considering the impact of globalization, focusing instead on the developed and developing world, what were formerly called the first and third worlds.

Most definitions of globalization emphasize the importance of global flows and linkages, the speed, scale and volume of which have become more intense (see Appadurai 2008; Tsing 2000). Anthropological perspectives probe in particular social and cultural processes, and flows of *people* and *ideas*, as well as goods and capital. This can perhaps most clearly be seen by contrasting economist Joseph Stiglitz's and anthropologist Ulf Hannerz's characterizations of globalization. Stiglitz (2002, 9), while more inclusive than many economists, privileges economic factors in his definition, including the lower cost of transportation and communication; he further specifies "the breaking down of artificial barriers to the flows of goods, services, capital, knowledge, and (to a lesser degree) people." Thus, he lists flows of "knowledge" and "people" last, and emphasizes ongoing limits on flows of people.[8] Hannerz, by contrast, focuses on the mobility of people, meanings and meaningful forms – in that order (1996, 19). Notably, people are mentioned first in his list. Anthropologists have studied the movements of migrants, tourists, refugees, diplomats, business people, journalists and NGO employees. Flows of people are also critical for understanding the influence of the EU, as well as understanding how the EU is perceived, and even how people shape what the EU is and can become.

The anthropological focus on cultural processes has also led to questions about homogenization and heterogenization (Appadurai 2008), and whether there is more or less culture within the global sphere (Hannerz 1996, 23–5). Most studies have moved beyond the simple assumption that dominates popular discourse that all people and all societies are becoming more alike. Anthropologists recognize fractal convergences and divergences in, for example, the way that Central Europe has adopted democratic and capitalist ideologies that nevertheless are differently shaped, understood and enacted throughout the region (see Dunn 2004; Verdery 1996).[9] Questions about the quantity and variety of cultural forms are equally relevant to studies of the EU. As a transnational organization, membership necessarily requires the ceding of some degree of national autonomy; new members have spent years harmonizing their political, economic and legal systems with EU standards in order to gain admittance. Nevertheless, each country has pursued these goals in its own way, setting its own priorities in response to national preferences, politics and values, making it important to study the resulting divergences among Central European countries (see Vachudova 2005).

These dynamics are consistent with insights by anthropologists that the local and global do not exist independent of each other, but are rather interconnected, understood in terms of each other, and even help to shape each other. It is not a simple matter of global processes and structures replacing local, situated cultures. Hannerz (1996) makes the point that the local is always viewed in relation to broader frames of reference, and Appadurai (2008) asserts that the local is itself constituted as a point of contrast to the global. Tsing (2000) makes an altogether different and more complex claim: that it is time to stop making the distinction between global *forces* and local *places*, wherein old and static localities become new and dynamic through global influences. Rather, we should be looking for relationships among global and local forces *and* global and local places. Tsing reminds us to be vigilant observers, attuned to the assumptions and hegemonic narratives that govern our participants' as well as our own thinking.

Interconnections between global and local help explain why close attention to a particular case is valuable. Case studies can reveal the ways in which the EU is differently understood, differently valued, and even takes on different shapes in different member states. This is particularly important with regard to EU expansion into Eastern Europe, where divergent pathways within and between countries also point to the limits of generalization about the postcommunist world. Differences among these countries that were masked by a common narrative of state socialism, as well as historical experiences of Soviet influence, communist ideology, authoritarian rule and a command economy, are increasingly exposed. For instance, despite the global economic crisis, the Polish economy has been thriving since Poland became a member of the EU, even as neighboring Hungary has nearly defaulted on its international loans. Furthermore, in public opinion surveys, Poland stands out as one of the most pro-EU new members, while simultaneously holding on to stronger-than-average national allegiances. I suggest that such distinctions can be explained, in part, by cultural patterns that are revealed in ordinary citizens' own explanations of their attachments, loyalties and experiences.

Anthropological Studies of Nation and Ethnicity

As I have already stated, conceptions of the Polish nation figure prominently in participants' reflections about Europe and the EU. In addition, much of the internal debate within the EU about what European identity is and can become has been conceptualized in relation to national identity. As Bellier and Wilson (2000b, 7) point out, "It is because of the constraints which nation and state-building place on the evolution of the EU project that the voluminous literature on nationalism may have much to tell us of the difficulties of culture and identity which face the EU." In this section, I review some approaches to the study of nation and ethnicity, and consider what they may contribute to EU studies.

Chronic indigenous struggles for Polish sovereignty meant debates about the concept of "nation" took on particular significance in Poland, and generated theories that have continued application within and beyond Poland. In particular, sociologist Stanisław Ossowski wrote extensively about *ojczyzna* (*patria* or fatherland), a term frequently substituted for *naród* (nation) in Polish discourse, which he treated as "the correlate of certain psychic attitudes, together with the cultural heritage of the social group" (1967, 203). He highlighted two levels of attachment: "ideological *ojczyzna*" corresponds to nation constructed through collective rhetorical forms, while "private *ojczyzna*" is based on direct experience of locality. Thus, he defined fatherland in terms of cultural and affective distinctions rather than territorial boundaries. These distinctions are relevant to my study because participants regularly made reference to both aspects of *ojczyzna* when discussing attachment to nation and to local region. "Europe" often stood in contrast to them, associated with more experientially distant connections.

The scholarly debate in anthropology about the category of "nation" has been profoundly influenced by constructivist models developed by Gellner (1983), Anderson ([1983] 1991) and Hobsbawm (1990). Gellner argues that states create nations. In other words, he challenges the folk perception that nations – people who share a common sense of who they are based on some combination of geographic, cultural and historical factors – are groups that emerge organically and only later establish states – political institutions – to represent and protect their interests. According to Gellner, political centralization must come first before such a sense of "groupness" can take hold, and states have an interest in promoting sentiments of attachment to the nation because they are a powerful means of legitimizing the state's authority to rule. From this perspective, states do most of the constructing of nations, so little would be gained from examining the perceptions and actions of citizens.

Anderson defines nation as "an imagined political community – and imagined as both inherently limited and sovereign" ([1983] 1991, 6). This idea of "imagined communities" has dominated the discussion about nation ever since it was published. It offers a compelling alternative to so-called "primordial" views which place the origin of nations so far in the past that national allegiance is seen as part of the fundamental makeup of members, and thus unquestioned and unchangeable (thereby making national conflicts intractable). By highlighting that nation is "imagined," Anderson does not mean it is not real or not important; rather he emphasizes that it is a social construct, built via public institutions such as schools and by means of cultural products such as novels and films.[10] Even though the sentiments and allegiances of members of imagined communities figure prominently in Anderson's formulation, and one of his key questions is to understand why people so often are willing to die for their nation, he does not examine individuals but rather aggregate beliefs and behavior.

Hobsbawm contributes to the constructivist perspective by emphasizing that there are no "objective criteria" for nations (1990, 5). Although nations usually invoke common heritage, culture, history, language, geographic region or religion, none of these factors are essential. What *must* in all cases be present, however, is a subjective criterion – some sense among people that they are indeed members of a nation. In other words, self-consciousness and self-categorization are necessary, and some combination of cultural, historical and geographic factors is usually used to explain members' perception of "nationness." Gellner, Anderson and Hobsbawm all note that modern nations emerged in eighteenth-century Europe as an instrument of nationalist (and statist) movements, and gained popular acceptance via mass printing, mass literacy and mass schooling. They engage in a rereading of history to demonstrate the ways in which power-seeking institutions and people naturalized the category of nation to promote particular power interests.

And here we come to a dilemma at the core of the constructivist perspective: even as their theories engage with subjectivities, they nevertheless sidestep close engagement with ordinary citizens. Instead, they focus on the interests of power-seeking institutions and people, and the particular texts, symbols, rituals, institutions and policies they manipulate to produce popular support. They tend to assume that most people simply adopt whatever dominant view is presented to them. In other words, constructivism tends to be based upon a kind of black-box approach to individuals; it assumes there is no way of knowing what people may be thinking and feeling, but nevertheless claims that public discourse reflects, and even determines, individuals' beliefs and allegiances. Although his project is to explain the ways in which nation is constructed "from above," Hobsbawm acknowledges the importance of analysis "from below [...] in terms of the assumptions, hopes, needs, longings and interests of ordinary people, which are not necessarily national and still less nationalist" (1990, 10). I focus on just such issues – what individuals actually think, feel and do, and how their everyday experiences shape their conceptions of Europe, nation and local region. I identify when and why categories of belonging become salient in their daily lives.

Another problem with constructivism, whether employed by nationalist leaders or by scholars, is that it is easy to slip into the assumption that nation can take any shape that suits the state or other power elites. This same assumption of malleability also enters into discourses and even policy of the EU, where it sometimes seems as though elites try to use symbols and rituals to persuade a skeptical public that they should support the EU, while failing to take into account the pragmatic realities of people's lives that might make them reluctant to do so. My point here is to emphasize that to be deemed legitimate, the deployment of national (and European) symbols must resonate with people's *a priori* beliefs, values and concerns. Poland's own history illustrates this well. National symbols have repeatedly been instrumental in reproducing Polish culture even as structures of leadership were in the hands of other national groups: the Russian, Prussian and Austrian empires from 1795–1918; the Nazis from 1939–45; and the Soviet-influenced communist state from 1945–89. Nominally a Polish government, the communist state struggled to gain legitimacy by employing Polish national symbols, but most Poles failed to be convinced that the state-socialist system was the rightful representative of the Polish nation (see Kubik 1994). Instead, these same symbols were more convincingly deployed by the opposition; or more to the point, the opposition's uses of these symbols resonated more with people's understandings and experiences, and thus contributed substantially to the ultimate failure of state socialism. Hayden (2007) comes to a similar conclusion about the limits of even well-intended imagining of other people's communities. Commenting upon academics' and journalists' efforts to reimagine postwar Bosnia as a unified community founded on ethnic diversity, he observes that Bosnians nevertheless divide themselves into distinct and oppositional nations. Hayden argues that international policy is likely to be more effective if it acknowledges this and works with it rather than ignoring it or seeking to change it.

I do not mean to suggest these examples support rigid adherence to primordial notions of nation; rather, they illustrate the limits of constructivism. Some nationalist discourses take hold and inspire passionate engagement (whether in wars or patriotic displays) while others fall flat. It is also of particular relevance to the study of the EU that in both of the above examples, national loyalties triumphed over internationalist movements. To understand why, it is necessary to look beyond top-down forces to what lies below, in everyday lives and in ordinary people's minds.

Some recent studies have engaged in compelling ways with the "everyday," but they nevertheless sidestep any claims about subjectivity. The most comprehensive ethnography of nation and ethnicity to date is Brubaker et al.'s (2006) study of Cluj, Transylvania.[11] Divided into two sections, it first examines "nationalist politics," from a top-down perspective akin to the constructivist approach outlined above, followed by a close study of "everyday ethnicity," the day-to-day lived experiences of ordinary people. The authors emphasize the close relationship between ethnicity and nationhood, or nationness (Hobsbawm's term). They see nationness as a particular subset of ethnicity that carries with it claims to political autonomy. Brubaker et al. point out that people are only rarely and intermittently self-reflexive about their ethnicity or nationality. This leads the authors to ask questions about salience, and through careful observation of everyday situations, they seek to pinpoint when ethnicity matters (2006, 15). They distinguish between situations where ethnicity is a marked or unmarked category. As a marked category, it is remarked upon and acted upon directly, as when Hungarian residents navigate within the majority Romanian social milieu. As an unmarked category, it functions "invisibly," much like Pierre Bourdieu's habitus (1977), as for example when Hungarians interact and speak Hungarian within Hungarian stores and schools. The authors note that ethnicity becomes marked most often in social spaces where different ethnicities come into contact. Furthermore, there is an "asymmetry of experience" in that ethnicity becomes salient for minorities more frequently than it does for the majority.

One of Brubaker et al.'s key observations is that, even in a context where ethnicity is highly charged in the public, political realm (as when the mayor of Cluj made anti-Hungarian assertions and placed Romanian symbols on Hungarian landmarks), it can remain peripheral to most people's everyday preoccupations and experiences. At the same time, they observe the myriad ways in which ethnicity becomes "a perspective on the world," and "a discursive resource" that takes on meaning in interaction with institutions and with other people (2006, 169). Questions of salience, marked and unmarked categories, and divergences between political rhetoric and everyday concerns are relevant, even in places like Poland that lack large ethnic minorities.

Fox and Miller-Idriss (2008) further define four ways in which nationhood is produced and reproduced in everyday life: talking, as a discursive construct; choosing, when decisions are made; performing, in ritual, symbolic contexts; and consuming, as shaped by tastes and preferences. These distinctions are useful for systematizing the study of everyday nationalism. Though everyday nationalism relies upon close attention to what citizens say and do, it is still not informed by a robust concept of thinking, acting agents. This is pretty remarkable considering all the attention paid to choosing, talking, consuming, imagining and experiencing. Without this attention to individuals and cognition, there is a limit to what these studies can say about *why* people do what they do or choose what they choose. Below, I explore what theories of self can contribute to the study of national and supranational imagined communities.

Anthropological Studies of Self

The concept of everyday ethnicity is valuable for bringing into focus the varied ways in which nation and ethnicity matter in everyday lives, and for showing the power these categories can have when they are so much a part of the fabric of the everyday social environment that they tend to remain outside the realm of conscious reflection and conversation. However, for my purposes here, this approach does not go far enough; it is unnecessarily dismissive of research methodologies that engage participants in direct reflection about the nation. Further, it dismisses out of hand the possibility of knowing what people think, but nevertheless makes inferences about what they imagine and what they feel. Brubaker et al. (2006) acknowledge that everyday categorization is both cognitive and discursive (or interactive), grounded in both mental and social practice, but conclude that it is impossible to access the cognitive because it is not directly observable. Further, they argue that experimental studies (and here it seems they include any study based on direct questioning) have little bearing on understandings of everyday experience (2006, 209). They describe ethnicity as "a modality of experience, rather than a thing" (207) and argue that it is more accurate to speak of doing rather than having ethnicity, and of becoming rather than being a member of an ethnicity (208). As such, they reject the idea of cognitive models, or even a concept of self, as sites for understanding belonging to a national or ethnic group.[12]

By contrast, my study centers upon individuals, whose thoughts, feelings and experiences reveal the ways in which collective identities take on meaning; in other words, I look at ways of doing *and* having "Polishness," and becoming *and* being Polish. I call this approach psychological to signal the attention paid to individuals, self, cognition, dispositions and affect. I examine how group categories are negotiated, and the extent to which individuals accept, reject or transform such categories. This perspective views people not just as black boxes shaped by external structures and filled by cultural symbols, but also as creative agents in their own lives, who sometimes have the power to resist and even change the structures and symbols they navigate within. Fortunately, much interesting work has been done that follows a similar trajectory – studies centered on "self," "person" and "subjectivities," including insights from cognitive anthropology and person-centered ethnography. What I take from them is a commitment to understanding what we can about inner lives, and practical methods for getting a pretty good idea what people think and feel.

In an important but often overlooked exploration of identity from the perspective of the self, Cohen (1994) argues that anthropologists must use their own self-consciousness to engage with and develop an understanding of the self-consciousness of the people they study. Not doing so, he asserts, "is to risk misunderstanding, and therefore misrepresenting, the people who we claim to know and who we represent to others" (1994, 4). According to Cohen, the self refers to the conscious, reflective "I" that provides experiential continuity, but that is also plastic, variable and complex. Thus, he seeks to reconcile concepts of the self as, on the one hand, stable and integrated, and on the other as contingent and shifting, by proposing a model of "the individual as essentially a basket of selves which come to the surface at different social moments as appropriate" (11).[13] This approach is different from others that focus on discrete "subject positions" because it takes into account the "basket" – the individual who holds various selves in relation to each other. Cohen emphasizes the creative dimension of self: "Culture does not impose meaning on individuals," he asserts, "it provides *form* which individuals substantiate themselves" (50, emphasis original).[14] Cohen also argues against describing the relation between self and society as disparate and oppositional. Rather, he makes the point that individuals often conceive of themselves in terms of their relationships to others. Cohen argues, "The self has primacy in the creation of locality, in rendering boundaries meaningful, in the interpretation of national identity" (132). My study explores the links between self and nation, and questions how, and to what degree, these links extend to Europe.

Just as Cohen argues we miss a crucial dimension of human experience if we abandon even trying to find out what others are thinking, D'Andrade (2008) contends that it is possible, and even fundamentally human, to be able to gain a reasonable understanding of other people's thoughts and feelings (see also Linger 1994, 2010).[15] Drawing from neurobiology, cognitive psychology and cognitive anthropology, D'Andrade argues that explaining cultural and social phenomena "always assumes an account of psychological processes" because individuals are what connect one collective variable to another. Any time researchers speculate about what people want, a psychological dimension is inferred. According to D'Andrade, there are many reasons why people do what they do, and it is not enough to look at cognitive content alone. Motivational systems, which are linked to affective processes, are required to turn thought into action (D'Andrade 2008, 135). He outlines a model of the mind that accounts for both cognition and emotion, each of which is processed differently but is just as important to our understanding and actions. Cognition involves rapid processing of numerous stimuli and ideas, while emotions are more limited in number than ideas, and are slower to change.[16] Also, there are numerous motivational systems, and taking them into account points toward a more developed way of exploring and understanding why people tend to form, and act upon, connections to places and categories of people. The most powerful motivational systems are based on attachment – the establishment, maintenance and enhancement of relationships to others – and self-interest – the drive to preserve and sustain oneself, and to get things. Most materialist theories focus on the latter motivational construct to the exclusion of all others. D'Andrade also identifies other common sources of motivation including, but not limited to, identity, abstract cognitive systems (this would include "isms" such as nationalism) and ethics.

D'Andrade puts forward a model of mind that accounts for both thought and emotion, and that rejects simplistic views based solely on rational self-interest, cultural symbols or external structural constraints. Relating this specifically to the issues I explore, attention to various motivational systems provides a more comprehensive model of the ways in which group affiliations at different scales are forged, and provides a useful lens for considering how local, national and European identities differ and relate to each other. As I have already noted, exposure to discourse and ideology is not enough for people to adopt associated national or supranational identities. Systems of motivation help explain why people respond the way they do to these constructs, and also to the institutions that give rise to them.

While cognitive anthropology has tended toward methodologies grounded in controlled experiments, "person-centered ethnography" provides the closest model for my ethnographic approach, centered on close engagement with specific respondents. The approach was developed by Levy (1973) and others who employ psychological interviewing techniques as well as psychoanalytic and cognitive analysis of subjects. In his groundbreaking study,

Levy interrogated Tahitians' experiences of "his [sic] body, his feelings, his sense of self, his needs for personal definition and integration, his understanding of what is going on around him as it involves himself," and how such aspects are related to the public world of "systematic relationships and formal arenas of community life" (1973, xvii–xix). Though he frames his work in terms of private (personal, interior) and public, he warns against overemphasizing the distinction: "There is personality and psychology in the most public behavior and culture in the most private" (xix). Levy looks for generalized patterns and contrasts in the "personally organized statements" respondents made during extensive, relatively open-ended interviews, in order to understand their *"experience as Tahitians"* (xxiv; emphasis original).

Although person-centered approaches share a commitment to understanding inner lives and intersubjective relations (the way in which meaning is communicated among people), in more recent years scholars have debated what exactly is meant by "self." Lester (2005, 37–45) distinguishes two perspectives with long philosophical and psychological roots: self as "seat of being," designating an authentic, unique, inalienable essence of an individual that is the locus of initiative and action; and self as "illusion of interiority," or a "construct through which power becomes inscribed in individual bodies." At issue is the degree to which cultural meaning (and personal agency) emanates from individuals, or conversely the extent to which political and social institutions control what people think and feel. The most interesting studies to date have proposed ways of integrating these two perspectives: selves are constructed out of inner processes, and are also subject to social hierarchies and discourses (see Lester 2005; Linger 2001). In an effort to find language that captures the "culturally constructed experience of interiority," (Lester 2005, 40) some recent studies have framed their work in terms of subjectivities and embodiment instead of selves and experience (see Biehl et al. 2007; Desjarlais 1997, 2003). Person-centered approaches have also moved away from a psychodynamic framework, favoring instead phenomenology and sensory experiences (Desjarlais 1997, 2003) and explanations grounded in political and historical circumstances (Borovoy 2005; Lester 2005). My work adopts this more phenomenological, historically grounded emphasis.

In sum, it should be clear that the conception of self employed here is not independent of cultural symbols, discourses, institutions or power structures. Rather, self is conceived in terms of individuals' *relationships* with other individuals, with collectivities and with the culturally shaped world around them. The approaches outlined in this section treat participants as thinking, feeling, articulate subjects who provide an important view into cultural realms. They also emphasize the *creative* self who makes meaning out of politically and socially shaped symbols and discourse, and who demonstrates agency when navigating social structures and institutions. Returning to the reflections that began this chapter, I contend that most participants made statements about a stable sense of self when discussing their attachment to Europe – "I'm by nature that kind of person, who loves mountains and valleys"; "I'm not a racist"; "I'm not the kind of person who identifies with the nation" – even as some also expressed thoughts and feelings that reflect a shift in their sense of who they are as a result of political transformations:

> I'm not sure what's changed inside me, maybe it's the EU, maybe it's because everything has opened, borders have opened, and you can cross the German border and they don't even check your passport. […] I feel the same solidarity [to Poland], but suddenly I also feel it toward other people in Europe. As if they have become closer to me.

Participants speak from the perspective of a continuous core self that engages with other people, ideas and institutions. Sometimes these engagements are transformative. More often, they are not; alternative viewpoints may be outright rejected, deemed unimportant or integrated into existing conceptions.

A Person-Centered Approach to European Integration and Collective Identities

To put it all together, this study explores Polish citizens' cognitive and emotional connections with categories of people and places, paying particular attention to the different kinds of loyalty expressed toward local, national and European scales. It focuses on the expression of collective identity in terms of psychological experiences of affiliation, attachment, sentiment, allegiance and identification. Person-centered ethnography (and psychologically attuned approaches in general) provides a methodology by which to study EU integration "from below" – a means of viewing ordinary people's assumptions, hopes, needs, motivations and interests as they engage creatively with historical and political dynamics of power shaped by processes of globalization, postcommunist liberalization and EU integration. Life stories offer a view into the processes by which building and imagining Europe can make Europe a marked category – one that individuals think of when they reflect on who they are – and perhaps more importantly an unmarked category – one that is taken for granted as a constitutive part of their behavioral environment. Close attention to individual lives, as revealed in personal life stories and via long-term ethnographic engagement, provides an avenue through which to explore the entitativity of Europe, and the processes by which the EU becomes part of people's reality.

What follows, then, is an account of the influence of EU expansion on collective identities as conceived and experienced by Polish individuals. The life stories of self-conscious, complex selves bounded by their corporeal bodies to particular, in many ways idiosyncratic, trajectories through life, provide vivid pictures of the diverse impacts of Poland's remarkable transformation from state socialism to EU integration. These stories are valuable for what they reveal about selfhood during a period of rapid social and political reform, and they also help us understand those broader social changes. Attention to individual lives reveals how social reforms matter in everyday lives, how they influence collective loyalties, and why some political claims and collective narratives are embraced while others are rejected. They also reveal the thoughts, feelings and experiences that motivate people to identify with their local region, their nation or with Europe, how these various levels of identification are mutually constitutive, and what those allegiances suggest about the kind of imagined community Europe is and can become.

There are different ways of integrating life stories into a monograph – having them stand alone in separate chapters (Levy 1973; Linger 2001; Pajo 2008), or weaving them into chapters that explore particular aspects of experience and social life (Borovoy 2005; Desjarlais 1997, 2003; Lester 2005).[17] Here, I start and end each chapter with a portrait of an individual whose story is particularly relevant to the theme addressed in the chapter. In addition, I draw liberally from multiple life stories throughout the book. The portraits help to show the way multiple influences and viewpoints can coalesce in individual lives. Drawing more selectively from life stories (as I did at the beginning of this introduction) helps to spotlight particular issues, and to show the various ways those issues become salient in multiple lives.

Chapters 2 and 3 consider a shift in temporal orientations, from past to present to future. Chapter 2 looks at the way the past has been deployed to shape the present, particularly in terms of messianic and heroic discourses at the heart of national mythology. I also examine how history figures in the stories participants tell about themselves, the nation and European integration. The chapter ends with an overview of the layered meanings attributed to the plane crash in 2010 that killed the Polish president near the site of the historic massacre at Katyn. Chapter 3 illustrates the tendency to focus on the present in the 1990s, and the future orientation that has become more common since. I link this shift in temporal orientation to the growth of stable institutions in Poland that, in part, are a product of the way the EU mediates member states' integration into global capitalism. The chapter concludes by considering how orientations and dispositions toward Poland's future may in turn influence processes of European integration. In Chapter 4, I explore spatial orientations, and the ways in which participants conceptualize their allegiances to local, national and European scales. I also show how European identity, when it is expressed at all, functions very differently from local and national identity.

Chapter 5 is the first of three chapters that focus on EU membership. It describes the EU's process of expansion into Eastern Europe, outlines participants' perceptions of European integration and explores the implications of their perceptions for the kind of legitimacy the EU is likely to gain in Poland. Chapter 6 looks at participants' experiences and reflections about economic migration and travel to other EU member countries, the circumstances they most commonly associated with EU membership. I view these encounters in terms of participants' aspirations to gain a higher position in an imagined hierarchy of nations via EU membership. Chapter 7 explores ways of using EU subsidies by participants involved in direct efforts to improve local conditions in the Bieszczady region. It shows how, even as these encounters make real the idea of Europe, social entrepreneurs and civil servants are more motivated by their local and national commitments than they are to the broader sphere of the EU. In Chapter 8, I conclude with reflections on the transformation of selfhood and national identity for Poles since I began my research in 1991, and the impact everyday thoughts and experiences can have on European identity.

Chapter 2

"WE HAVE ALWAYS BEEN IN EUROPE": DEPLOYING THE PAST TO SHAPE THE PRESENT

Bartek: Historical Consciousness in the Twenty-First Century

When we met in 1992, Bartek was in the academically demanding science track at the lyceum in Lesko.[1] He was not an especially motivated student, but he loved to explore the outdoors and dreamed of becoming a mountain tour guide one day. In the interview I recorded in 2005, he invoked national history to explain Polish identity and Polish responses to structural and ideological changes associated with European integration. Still, he made it clear that he was far more interested in the history of the Bieszczady region than in Polish, European or world history:

> A lot has changed since high school, that's for sure. I had a hard time getting into university. Right after finishing lyceum, I tried to study geography, but I didn't get in. Then, I got into a chemistry program, and even though it was really hard I did well my first semester. It's just that I lived in the dorm with guys studying physical education and I decided that's what I would rather do. So I quit and waited a year and I passed the exams to study physical education. You can say I was a year behind, but I'm still satisfied with what I did.
>
> I didn't have a hard time finding a job in Lesko. My parents are teachers so I grew up in a teaching environment. But maybe that has nothing to do with it; when I finished university, schools were hiring because of a baby boom. I know it would be harder now because there are a lot fewer children.
>
> I definitely think things have gotten better in Poland ... but it's hard for me to say because essentially I don't know if it was good or bad in the 1970s during what's called communism. You'd have to ask my parents. But I definitely can say that things are better for me because I have a job, my wife has a job. And like I've told you, I also became a tour guide. I know that if things turn bad, I still have an arrangement with the tourist agency and they'll use me even on weekends or vacations, which gives me a solid opportunity to earn money.

Do ideas like patriotism and *ojczyzna* [fatherland] still matter in Poland? I think that they definitely do, but these ideas are often misinterpreted – by Nazis, skinheads, nationalist parties like Młodzież Wszechpolska [All-Polish Youth], the extreme Right. Politicians use words like patriotism, *ojczyzna*, church, Catholicism, to win elections. This annoys me. But I think that most people feel like patriots.

I feel like a "local patriot." Do you remember what happened when there was the administrative reform [in 1998]? Lesko is a historic city with traditions; it was supposed to become a *powiat* [a local administrative district] like it was before the war. But when the maps were released it instead became part of Powiat Ustrzyki.[2] Then, all the residents somehow united patriotically. For weeks, they blocked roads throughout Bieszczady. Local officials traveled to Warsaw; it didn't matter if one was a communist and the other a right-winger. And can you imagine? They won that *powiat* for Lesko.

I definitely voted in favor of Poland's membership in the EU. I consider EU membership a kind of opening up. You can't be eternally closed between Russia or Ukraine and Western Europe, you see?

How attached do I feel to Poland? Infinitely more than I do to Europe. Growing up in Poland is definitely an influence, as is Polish history – those two world wars, the control of the Soviet Union, to say nothing of the partitions in the eighteenth and nineteenth centuries. Our historical consciousness further reinforces the feeling that at last we're Poland, that at last we can feel united together, that we mean something in the world.

How attached do I feel to this region? Very much; even more than I do to the country. It's because of my love for mountains. From childhood, my father would take me to the mountains. I have spent a lot of time in the mountains, and I have read a great deal about their history. The history I learned in school about Poland and Europe – you know, the most important things, the dates – were boring to me. I learned them because I had to, but I learned the history of this region because it interested me.

It has never occurred to me to leave Lesko. I feel good here. This is where I was born, where I grew up. My parents as well. My mother's family is from the Kresy [the region east of the contemporary border that historically was part of Poland], because my grandfather was from near Sambor, in what is now Ukraine. My mother feels very patriotic. My grandmother was in "Sokół," a gymnastics society and paramilitary organization before the war,[3] so it probably went from my grandmother to my mother. I definitely got this patriotism somehow from my family roots.

To now feel patriotism to the EU, to be able to answer the question if I'm a European, I think it will require some time to pass. Because in history classes, even during communist times, they still told us we're Poles. They taught us that Germans attacked Poland, and Poles fought heroically. I know from my grandmother's stories that the war [World War II] lasted until 1947 in Bieszczady.

Because Ukrainian partisans fought. It's enraging that Poles were murdered. Wherever you look, Poles always suffered. That's why I say that for the EU, a little time must pass still. Maybe people have to travel, make contacts and feel that the Germans and the British are not that rich, and we're not so far behind. The EU also has to somehow prove that that it depends on Poland, that it's holding out a hand, you see? It's hard to convince anyone with books or television that they're European. We need to see it and feel it.

In his life story, Bartek articulated a sense of self that is deeply rooted in history, place and family. His family's historical connection to the Bieszczady region figures strongly in his reflections. He also expressed attachment to the nation, and linked Polish identity to national consciousness born of a history of oppression. He referred to common elements of what I describe below as Polish national mythology, including Poland's historical position between Eastern and Western powers, and heroism in the face of foreign occupation and communist domination. He also criticized the misuse of patriotism by political extremists. For Bartek, identity is grounded in emotional attachment – he feels Polish, but his deepest connection is to his native Bieszczady Mountains. His closest experience of patriotic action was when his town fought to become a regional political center. He linked his "local patriotism" to family history – his grandmother's defense of Poland's claim over Bieszczady, his mother's patriotism and his father's experiences as a hiker and mountain tour guide.

Bartek's life story also provides a glimpse into the way Europe fits into historical narratives of place, and the degree to which the past is remembered, evoked and deployed such that an emotional connection to Europe (and by extension the EU) might emerge. For Bartek, as with nearly all participants in my study, history provides at best an ambiguous basis for "feeling European." He is supportive of European integration, largely because of the benefits it brings Poland and, by extension, the Bieszczady region. It provides a way out of the historical isolation between Eastern and Western powers that has continually threatened Polish autonomy, and it provides a pathway for social advancement within the global imaginary of nations. Nevertheless, the memory of past abuse by other European countries as well as continued economic inequalities between EU member states mean that it will still take some time for emotional attachment to "Europe" to grow, and for Bartek to truly "feel European."

Deploying the Past to Shape the Present

The concept of collective memory is useful for explaining how the past can become a powerful motivational force in the present. Shared stories, commemorations and monuments can evoke traumatic or deeply moving historical events in ways that produce in contemporary witnesses a sense of connection to particular interpretations of the past (Irwin-Zarecka 1994). This chapter explores the ways in which the past is remembered, evoked and deployed in Polish popular discourses, and in participants' life stories, and how these historical narratives reinscribe, revise and reinvent group identities at various regional scales – European, national and local. It considers the ways in which the profound changes of the past twenty years have shaped participants' world views, particularly in relation to the way they tend to regard the past, and make use of history to understand the present. The chapter also considers how orientations toward Poland's history, and perspectives on historical relations between Poland and Europe, may in turn influence views of contemporary processes of European integration. Participants' reflections demonstrate they are not just conduits for collective representations passed on through national mythology or official propaganda; rather they are creative selves who engage with and make meaning of the stories they are told.

I begin with an overview of the narratives that constitute national mythology, including the motifs of Polish messianism and heroism. I consider the conditions that gave rise to this particular way of telling the story of the nation, and then review the chronology of Polish history as it is commonly told. I argue that the national mythology is important because Polish citizens know these stories and use them as reference points in their personal narratives, even when they reject some elements and prioritize other narratives. How they negotiate national mythology and associated counternarratives also influences responses to European integration. These various themes converged in the controversy that erupted over the proper way to commemorate President Kaczyński after he died in a plane crash in 2010. I explain the social divisions this controversy exposed in terms of associated tensions between past and future orientations.

National Mythology: Polish Messianism and the Heroic Ideal

Poland's history is often linked to a narrative, or what Zubrzycki (2011) calls "national mythology." She outlines the mythology's paradigmatic elements as follows:

> Essentially and eternally Catholic, Poland is the bulwark of Christendom defending Europe against the infidel (however defined). A nation assailed by dangerous neighbors, its identity is conserved and guarded by its defender, the Roman Catholic Church, and shielded by its Queen, the miraculous Black Madonna, Our Lady of Częstochowa. Christ among nations, it was martyred

for the sins of the world and resurrected for the world's salvation. Last but not least, it is a nation that has given the world a Pope – deferentially referred to as the "Pope of the Millenium [sic]" – and rid the Western world of communism. (Zubrzycki 2011, 25–6)

Zubrzycki emphasizes two intertwined component myths that she says are at the core of Poland's national mythology: one of Poland's Catholicism, and the other of "messianic martyrdom."

While these elements are certainly foundational, here I consider as well other elements that are equally fundamental to stories about the nation, including especially Poland's place between East and West (Galbraith 2004) and what I have called the "Polish heroic ideal" (Galbraith 1997). These paradigmatic elements can be summarized as follows:

Fiercely proud and independent, the Polish people have championed values of liberty, national self-determination, and democracy. Located geographically and spiritually at the "heart of Europe," Poland is uniquely positioned to model these values to other nations, and even to defend them for all of humanity. However, without natural barriers to the east or west, Poland's fertile plains have also been vulnerable to invasions by dangerous neighbors. Even in the face of radically shifting borders, including times when Poland disappeared from the map, Poland has survived as a nation because of the heroic sacrifices of Poles who refused to compromise values of liberty and national autonomy.

Though grounded in many of the same historic events as the first, this second version of national mythology highlights the role of the Polish people, and in particular the heroic patriot who makes personal sacrifices for the good of the nation. Importantly, this narrative highlights individual agents; it prescribes for Polish citizens a way of being in the world linked to cognitive and emotional connections to the nation, and outlines the actions ideally expected of members of the imagined national community. Fundamental as well is the claim that Poland is not only within Europe, but also has played a critical role in defending European territory and values.

Thinking about history in terms of a framing mythology emphasizes how the past is a cultural construction; it explains how the nation came to be, and naturalizes associated beliefs and values. Thus mythologized, history also becomes operationalized in the social imaginary as a model for the present and the future. National mythology is linked to the development of the modern concept of nation. Although the expression "nation-state" assumes an unproblematic connection between "nation" and "state," for much of Poland's modern history, the boundaries of nation and state were not the same.

In fact, Poland lost its sovereignty just as the homogeneous nation-state ideal was taking hold in Europe around the turn of the eighteenth to the nineteenth century. The national community was instead championed by writers, artists, intellectuals and freedom fighters. In other words, Poland persisted, and in fact flourished as a cultural entity, even in the absence of an autonomous state. When Poland regained statehood in 1918, as part of the realignment of European power after World War I, nation and state boundaries still differed, but in another manner; ethnic Ukrainians, Germans, Lithuanians and Jews comprised 30 per cent of the population within the new state borders. Additionally, large populations of ethnic Poles lived outside the boundaries of the Polish state.

According to national mythology, Poland's origin begins much earlier than the eighteenth century, with the conversion of King Mieszko I to Catholicism in 966 during a period of territorial expansion. The historical narrative links the beginning of Poland with the Catholic faith, and with the politics of territorial growth via warfare. The mythology also highlights the "Golden Age" from 1466 to 1576, when the Polish–Lithuanian kingdom achieved its greatest control of territory, extending beyond the contemporary cities of Riga, Smolensk and Kiev (now in Lithuania, Russia and Ukraine, respectively). Nevertheless, as Western Europe became increasingly centralized, urbanized and industrialized, Eastern Europe remained relatively decentralized and agrarian, and the Polish nobility, comprising about eight to ten per cent of the population, retained considerable autonomy. Their resistance to centralization led to three democratic innovations that are remembered in national mythology as evidence of Poland's privileged status among nations, or (sometimes simultaneously) are lamented for making the weakened Polish state vulnerable to attack. Starting in 1572, kings were elected by a parliament composed of nobles and clergymen. Second, the parliament instituted the *liberum veto*, whereby a single member could defeat any piece of legislation by voting against it. Third, in 1791, inspired by political reforms in the US and France, the parliament ratified a new constitution that laid the groundwork for extending democratic liberties. The Russian Empire, threatened by these political reforms and taking advantage of a request for assistance from Polish nobles opposed to the new constitution, asserted control over Polish territory. The neighboring Prussian and Austrian empires divided the rest of Poland between themselves, and Poland ceased to be an autonomous political entity for 123 years, a period commonly called the Partitions.[4]

The stories and myths that came to define Polish national identity in the nineteenth century were built on the foundation of foreign rule, which was conceptualized in Polish discourse as a lack of freedom or even imprisonment. In fact, it would be fair to say that defining the nation in opposition to outside,

Figure 2.1. *King Jan III Sobieski Sending Message of Victory to the Pope* by Jan Matejko, 1880

oppressive states contributed to the persistence of the Polish "imagined community" throughout the nineteenth and much of the twentieth centuries (see Dabrowski 2004). The national mythology and associated symbols, such as the Black Madonna of Czestochowa, evoked in many Poles a visceral, emotional connection that was considered all the more precious because it had to be expressed in secret. Artists of the period encouraged such national sentiments by looking backward to moments in Polish history that exemplified Poland's central position within Europe, when Poles defended Christianity and freedom. This can be seen, for instance, in Jan Matejko's painting, *King Jan III Sobieski Sending Message of Victory to the Pope* (figure 2.1). Painted in 1880, the artist imagined the culmination of the Battle of Vienna in 1683, when the Polish king defeated the Turks, saving the city from invasion, and by extension "saving" Europe from Islam. The painting depicts the king backed by his winged hussars, cavalrymen who according to legend charged into battle wearing massive wings made of wood and feathers.

As Koczanowicz notes, "Any struggle for the past is in fact a struggle for the future" (2008, 20). Constructions of the past were wielded as models for the future, designed to spur action in the present. Significantly, those who advanced romantic messianism in the nineteenth century, like the freedom fighter Tadeusz Kościuszko and the poet Adam Mickiewicz, lived much of their lives in exile. Fueled by nostalgia for a distant homeland, the past became a vehicle for representing the long-term persistence of the Polish nation and its key values like freedom, national pride, heroism, Catholicism and resilience in the face of impossible odds. This mythology placed Poland firmly at the heart of Europe as a protector of every nation's right to sovereignty, and the slogan "For our freedom and yours" became popular among Poles who participated in insurrections against imperial powers throughout Europe.[5] The challenge for national activists was justifying the relevance of a distinct Polish identity in the absence of supporting political institutions. As successive insurrections failed, these defeats themselves became elements of national mythology, illustrating Poland's suffering and confirming the nation's role as the "Christ of Nations." The mythology they constructed placed reality at odds with truth, and asserted that things were not as they should be – Poland should be free.

After a brief period of sovereignty between the world wars, Poland again lost its autonomy during Nazi occupation and state socialism; the national mythology took on renewed relevance, and activists once again employed works of art as potent national symbols and vehicles for motivating the fight for freedom. Poles became skilled at what Bakhtin (1981) called "double-voiced discourse" in which they learned to underlay official, sanctioned communication with implicit, proscribed meanings. Nationalist literature continued to be featured in school curricula, on the surface taught as historical classics, but simultaneously evoking patriotic sentiments and keeping alive the hope that Poland would one day be free again (Kubik 1994). A prime example of the power of the romantic classics was the staging of Adam Mickiewicz's play *Dziady* (*Forefather's Eve*) that sparked student protests in 1968. National mythology, grounded in Polish romanticism, also captured the imagination of non-Poles – most influentially, British historian Norman Davies. Regarding the Solidarity movement, he asserted, "On balance, recent events have confirmed that Polish Romantics had a more profound understanding than their Positivist rivals of their own and their country's nature, and that, in the last analysis, they are more realistic than the self-professed 'realists'" (1986, x). Similarly, Michael Kaufman, a foreign correspondent in Poland during the 1980s, commented, "Poles shield themselves with a living past," and "from childhood Poles are nurtured on legends of daring deeds and tragic hopes" (1989, 9, 47–8). These scholars have been instrumental in reinscribing historical narratives celebrating the Poles' struggle for national self-determination.

The romantic (or idealist) and the positivist (or realist) have often been posed as oppositional ideologies that have traded dominance at various periods in Polish history. The "realist" counternarrative advocates working within the existing system – whether the Partition powers of the nineteenth century, the communist party of the twentieth century, or the European Union of the twenty-first century – to advance Polish interests via economic modernization. Positivists promoted what has been called "organic work" – doing whatever needs to be done to grow the economy and educate the majority, including setting aside unrealistic efforts to liberate the nation (Dabrowski 2004). Such pragmatic reforms were seen in the nineteenth century as a way of promoting national consciousness among the rural majority, who tended to identify more closely with their local communities and their religious affiliation than with the ideological nation. From a romantic perspective, positivism was condemned on the grounds that accepting Poland's occupation meant giving up on the very thing that defines Poland as a nation – the expectation of sovereignty. This point of view made compromise a bad word, akin to "being compromised." Realists, by contrast, condemned idealists as hot-headed extremists insensitive to the havoc they cause for the majority of the population. Dabrowski, however, points out how often idealism and realism have worked in tandem. In particular, she shows how nineteenth-century nationalist commemorative practices were "a constructive, creative, yet intensely national variant of organic work – an attempt at national modernization, Polish style" (2004, 15). Similarly, Wood (2010) argues that in early nineteenth-century Krakow, narratives of the city's nationalist history was often used in the service of modernization projects designed to bring a European standard of urban comfort and safety.[6]

Positivism and romanticism, and possible convergences between them, have been applied to other contemporary issues. For example, throughout the 1990s and 2000s, a hot area of debate has been whether former president Jaruzelski's decision to declare martial law and suppress the Solidarity movement in 1981 was a traitorous betrayal of the Polish people, or an act of pragmatic realism. Jaruzelski himself claims to be a patriot, and defends his actions as a way of preventing a far more brutal attack against the nation by Soviet forces. In other words, he sees himself as a hybrid between realist and idealist. Notably, the Polish population has remained divided as to whether Jaruzelski's actions were justified, but there has never been the sustained political will to prosecute him for his actions. In fact, political debates about reconciliation and lustration (the practice of exposing contemporary leaders' ties to the former regime) have been pivotal in party platforms since 1989 (Koczanowicz 2008).

My point in reviewing the national mythology is not to suggest that participants uncritically accept narratives about Polish messianism or self-sacrificing heroism, but rather to show they are familiar with these stories. At minimum, they learned about them while studying classic romantic texts in Polish literature classes, or heard stories of national valor and defeat from family members, some of whom were personally engaged in the Solidarity trade union, earlier protest movements or even World War II resistance. Perhaps not surprisingly, as participants have grown accustomed to living within a free country, these romantic narratives have been challenged by revisionist histories.

National Mythologies in Everyday Life

While it is valuable to identify the narrative contours of national mythology, this by itself reveals little about the day-to-day salience of these collective representations. Person-centered ethnography can show the ways in which narratives about the past are received and used by individuals in their everyday lives, especially in relation to the constellations of debate that surround them. As I have said, participants in my study know these stories, but what do they *do* with them? Below, I consider how, and under what circumstances, Polish national mythology and opposing counternarratives figure in participants' life stories. For the most part, participants focus on the present and the future more than they do on the past, but nevertheless, historical narratives often function as reference points in their reflections about nation, patriotism, democratization and European integration. I begin with a vignette from a high school classroom in 1993 that illustrates both the reinscription and contestation of mythological themes in a lesson about Polish romantic literature.

In the early 1990s, I had the opportunity to observe how national mythology was being taught, and also how students reacted to those lessons. For instance, at a technical school in Krakow, the Polish teacher, Pani Sułkowska,[7] reviewed the day's theme: "The portrait of Polish society and its evaluation in part 3, scene 3 of *Dziady* [*Forefathers' Eve*]." Romantic poet Adam Mickiewicz wrote part 3 of the play in November 1830 following an unsuccessful insurrection against Russian rule, and it has periodically functioned to reinscribe perceptions of Poland as the "Christ of Nations," suffering quietly but keeping the hope of freedom alive under the surface.

The lesson unfolded as follows: The class was reminded that part 3 of *Dziady* is set in Poland when it was under control of the Russian czar. The poor Poles stand by the door, representing their marginality, where they debate what they can and should do about Russian domination. Pani Sułkowska asked, "A romantic drama need not have a sharp connection with what?" and the students responded in unison, "Reality." From the classroom discussion, a portrait emerged of Poland without freedom, in which direct armed opposition to the czar would lead to death. Instead, poetry becomes the most effective form of protest because it keeps the goal of freedom alive until armed conflict is possible. One student pointed out the messianic nature of the story. When asked to explain, he replied, "Though Poland lives in the land of darkness, God sees their suffering and will reward them. Since God is the highest authority, it is not important for others to know they are heroes."

The class also discussed a passage which compares the nation to lava: cold, hard and dry on the surface, while the fire inside does not cool for one hundred years. Pani Sułkowska encouraged students to reflect on the symbolic significance of the passage. One volunteered that although the nation may appear stable on the outside, inside it is hot and ready to burst. Another explained that the nation is ready to fight when aroused. Pani Sułkowska prompted them, "They never agree to…" and a student finished, "*niewola*" (slavery or captivity). When asked to relate the lava simile to contemporary Poland, students identified instability, political disagreement and negative orientations toward government. Pani Sułkowska suggested this means the fire is on the outside now. She concluded by asking whether Poles can unite only in tragic situations. No one answered so she volunteered that the situation need not be tragic, though often Poles do not unite unless times become difficult.

The symbols and images discussed by the class resonate with the romantic national mythology, including the messianic narrative of Poland's suffering, which goes unnoticed except by God, and the heroism of the people who refuse to submit to captivity. Students were taught that fighting may take many forms, and that sometimes the most effective strategy is to appear compliant (like the poor Poles standing at the door) until an opportunity arises to take more radical action (like the lava ready to burst). According to Pani Sułkowska, the passage highlights the value of waiting, and in that time building awareness through conversation and poetry. Further, students reiterated that romanticism need have nothing to do with reality, but rather may be equated with feelings greater than life and death, or even a kind of ecstatic insanity.

Pani Sułkowska's students also questioned the relevance of messianic symbolism to the post-1989 situation. Their concerns about instability illustrate the failure of the play to provide a model for what should happen after the goal of national autonomy is achieved and there is no longer an outside enemy to fight. In 1993, Poland's past (and future) was no longer in the hands of poets and others whose convictions seemed to defy what was possible in the real world. Instead, many of the people I met felt it was time for pragmatic "organic work" to rebuild the economy, as expressed in assertions like "It's time to get back to work" and "The best way to show patriotism is to work hard." Most had expected their lives would get easier when communism fell, and hoped it would not take long to achieve the higher standard of living they saw in capitalist countries. Few were prepared for unemployment or skyrocketing inflation, and they complained regularly about the daily frustration of finally seeing material goods available in stores but having no money to buy them. They also complained about democratically elected officials who squabbled among themselves and seemed more interested in their own well-being than that of the nation as a whole. As Pani Sułkowska suggested, the "fire was on the outside," as Poles used their newfound freedom to criticize leaders for their shortcomings and complain about economic insecurity.

By 2005, although complaints about insecurity and disorder were still commonly expressed, participants' daily lives had settled into routines that signaled greater political and economic stability. On a national level, democratic institutions were assured and the economy was growing. On an individual level, most participants had their own homes, jobs, spouses and children; they were meeting their basic expenses, and many were even thriving. Though it had been a long time since their school lessons about romantic poetry, elements of the national mythology nevertheless emerged in some life stories. Below, I cite instances in which participants talked about the past, and I consider when and how they associated historical narratives with the present and the future.

Corruption of a glorious past

In keeping with the national mythology, participants commonly identified sacrificing oneself for the nation as the ultimate expression of patriotism, though they usually associated such acts with older generations. For instance, Krzysiek, who lives in Lesko, commented:

> In the past there were great people in Poland. They gave their lives for Polish independence, and they gave up their entire fortunes. Sometimes I listen to patriotic songs and tears come to my eyes. But then I think: so much blood was shed, but would they want Poland like it is now – when, for instance, many who fought for Poland now get a retirement pension of just four or five hundred zloty [per month; about one hundred and fifty dollars], which isn't even enough for medicines for an old man who survived Siberia, or a camp somewhere, who fought on the front and was wounded?

Similarly Grzesiek, a computer repairman in Krakow, lamented:

> We're a country that is a gray sheet stretched between Germany and Russia. We're nothing. And it's a shame to me because during both the First and Second World Wars, people devoted their own lives, they devoted everything so that Poland would exist, so that it would be a country that mattered. After all, we have our own history, we have people who are now retirees and really no one listens to them anymore.

Krzysiek and Grzesiek expressed regret that heroism has no place in the present and the sacrifices of the past are not honored in the present. On the contrary, those who practiced heroic acts are now cast aside; they receive pensions that are too small to live on, and "no one listens to them anymore." Their comments suggest a kind of moral bankruptcy has accompanied the achievement of national autonomy.

Participants place themselves on the cusp of the postcommunist transformation; sometimes they associate themselves with the generation that remembers, other times they claim they were too young to experience any trials themselves. Jurek, an architect in Krakow, noted, "I believe that I am the last generation that can feel something, because I physically went through martial law, and by extension [through my grandfather] earlier events like the Polish Uprising, where people died." Others said that younger generations have a different attitude toward the past because they lack a direct connection to the historic events that shaped Polish national identity. For instance, Marzena, a banker in Warsaw, told me she does not identify with narratives of Polish heroism: "Sometimes, when my husband and I see the traces of those old folks who were soldiers in World War II, it seems funny. When you think that they were in a position to sacrifice their lives for the fatherland … that's something we just don't understand. So many years have passed since the war. I haven't had any drastic trials where I could prove my patriotism." Marzena takes a different view of the same people Krzysiek and Grzesiek regard as neglected heroes – she sees them as archaic holdovers of another era.

Participants also complained that history has become a tool wielded by political extremists (as Bartek noted at the beginning of the chapter). Ewelina, a lawyer in Krakow, criticized "extreme parties that use history for effect." She blamed perpetual political scandals and bribery on the "historical habit from fifty years of being told that stealing means you're more capable than others" – an allusion to state socialism, when breaking the rules was often seen as the only way to get things done (see Sampson 1985–86; Wedel 1986). Similarly, Ania, an artist in Krakow, complained, "Instead of building something, we continually fight with the past," in reference to ongoing efforts by some politicians to prove that key Solidarity figures like Lech Walesa collaborated with the communist leadership during state socialism. Grzesiek remarked, "It would be great to have a government that reacted appropriately, that made us someone in the world. We have such a history, but we sold it for free, we threw it in the trash." He invoked an image of a glorious past that has been sullied by the people currently in charge. Most of these comments evoke a sense that contemporary Poles do not measure up to the ideals contained in national mythology; participants emphasize how political and economic transformations have provided little reward for heroism and ethical social engagement.

The history that matters is personal

Though some participants expressed an interest in formal historical accounts, more commonly the history they cared about was conveyed to them by their grandparents. The pivotal event in stories passed down through families is usually World War II. Jurek explained, "We had that continuity [with the past] through our grandparents – they told us about it, not our parents who are already a postwar generation." Similarly, Halina, a farmer in Bieszczady, said, "My parents and grandparents lived and fought for Poland. That emotional attachment is very strong. I think that even though not every Pole shows it, in the event of any kind of trouble, they'll unite." The concept of "memory households" is useful for understanding how the home can become a symbolic "nest" of objects and stories attaching meaning to memory (Irwin-Zarecka 1994, 88).

Notably, the history that is remembered by many residents of Bieszczady diverges from the national mythology because it hinges on events that are particular to the region, especially the shifting borders and forced relocations of the mid-twentieth century. As Joasia, a librarian in Bieszczady, explained, "We still have this mentality, because our grandparents took part in World War II, so we remember it from their stories. My grandmother was removed to Kazakhstan and spent six years there as a small child, and was essentially a prisoner. My nephew's generation won't know that because our parents, their grandparents, were born after the war. So their mentality will be completely different." Maciek, who grew up in a village near the Ukrainian border, told me:

> My parents are Poles from the region near Lviv, what we call the Kresy. Also, my grandparents were removed to the region near the Black Sea during the war, and then later they were moved here in 1951. And so, wherever they settled, they suddenly lost their land and home, and they constantly lived out of their suitcases. My parents met here [in Poland], but they still miss the land they came from – near Lviv, Krystynopol, Sokol, Ostrów – because that is where they were born and where they grew up.

Refrains about suffering are consistent with national mythology, though these residents' memories center on the pain of dislocation, which is a particular element of Bieszczady history.

Considering the large prewar Jewish population in Bieszczady, the absence of Jews from this kind of family memory is striking. No one has ever shared with me personal recollections involving Jews, nor has anyone from Bieszczady ever hinted to me that they have any Jewish heritage, even in Lesko, where the historic synagogue is larger than the Catholic Church, and the Jewish cemetery abuts a housing development near the town center. As Irwin-Zarecka says, "The absence of memory is just as socially constructed as memory itself." She calls the absence of Jews in Polish collective memory a "memory void" because Jews were deemed irrelevant to the trajectory of Polish history from the start (1994, 116). Furthermore, Poles have found it hard to reconcile their own narrative of suffering at the hands of other ethnic groups with Jewish narratives of suffering, sometimes at the hands of Poles.

For those with Ukrainian ancestry, historical dislocations were made worse by the repression of ethnic minorities after the war ended (see Hann 1998; Buzalka 2007). Darek, a devout Catholic who was born and raised in a tiny village, struggles with his identity; his father is an ethnic Ukrainian who in 1946 was expelled from Bieszczady and forced to live in the territory Poland obtained from Germany after the war. He eventually made his way back to Bieszczady in the 1960s, despite legal restrictions against returning and other kinds of oppression. For instance, he was given the worst jobs at the state farm where he worked, and was compelled to keep his native language and Greek Catholic faith private. This family legacy leaves Darek with ambivalent feelings about Poland, but a very strong sense of attachment to the Bieszczady region that his father struggled so long to return to. He laughed when I asked him about European identity, saying, "I've never thought about it. Not only is Poland on the edge of Europe, we live on the edge of Poland." These stories show that the history that matters most is personal, reflecting and reinscribing attachment to family and to place. The realm of intimacy is sometimes extended to the nation but almost never to broader geographic scales.

Past and future in Europe

Of course, critical to my project is the manner in which Europe figures in narratives of the past, and the extent to which historical connections between Poland and Europe provide a rationale for EU integration. As I have illustrated, participants tend to assume an organic connection to the history, traditions and culture of their native place. The locus of those attachments is commonly national or local. By contrast, participants tend to regard the connection to Europe, and even more so the EU, as artificial and shallow. They neither want a united Europe to replace national distinctions, nor do they believe that European identity can replace national identity. Robert, a teacher in Bieszczady, stressed: "Even as members of the EU, everyone should have that feeling of national attachment. Because the EU is an artificial creation; essentially, what kind of history, what kind of culture is there that's general to all of Europe? I believe it's easier to understand the history of our own country than the history, culture and problems of another nation." Similarly, Bartek said, "To now feel patriotism to the EU, to be able to tell you whether or not I'm a European, I think it will require a little time to pass."

Bartek's remarks at the beginning of the chapter also illustrate another problem participants confront when imagining a united Europe: historic rivalries with other member states. Bogdan, a regional government employee from Bieszczady, told me that Poland has gained nothing from past alliances, whether the Warsaw Pact or NATO, and he expects the EU to crumble in a few years because of internal rivalries. Joasia commented on Poland's historic place between larger powers, "We always were somewhere in the middle and got a beating, looking at past history." She also expressed hesitancy about an alliance with Germany: "Can I feel any sort of attachment to Germany? Due to all those historical events, I am very cautious. I still remember through my grandparents, even though I was born a long time after the war." Similarly, Agata's husband remarked, "I come from Silesia, where there was the Polish–German conflict. And still today there are people there who can't forgive, and there's nothing we can do about it." Jurek, an architect in Krakow, said, "I can't forget what the Germans did, but I can forgive them." Memories of historical conflicts with European neighbors, the fundamental condition that shaped national mythology, remain impediments to European integration.

A few participants invoked messianism in their comments about historical relations between Poland and Europe. Jurek commented, "Historically, we always defended Europe. And the funny thing is we always end up losing. For hundreds of years, we have defended Europe against Islam, against communism, and we're always the nation that gets kicked in the butt; we aren't able to take advantage of it." Similarly Wiola, a civil servant in Bieszczady, said: "I feel that for some time we were orphaned by Europe. Through an adverse combination of events, we ended up under Russian influence. It was as if Europe turned its back on us after the Second World War, even though Poland fought for Europe and the whole world. We helped other countries fight against their enemies, but later, Europe somehow forgot about how much they owe Poland."

Wiola's reference to orphanhood is telling because it signals how kinship metaphors can work against the development of European identity. European integration is suspect because Poland's past suffering for Europe is neither recognized nor valued, contributing to participants' apprehension that Poland may not gain the place it deserves in Europe. Wojtek, a professor in Krakow, took this one step further: "Our cultural contribution isn't proportional to our potential, because we could give more to Europe, and Europe could take more from us." Exemplifying "in-group projection" (Mummendey and Waldzus 2004), he saw Poland as a role model (or in the language of national mythology, "savior") for other member nations that had lost their moral compass. These evocations of national mythology signal Poland's rightful membership in Europe, but also point to potential conflicts because the EU is not necessarily taking the shape imagined; Poland's traditional, Christian values can be difficult to reconcile with EU values of diversity and neoliberal capitalism.

Less commonly, participants indicated a sense of shared fate with the rest of Europe, as for instance, when Ania remarked:

> When they destroyed the Berlin Wall, all of Europe felt relieved to put that whole history behind them. Because something opened: a new opportunity, a new society. Those who were Nazis and fascists died and were left in the past, and now there is a chance for us. I think it gave Poles a lot and it also changed our attitudes toward Germans. We came to see that it wasn't only us who suffered, who were poor, under communism. At this point, I really have the feeling that I could easily live somewhere else and I won't miss Poland, or feel that I'm missing something or that my country is losing out on something. Because that patriotism has changed, in fact, into more global thoughts. It's very interesting; I haven't thought about it this way before, but I could easily live abroad.

Because the European Union has opened everything up, especially borders, Ania has started to feel more connected to Europe than she used to.

Similarly, Paweł, a sales manager in Bieszczady, characterized EU integration as a historic opportunity:

> I believe that all of the effort, the transformation so to speak, the changed regulations that were forced on us so that Poland could enter the EU, made it possible to organize many things that lay fallow, were not done at all, or were done poorly over those fifty years in the Eastern Bloc. That's why I think it was the only way, a reasonable solution; it was a "marriage of convenience." But it wasn't an accident, or blind reverie. We always wanted to be in the West.

Others suggested EU membership will be a good thing eventually, but Poland is not rich enough or strong enough to be fully accepted yet. Most emphasized the importance of preserving the historical and cultural distinctiveness of the Polish nation, and of all member nations. While longstanding antipathies are considered by many to be something that needs to be overcome, most also feel that cultural differences are here to stay and should be celebrated. Such comments suggest that orientations toward Europe are transforming, and perhaps also strengthening, but also that there is little support for a federalist model of the EU. Growing support seems to be linked to the promise of benefit for participants *as* Poles.

In sum, I have outlined three patterns in references to the past. First, participants tend to argue that traditional Polish heroism and messianism have little use in contemporary social, political and economic situations. The heroes of the past have been forgotten, and patriotic discourse has become corrupted by political extremists. Second, the history that is most readily remembered, evoked and deployed in everyday life is personal; if participants feel a connection to the past, it is because they identify with the hardship and suffering experienced by their parents and grandparents. This realm of intimacy can extend beyond families, as when memories reinscribe attachment to place (local region or nation). Third, allusions to the past only rarely invoke a sense of connection to Europe; more often, they point to historical rivalries and prejudices that impede European integration. Nevertheless, messianic references position Poland firmly within Europe; indeed, Poland is conceived as the "Savior of Europe," even though her sacrifices have gone unrecognized and unrewarded.

In the next section, I consider a recent crisis in Poland in which historical narratives took on new life. Rather than simply reinscribing national mythology, however, the ensuing public commemorations became a battleground for rival political and social groups over how to define the Polish nation – in terms of the past (associated with tradition, Catholicism and historical rivalries) or in terms of the future (associated with European integration).

The Smolensk Disaster

On 10 April 2010, a plane crash killed President Lech Kaczyński and 95 other people as they landed at a military airport in Smolensk, Russia. They were on their way to the Katyn Forest to commemorate the 70th anniversary of the murder of over 20,000 Polish officers and intellectuals by Soviet forces. Many observers, both inside and outside of Poland, noted uncanny parallels between the massacre of the Polish elite in 1940 and the death of the contemporary political elite. Some passengers were even descendants of the original Katyn victims, which added to the sense that history was repeating itself. It would also have been consistent with the historic events at Katyn, and narratives of Polish messianism generally, to infer that Russia had engineered the crash, just as the Soviet Union was responsible for the deaths 70 years earlier.

In fact, much public discourse, as well as most participants in this study, has taken the narrative in a different direction, lending support to my general observation that a future-oriented perspective, rather than a past-oriented one, has gained prominence in Poland (a point I develop in Chapter 3). Nevertheless, the national mythology of suffering at the hands of foreign enemies remains salient in reactions to the Smolensk disaster, fueled by a vocal minority aligned with certain political interests. The public, often heated, dispute about the larger significance of the tragedy has exposed and deepened fractures in Polish society that divide winners and losers in Poland's transformation, old and young citizens, religious and secular forces, and traditional (past-oriented) and modern (forward-looking) inclinations of citizens. The outcome of this debate is important as a bellwether of popular support for future trends in Poland – toward nationalism or integration.[8] I turn now to the history of the 1940 massacre at Katyn, and its symbolic significance over the past 70 years.

History of Katyn

The Katyn massacre has long been a sensitive topic for Poles, reflecting the complex relationship between Russia and Poland, and symbolizing a long history of rivalry, betrayal, oppression and suffering. Though commonly used in the singular, "Katyn" denotes a series of mass executions that occurred in a number of locations in and near the Katyn Forest. The victims included officers in the Polish army who were taken prisoner in 1939, as well as members of the Polish intellectual elite arrested for supposed offenses against the Soviet Union. For years, the Soviet authorities claimed the massacre was perpetrated by the Nazis, and the exact numbers of dead and locations of their graves remained shrouded in secrecy. The Polish state, as a satellite of the Soviet Union, could not dispute these statements directly, although it was generally known that the Soviets were responsible for the deaths. Only in 1990, after Poland had already made its historic break with state socialism, did Soviet president Mikhail Gorbachev admit that the Soviet secret police performed the executions. Slowly since then, historical records have been declassified and released by Russia. This gradual disclosure has helped to keep "Katyn" in the news, and a common topic of discussion. Public awareness was further promoted by Academy Award-winning director Andrzej Wajda's film *Katyń*, released in 2007.[9]

The memory of historic events at Katyn has reinscribed national mythological themes of Polish suffering at the hands of deceitful neighbors and sacrifices that have largely gone unrecognized outside of Poland. According to Niżyńska, Katyn "became a symbolic national trauma, a center of gravity in the Polish sense of historical injustice that absorbed and conflated other traumas involving Russia and the sanitization of history" (2011, 470). When the plane crash occurred at essentially the same location in 2010, she observed in herself and others what she calls the "shock of the symbolic absurd" (469). Specifically:

> [It] activated a deeply rooted, almost knee-jerk emotional response that redirected the crash from the empirical plane of the "here and now" to the realm of symbolic imagination, which culturally linked Polish national identity to the experience of pain, suffering, and loss. I could sense the overwhelming emotional power of this imagination as it moved the crash beyond the dimension of a singular tragic event into an "absurd" realm of repeating the "Polish complex."

What was "absurd" about the crash was precisely the clash between a rational understanding of incommensurability between the Katyn forest massacre of 1940 and the plane crash of 2010 and the chain of mental images, associations, symbols, and subliminal cultural resonances that the very place of the crash automatically triggered. (Niżyńska 2011, 470)

Niżyńska describes her surprise that the plane crash activated in her patriotic sentiments that she would normally disparage as a forward-looking, rational, urban, educated Pole. It points to the power of what might be called from a cognitive perspective "fast thinking," linked to emotional connections, even in the face of contrasting "slow thinking," grounded in reasonable assessments of the facts (D'Andrade 2008; Kahneman 2011). National identity seems able to generate these "fast" emotional responses, bolstered by traumatic collective memories inscribed in national mythology.

Despite the uncanny associations with the 1940 massacre, the orderly transition after the 2010 plane crash confirmed the stability of the Polish political system. Just as official protocols dictated, elections for the new president occurred within three months, and Bronisław Komorowski, acting president and candidate of the Civic Platform Party (Platform Obywatelska; PO), defeated Lech Kaczyński's twin brother Jarosław, the candidate of the Law and Justice Party (Prawo i Społeczeństwo; PiS). Key politicians from both parties accepted Russia's expressions of sympathy for the Smolensk tragedy, and responded with conciliatory rhetoric of their own (Niżyńska 2011, 475–6). Nevertheless, it did not take long for the political divisions between the PO and PiS to resurface, exposing deep fractures in Polish society. Participants' claims about the cause of the accident and their criticism of ensuing commemorative acts demonstrate their reluctance to explain the tragedy in terms of national mythology, and suggest a willingness to consider a future within an integrated Europe.

Commemoration and controversy

The power of ethnographic fieldwork is that careful observation and listening can reveal issues of importance that might not find their way into a formal interview protocol. During my visit to Poland in 2011, the issue everyone was talking about was the Smolensk disaster and the social controversy over its commemoration. In fact, it came up in one of the first conversations I had that summer, when I told Basia, who works at a multinational corporation in Warsaw, about the ideas I was developing with regard to past and future orientations. She suggested that the tension between looking back and looking forward have been exposed in disputes about the proper way to commemorate the disaster, and social divisions have been further polarized by rivalries between political parties. Specifically, PiS champions tradition and nationalism, and resists change, neoliberalism and the EU, while future-oriented political parties like PO support EU integration.

Although PiS frames the Smolensk disaster in terms consistent with national mythology, public responses to the tragedy have been more varied. As described in a recent article in the *Guardian*, "While the immediate reaction to the catastrophe showed that national identity and symbols are important to Poles, the ensuing events also revealed how strongly they differ when it comes to the values around which this identity should be built" (Adekoya 2011). Niżyńska points out:

> [Jarosław] Kaczyński's ideology of Polish identity as focused on the memory and celebration of historical traumas presupposed a deep distrust of Russia and Germany. Consequently, Poland's accession to the European Union was suspect to Kaczyński, as the Union represented the danger of tranquilizing the national memory and its quiet pacification for the sake of reconciliation between Union members. (Niżyńska 2011, 473)

During the summer of 2011, however, only 17 per cent of those surveyed in a CBOS (Centrum Badania Opinii Społecznej; Public Opinion Research Center) poll expressed the intention of voting for PiS, while 38 per cent said they plan to vote for the rival PO party in the fall parliamentary elections (Pankowski 2011, 2).[10] Public commentary at the time suggested that declining support for PiS might be due to the growing perception that the party holds extremist viewpoints, and concern that Jarosław Kaczyński, the party's leader and twin brother of the deceased president, is out of control. Similarly, Basia and Piotr, a sales manager in Krakow, both said they believe Jarosław is mentally unbalanced, and this has become more apparent now that his less contentious brother is no longer around to moderate his more extreme ideas. Piotr commented that Jarosław was recently urged to undergo a psychological evaluation (see Siedlecka 2011). Basia told me Jarosław has alienated the most moderate members of PiS, and even kicked some of them out of the party. Other participants, who in the past held favorable views of PiS, blamed the party for the growing divisions among Poles.

Returning to the days immediately following the plane crash, sharp divisions shattered the unity forged from collective grief when it was announced that President Kaczyński and his wife would be buried in Krakow's Wawel Cathedral, the resting place of Polish kings. There was a public outcry against treating Kaczyński as a national hero who died a martyr's death; before the accident, he had generally been regarded as a mediocre and divisive leader.

For example, Ania told me she did not like Kaczyński because he incited conflict and disagreement. In death, she said, he has divided the country even more. Many boycotted the funeral in protest. Ewelina, a lawyer in Krakow, explained that she shared the collective sense of mourning for all the people who died in the plane crash, but that changed when plans for the funeral were announced. She said that burying the Kaczyńskis at Wawel turned the funeral into a political spectacle in which PiS sought to gain prominence. Ewelina also thinks the Catholic Church lost some of its authority by supporting the interment at Wawel Cathedral, because it linked the church with PiS, which is increasingly seen as a fringe party. Nevertheless, because Ewelina's children attend a Catholic school and many of the parents and administrators are socially conservative PiS supporters, her husband took their children to the funeral. She refused to go, but she did not want her children to experience ostracism at school for not attending. In this way, she contributed to the social reproduction of national mythology for the next generation, even as she shaped a counternarrative about these events in the privacy of her memory household.

A second site of commemoration also became a flash point for disputes about national and religious symbols. In Warsaw, a group of scouts erected a wooden cross outside the presidential palace. What ensued was a heated debate, both in the media and at the site of the cross, over the appropriateness of a religious symbol in a civic space. The fact that anyone even questioned the public use of a cross illustrates a marked shift in perception of the role of the Catholic Church in civic life, considering that national commemorations routinely begin with a public Mass, and crosses adorn any number of public monuments.[11] Supporters argued that a cross is an appropriate symbol because Poland is a predominantly Catholic country. Opponents mocked the so-called "defenders of the cross" who continued to mourn and pray at the site; they called for the cross to be moved to a location associated with the Catholic Church. On 3 August 2010 a riot nearly broke out when clergymen came to transfer the cross to a nearby church. The cross remained until late September, protected by a constant vigil composed mainly of elderly female PiS supporters. The most active opponents of the defenders of the cross were by and large younger men and women. Basia, who lives in Warsaw, told me that when she walked by the site in June 2011, she heard a young man making such vitriolic religious comments that she wondered if he was crazy. Basia is herself deeply religious, but she found what he had to say, and the way he said it, very off-putting. She cannot identify with such incendiary commentary. Even though the cross has been removed, I witnessed people still gathered where it used to stand as recently as April 2013; they held a large wooden cross and recited prayers (figure 2.2).

Figure 2.2. Warsaw, April 2013. The "defenders of the cross" return to the presidential palace to commemorate President Lech Kaczyński's death in a plane crash near Katyn

The debates surrounding the Smolensk disaster demonstrate the continued relevance of national mythology, and also reveal the constellations of debate surrounding the traditional portrayal of the Polish nation. Although mythological themes of suffering, threatening neighbors and heroism were deployed, significant segments of the Polish population pushed back against such symbolism. Notably, public debate about appropriate ways of memorializing the Smolensk tragedy is far more confrontational than the opinions expressed by participants in my study. I am reminded of Brubaker et al.'s (2006) observations of the way ordinary citizens reacted to the anti-Hungarian rhetoric and actions of the mayor in Cluj, Romania. For the most part, both ethnic Hungarian and Romanian residents ignored them, and just went about their daily lives. Similarly, in 2011 participants in my study were more likely to talk about their new homes, their children and the general improvement in their lives. If they talked about the political divisions exposed by conflicts over commemorations, it was to criticize radical and divisive forces and condemn the politicians who encourage them.

A country divided? Competing explanations of the tragedy

The question of who was responsible for the plane crash was a central topic in the news during the summer of 2011 (see for example Stankiewicz and Śmiłowicz 2011), and it resonated with participants in a way that other contemporary issues did not. For example, on 1 July, the Polish prime minister Donald Tusk took over the presidency of the EU Council, but only two participants mentioned it during my visit. This key position of leadership in the EU is rotated among member countries for six-month terms, and this was the first time Poland had taken its turn. The contrasting levels of interest in these two concurrent events is consistent with my observation that attachment to nation remains in many ways far more meaningful than a more distant sense of connection with "Europe" (a point I develop in Chapter 4). The constellations of debate about the causes of the crash centered on the question of Russian responsibility on the one hand and Polish carelessness on the other.

Although conspiracy theories have only become more elaborate over time, participants in my study were most likely to blame the pilots and the contemporary state of Polish government and politics for the plane crash, while also maintaining some suspicion about Russian involvement. Piotr said he has no doubt that the bulk of responsibility should be placed on the pilots. As he explained, he knows how pilots are because his father was one; they are prone to arrogance. He thinks the ones flying to Smolensk probably overestimated their own abilities and chose to ignore warnings that the fog was too thick to land safely. Piotr said he is disgusted by the way some people, especially members of PiS, look for conspiracy.[12] Clearly, he says, it was a matter of mistaken bravura on the part of the pilots. Others also pointed fingers at the cockpit crew, but for a different reason. They told me there was an earlier incident in Georgia, in which a pilot refused to land under dangerous conditions, despite the president's demand that he did. As a consequence, the pilot received a reprimand and was never recruited to fly the president's plane again. The pilot in charge of the flight to Smolensk had been the second in command on that flight to Georgia. I was told, "You can draw your own conclusions from that." Similarly, Dominik, a business owner in Krakow, called Polish political authorities "careless" – too caught up in their own power plays to pay attention to hazards others pointed out to them. Thus, some attributed the accident to the hubris of politicians, including the president, whom they suspected had insisted the pilots land as scheduled.

Another area of debate was whether Russians were in some way responsible and whether the Polish government was complicit in a cover-up. None of the participants in my study claimed that the crash was deliberately caused by Russia, but several suggested that Russia (or Russians) might have contributed indirectly to the accident. Marcin, a business owner in Bieszczady, explained that it does not sit well with him that a Russian task force conducted the accident investigation. He asked, "If your neighbor ran over your child, would you trust him to take charge of the investigation into what had happened?" He said he has no doubt the Polish pilots were at fault, but he is also sure that the Russians were in some way responsible. Poles (he made a point of attributing this position to Poles generally, not just himself) are not sure the role of Russians in the accident will ever be addressed fairly because even the Polish report is based on data collected by the Russian task force. Ania, an artist from Krakow, remarked that even though there was no conspiracy, she thinks the people in the control tower probably said something that made the pilot decide to land. Aneta, a television producer, called this kind of speculation "sick," and told me a joke:

A Frenchman, a German, and a Pole are on a plane that is about to crash. The Frenchman is told to jump out of the plane; he refuses until he is told, "But it is very fashionable to jump." So he jumps. Then, the German is told to jump; he refuses until he is told, "I order you to jump." So he jumps. The Pole is told, "You won't jump; you're chicken." So, of course, he jumps.

What spurs the Pole to action is a challenge of his bravery. Aneta is critical of national stereotypes (see her portrait below), but she nevertheless reproduces them in this joke.

Taking yet another position in the constellations of debate surrounding the tragedy, Ania said that she expects that Vladimir Putin and the Russians were glad the accident happened because it diverted attention from the anniversary of the Katyn massacre; instead, everyone was talking about the plane crash. Another of my participants said just the opposite: if Russia's goal was to minimize global attention on the anniversary of Katyn, they would not have engineered a plane crash that would conjure up eerie parallels with the past.

Taken together, these comments reflect a general suspicion of Russians, but they are a far cry from more radical claims about a deliberate plot by Russia.

To summarize, although the context and circumstances of the crash that killed President Kaczyński have provided fodder for conspiracy theories linking the event to historical narratives of Polish suffering at the hands of duplicitous neighbors, most participants explain the event instead in terms of Polish leaders' suspicion and hubris, and pilot errors and incompetence (sometimes also combined with stories of continued Russian–Polish distrust). They are far more inclined to think about the contemporary implications of the disaster and how to move forward than they are to dwell upon parallels with past events. In other words, they are reluctant to seek meaning in connections with the past, preferring instead to look toward the future.

Moving Forward

My approach in this chapter has not been to outline the events that constitute Polish history, but rather to highlight how the past is remembered, evoked and deployed in ways that reinscribe, revise and reinvent group identities. I have examined the history participants refer to in the stories they tell about themselves, and how elements of national mythology shape their self-identity as Poles. I think it is fair to say that all participants have some familiarity with motifs of Polish heroism and messianic martyrdom. They grew up hearing these narratives, both at home and at school. Most have on occasion been moved by them, especially in relation to stories of trauma, dislocation and suffering passed down in families. That is to say, they have internalized emotional attachments to the nation, sometimes even in spite of their more conscious, rational rejection of mythological themes. This comes out particularly in Aneta's life story, recounted below.

Although national mythology is deeply embedded in Polish culture, responses to the death of the president and ensuing controversies about the proper forms of commemoration expose deep social and political divisions. There is no consensus about the relevance of Polish exceptionalism or even about just what should constitute the dominant narrative about the Polish nation. And yet, no narrative with the same emotional weight bolsters attachment to the broader sphere of Europe. I have discussed the competing, and sometimes complementary, strands of romanticism and positivism, and tradition and modernization. As I describe in the next chapter, the orientation toward the past has been challenged, first by the present orientation of late state socialism and the early postcommunist period, and then by a growing future orientation as Poland has become integrated into the EU.

Aneta: Not the Christ of Nations Anymore

Even at 17, when I first met Aneta, she was outgoing and spirited; she liked to be at the center of action, whether she was acting in a youth theater group or just joking around with friends. She told me she felt more mature than her classmates because of her experience in the US, where she spent a year with her uncle's family. When I spoke with her again in 1999, she told me she feels she grew up faster than most of her friends from high school because, rather than just going to university and postponing adulthood, she moved to Warsaw to work on film and television productions. She feeds on the intensity of this kind of work – the long hours and the freedom and uncertainty of freelance employment. Aneta is familiar with messianic nationalism from her upbringing in an elite Krakow family, and from her schooling at a historic lyceum. Though these feelings of attachment bubble up occasionally, more often she laughs at such sentiments, preferring instead to identify with a forward-looking, creative, cosmopolitan social world that transcends national boundaries.

In the years I have known Aneta, she has continually reinvented herself as she has made new friends and pursued new opportunities. Consistent throughout, however, have been her creative drive, cynical humor and fierce independence. She shrewdly brokered an opportunity in the 1990s to work with a German director into a career involving a wide range of media, including music videos, independent films and television productions. Aneta insists that she is disillusioned with politics, even though some of her productions touch on political themes. When I reminded her that in high school she had worked on political campaigns and even said she wanted to be a diplomat, she laughed it off as a phase she went through, when she had a boyfriend who was interested in politics.

In 2005, she explained:

I think that we were complete fools, completely immature back then. The only thing that surprises me is that I thought that once I turn 30, I'll have children; but among my circle of friends, our generation is different from our parents' generation. At our age, namely 30, we live as if we were 25. We push aside questions about responsibility. I keep thinking there is still so much to do, so many things to see, and that there is time for everything.

I began to work in 1997, when there was a lot of money in the kind of television I do. We were 21, 22, we were total brats and we created things that were popular then – music videos and programs – without any knowledge or understanding. We earned a lot of money. Then everything collapsed. That was when I returned to Krakow and I went back to university. Because there was no work at all. It was really difficult in Warsaw; people were laid off.

That's when I began to travel to the US, and to work at [Polish film] festivals, and then as a nanny. And then in 2003, I moved back to Warsaw. And now I see that it's better again. I don't know if it's because we're in the EU, or if it's a natural thing that after a period of decline everything grows again? But I'd say that we all grew up a bit and learned how to work, and respect each other; we now know what we want to do. Now things are better, but I can't talk for all of Poland. So I can only talk about the tiny circle in which I live. We in Warsaw are not representative; it's like a little Polish New York. Everything is faster, more expensive and salaries are higher. In Krakow, I could live really well on what I earn, but here I don't have my own apartment, I don't have a car, I don't even have insurance.

I lived in the States a total of three years, and I could have stayed because I had a boyfriend who wanted to marry me. But I didn't want to. In my opinion, out of all the European cities, I could do the things that I do here only in Berlin or London, because they are connected with film, culture and new media. But I don't think I could live in America. It would be easier there because there is more movement of this kind of thing in young art circles. But is it worthwhile? Maybe it's better to create something from the ground up in Poland. Why push there? Still, many people, my acquaintances, emigrated. Many live in London and have good jobs.

Throughout our whole education, we learned about romantic culture from the Partition period and the nineteenth century. We were raised with the feeling that Poland really is a very special country, that we are such wonderful patriots, and Poland is the "Christ of Nations." And I think that a very important life lesson is to recognize that this is garbage [laugh]. Because every country is very special, and things like the revolutions that happened in Poland happen everywhere.

Sometimes I think I am tossed between such different feelings. On the one hand I have a sense of attachment to my Polishness, and sometimes when I'm abroad I get the feeling, "I have to return to Poland, I love my country" [laugh]. But I have ambivalent feelings toward Poland ... I'm neither proud nor am I embarrassed. It's funny that patriotic songs can move us, who knows why; but these are just momentary feelings. I like this country. I live well here. But I'm nothing like a nationalist.

Do I think EU membership will bring Poland more advantages or disadvantages? Advantages, definitely. I think that young people especially are benefiting. Maybe EU membership will even help overcome the myth of the specialness of Poles, and of our nationalist mythology, if it turns out that in fact we're all similar to each other. That's the first good step.

By 2011, Aneta had expanded her repertoire of accomplishments to include two published books in the genre she calls "documentary fiction." In these narratives, she portrays herself as irreverent, fun loving and critical of most of the people and places she encounters. I was surprised she moved back to Krakow because she has often criticized its provinciality and insularity, but when I asked her about it, she explained she took advantage of an opportunity to finally return. After publishing her books, she was invited to write for television. This is something she can do in Krakow, and take brief trips to Warsaw when necessary. In her life story, Aneta tacks between criticism of the nation and bewilderment when she nevertheless catches herself feeling sentiments of attachment (not unlike the emotions Niżyńska expressed in relation to the Smolensk disaster). At times, she seems to be fighting with herself about what she believes, and is startled when she becomes aware of the unmarked ways in which the nation is salient to her sense of self.

None of the participants accept unambiguously the messianic narrative about Polish culture. While references to Polish history were made in life stories, usually when discussing topics like patriotism, attachment to place and democracy, ideas of Poland's "specialness" (to borrow Aneta's word) were often contested or even rejected. Sometimes, as we have seen with Bartek, alternative narratives more closely associated with a specific region of Poland have greater emotional force and everyday relevance than the national narrative. In life stories, we witness the creative self in the process of making meaning. The nation is salient, even as a focus of resistance. Europe is less so, though it can function as a point of contrast, or less often solidarity.

Chapter 3

"UNBELIEVABLE! POLES ARE HAPPY": LOOKING TOWARD THE FUTURE

Józef: Building a Future

Józef's ancestors lived for generations in a mountain village that was flooded when the massive Solina dam was built by the state-socialist government in the late 1960s. Józef grew up on the edge of the reservoir, where displaced residents were relocated. The child of farmers, he attended the agricultural high school in Lesko. As he describes below, his decision to get a higher education was not part of a life plan. Rather, he responded to historical circumstances, made decisions based on his friendships, and took advantage of chance opportunities. Like most of the participants in this study, during his teens and early twenties, Józef and his close friends Przemek, Darek and Maciek tended not to think about the future. While it seemed likely that state socialism was a thing of the past, there was still a great deal of uncertainty about the direction the country would take. Instead, Józef adopted a "wait and see" attitude, and remained open to whatever opportunities came his way. This strategy worked for him in that, by the time he graduated from college, he managed to land a good job in public administration. Over the years, he has gained a position of prominence in local government, and built a spacious home on a hill overlooking his native village, where he lives with his wife and three children.

In 2005, he told his story as follows:

> When I was in school, I was one of those kids who didn't know what I wanted to do. I didn't know what I was capable of doing. I was lucky to find my way to the university, and later to my job. After we finished technical [high] school, none of my friends had any concrete plans. One day, Przemek and I decided to go to Rzeszów and look for a university. We didn't know what else to do. We ended up submitting our papers at the WSP [Wyższa Szkoła Pedagogiczna; teachers college], where we had heard it was easy to get into. Darek and Maciek ended up going to the Studium Medyczne [a two-year medical college] in Sanok. Then,

Przemek heard about the possibility of getting into the Akademia Rolnicza [agricultural university] in the economics program, so he went and took the exam. So I borrowed my papers from the WSP, and applied at the Akademia Rolnicza, too. I passed the entrance exam, which was very easy, and ended up spending five more years studying with Przemek. It is always more pleasant when you have someone you know around.

After finishing their program, Darek and Maciek both managed to get jobs as nurses. After I graduated, I sat at home for six months. Again I had no idea what I was going to do. Then, a local government official mentioned that a position was available at the regional office nearby and maybe I should go and ask about it. So I went, and got the job. Even though my education is in agriculture, 80 per cent of my position involves matters associated with forestry, and only 20 per cent associated with agriculture. I'm also responsible for tourist information, things like brochures about the region. Przemek got a job in Bieszczady as well, at the power plant at the Solina dam. I like my job because I have the freedom to go into the field when I'm tired of sitting at my desk.

I feel like a European and a Pole. And I don't have any complexes that others are German or French. I am a Pole. Do I have a strong attachment to Europe? Maybe I don't yet. We've only been in Europe for a year, so maybe we haven't learned to identify with Europe yet. But I think it has some kind of influence, that we will feel European. Maybe not us so much, but our children will, more likely. There are still problems with understanding each other. I don't know English or German, so I can't speak freely with others. Maybe this puts the brakes on feeling I'm European.

I must admit, I feel even more attached to this region than to Europe or Poland. This is my "little fatherland" [mała ojczyzna]. This village is like the shirt closest to my body. I wouldn't trade these views for anything. The landscape is distinct, the people are open. Of course it's still necessary to work to make it great. I'm trying to make it better.

When I visited Józef in 2011, his economic situation and his outlook on the future had continued to improve. In addition to his new home, he had two cabins to rent to tourists, and a new car big enough to fit three child seats in the back. He explained:[1]

My wife and I had the good fortune to both find work nearby. Many people in this village live off of the two-month tourist season, and just sit around for the rest of the year. What kind of life is that? Maybe our salaries aren't the highest, but we have been able to earn enough to pay for our home and car, and to support our three children.

Tourism in my village has grown steadily. There are now 800 places for tourists, compared to a permanent population of just 230 residents. No one really farms anymore. Maybe older people have one cow, but it doesn't pay. Many people leave and don't come back, especially if they have families abroad, they have jobs and their kids go to school. But many are investing here also, building cabins to make some money, and also to have a place to come back to one day, even if it's for their retirement. Compared with other European countries, Poland has nothing to be ashamed of at this point. We have always compared ourselves with Germany, the highest standard [in Europe]. But, with our recent economic growth, Poland has nearly reached the standard of countries like Greece, Italy and Portugal. And a friend who has lived in England told me you can drive out of London and find living conditions worse than in Poland. Poles have nothing to be ashamed of. The global crisis hasn't affected Poland so much. Most people don't feel it because Poland has such a large internal market. Furthermore, everyone is building right now.

Józef's life story illustrates a striking shift in temporality from a present orientation to a future orientation. When I shared my ideas for this chapter with him, he explained the present orientation of his youth in terms of the uncertainty people were experiencing. He also suggested age is a factor; now that they are older, it has become more important to think about the future. In addition, he said they have to plan for things like retirement and insurance coverage because they can no longer count on state social welfare provisions.

Unbelievable! Poles Are Happy!

The point I make in this chapter is that since 1989, the tendency to explain the present in terms of the past has been superseded, initially by preoccupation with the present, and more recently by future-oriented perspectives. Briefly, when participants were in high school in the early 1990s, political and economic insecurity made them reluctant to look forward or backward to explain their lives or their nation. Instead, they focused on the present; they adopted a "wait and see" attitude and sought ways of prolonging their youth (often by staying in school) until the situation in Poland stabilized. By 2000, most were settling into adult roles, with full-time jobs and spouses, but still unsure about their future as Poland established its position within global capitalism (as illustrated, for example, in their reluctance to have children despite the high value they placed on parenthood and family).[2] Since Poland joined the EU, there has been a marked shift toward future-oriented perspectives. With notable exceptions that I describe below, they have plans and expectations, and confidence that economic advancement in Poland will continue. Thus, accompanying this change in temporality is a corresponding shift in dispositions, which I argue are influenced by Poland's improved standing within a social imaginary of world countries, and associated real-world opportunities in everyday lives.

Figure 3.1. "Unbelievable! Poles Are Happy!" *Polityka* cover, 13–19 July 2011

Participants in my study seemed surprised by this development. In fact, surprise appears to be a common reaction, as illustrated by a recent cover of the weekly news magazine *Polityka* (figure 3.1), whose headline reads "Unbelievable! Poles Are Happy!" (Żakowski 2011).

Reviewing my field notes from the summer of 2011, I was struck by the answers I received when I asked whether Poles are happy people:

> Danuta, a school teacher in Bieszczady, said that maybe people are becoming happier, but they still complain. Even when things are good, they complain about what they still don't have.

> I asked Halina, a farmer in Bieszczady, if she thinks Poles are happy people. She paused, and replied slowly that she's happy. She has a good husband, and a good marriage. But for many, life is very hard. She gave the example of retirees living on miniscule pensions (450 zloty per month). "How can you live on that? They do because they have to."

I asked Ania, an artist in Krakow, if she thinks Poles are happy people. She hesitated, but said they should be. They live better and better.

I asked Michał, a real estate broker in Krakow, about the article that said that Poles are happy. He said he can't complain, with a small smile on his face.

Dominik, a business owner in Krakow, responded, "I'm happy. Poles like to complain, but in fact, things are okay."

These responses do not reflect the "dark Slavic soul" that has historically been associated with experiences of oppression and foreign domination. It is still notable, however, that although participants agreed with the claim that "Poles are happy people," they usually hesitated to admit it. Most felt the need to point out that others are still struggling, or that Poles tend to complain. Nevertheless, they attributed this newfound happiness to better economic conditions, and the sense that their situation would continue to improve.

My visit in 2011 was important for a number of reasons. I wanted to see how participants in my study were doing (after all, I consider most of them friends). I was pleased to see that most were getting along just fine, and also that they were at a relatively stable point in their lives. Few had changed their place of employment since we last met in 2008, though some had moved into new homes and had more children. I had neither an interview protocol nor even a concrete set of topics to discuss with them. Instead, I relied on the inductive method that is characteristic of ethnographic fieldwork; through participant observation, certain key social issues emerged as central preoccupations of the people I encountered. Mostly, we talked about family, children, jobs and home renovations. These discussions confirmed to me that most participants had experienced a profound shift in temporal orientation, toward the future rather than the past. This chapter links the emergent orientation toward the future to the growth of stable political and economic institutions. Poland's processes of democratization and market liberalization predated EU conditionality, but they have been further nurtured by European integration. Person-centered analysis suggests that positive dispositions toward the future may in turn lend legitimacy to participation in the EU, as long as European integration promotes individuals' ability to work toward their personal life goals.

The 1990s: Living in the Present

The failure of state socialism was broadly understood in economic terms – the inefficiency of state-run industries, the growing consumer economy in the West, and the inability of the command economy to satisfy citizens' wants and

Figure 3.2. The liquidated state farm in Lesko was still empty and for sale in 2008

needs. Still, the shortcomings of the former regime did not prepare people for the deprivations of the transition to global capitalism. The new government instituted "shock therapy," the idea being to simultaneously open markets, float the currency on international exchanges, withdraw government regulation of the economy, liquidate unprofitable state industries and privatize the viable industries (Balcerowicz 1994; Sachs 1993). Economic advisors knew this would be painful to most citizens, but they promised the economy would start to work on its own before any organized opposition took shape (Balcerowicz 1994, 54). In fact, the dismantling of the command economy and development of global capitalist structures was far more complex and lengthy than early reformers promised, and years later former state enterprises still stood empty (figure 3.2). In the early 1990s, people throughout the postsocialist region did not know what to expect of the future. New political and economic institutions were still being established, and the relationship between the government and citizens was being redefined (see Galbraith 2000, 2003b; Kideckel 2008; Verdery 1996; West 2001).

With regard to issues of security, it would be hard to overstate the profound transformation in people's lives when, following the fall of state socialism, social services and social supports were curtailed. Under state socialism, the government assumed responsibility for insuring that all capable adults had a job, healthcare and even vacations to the mountains or the sea coast. Since 1989, the trend has been to pass responsibility from the public sector to the private sector. Correspondingly, new expectations have been placed on individuals to take responsibility for their own well-being, what Dunn (2004) describes as the remaking of persons, produced by government policies of privatization and economic liberalization. At the root of much social anxiety about these reforms is what has been called the "privatization of risk," a key characteristic of neoliberal contexts generally (see Beck 1992; Giddens 1991). The expansion of a "risk society" (Beck 1992) is felt particularly strongly in postcommunist contexts due to the rapid retreat of guarantees formerly provided by paternalistic states (see Dunn 2004).

Social and economic instability was particularly critical for young adults trying to decide what career path to follow. Because unemployment rates for recent high school graduates hovered around fifty per cent, many decided to stay in school as long as they could. At worst, this would postpone their entrance into the ranks of the unemployed, and at best the economy would improve and they might actually learn skills that would enable them to get jobs. Participants said they prefer not to think too seriously about the future, and in this way maintained a generalized sense that conditions were bound to get better. "Things have to get better because they can't get any worse," they explained. Many, like Józef, adopted a "wait and see" attitude, hoping that once they finished school or university conditions would stabilize and a "normal" life would be possible.[3] A person-centered approach reveals how participants adjusted, not by adopting traits commonly rewarded in global capitalism, but rather by falling back on tactics developed during state socialism.

A number of studies note the preoccupation with the present during state socialism; people were so busy seeking out scarce resources, standing in line and making do with what they were able to acquire, they had little time to reflect upon much else, including political protest (Ries 1997; Wedel 1986). In a 1993 interview in *Gazeta Wyborcza*, sociologist Elżbieta Tarkowska presented a compelling argument why, even after the fall of state socialism, Poles tended to perceive linear time differently than is typical in the West: "[Poles have] an unusually shortened perspective on the future; they live primarily in the present, they fear what might come in the future, and because of this they have an emotional relationship with the past. The most important consequence comes from this blocked future. We cannot think of it. It paralyzes us" (Bogucka 1993, 8). Tarkowska characterized this shortened time depth as a response to crises that have both historical and psychological dimensions. Those who face difficult and uncertain conditions in the present, such as war, political oppression or unemployment, tend not to think about the future for two reasons. First, most of their energy is expended on figuring out how to get by in the present, and second, they are afraid to anticipate what the future may be like. Tarkowska contrasted this with Americans, whom she characterized as compulsively future-oriented; they plan everything from careers to vacations to starting a family, and devote much of their energy to achieving goals. She asserted that Americans are able to make plans because they have a stable notion of what conditions will be like in the future, and can therefore make informed decisions about the likely outcome of their choices.

It was exactly this kind of certainty about present and future that participants lacked in the 1990s, making it difficult for them to pursue concrete plans. The irony, of course, is that champions of global capitalism promised a better life – one characterized by greater opportunity and affluence – and at the same time pushed Poland (and other postsocialist countries) toward a "risk society" in which the state withdraws provisions for the social welfare of citizens (see Beck 1992). I am reminded of a conversation I had with some girls in Lesko who were preparing for *matura* (their final exams) at a technical high school in 1993. We were having cokes and pretzels at a cafe in the town's castle. Mostly, the students were preoccupied with their final exams, but they also made vague comments about what they were going to do after graduation. I remarked that I never would have guessed how much Poland would change in the four years between my first visit in 1986 and my second in 1990. I wondered what Poland will be like in another four years. Julia laughed and responded, "I don't like to speculate about what might happen tomorrow or next week, let alone several years from now." She explained that thinking about the future just underlines the uncertainty they face. When asked about the future, high school students most often commented that they just wanted to enjoy themselves while they still had few responsibilities (they talked about it in terms of *beztroska młodości*, the carelessness of youth). Another characteristic response was that they prefer not to think about the future because they see everything "in dark colors" (*w ciemnych kolorach*). Nevertheless, usually when we talked in private, they lamented about the limited choices open to them, and expressed a sense of powerlessness to control their fate.

During a group interview in 1992, students attending a college preparatory high school in Lesko described some of their friends as follows:

JANEK: Our friends who finished trade school already have jobs, or they collect *zasiłek* [unemployment compensation] and they just sit around now, and get their 700,000 zloty.[4] And for most ...
ANDRZEJ: It's vegetation.
JANEK: It's a kind of vegetation, living day-to-day.
ANDRZEJ: Lately apathy has grown in Poland.

JANEK: A social apathy, Andrzej's right. We still somehow have hope that
            after we finish our studies, maybe after five years something will
            change.
PRZEMEK: It will be better.
JANEK: But there are very many people who sit on unemployment after
            trade school, and there's nothing [no social programs] to help them.
            The majority just wanders the streets.

Unemployment was described with metaphors of immobility and lack of
direction – vegetation, sitting, living day-to-day and wandering the streets. It
was not what people chose, but rather what happened to them because neither
a job nor special training programs were available. Lyceum students felt less
directly threatened by unemployment because they had chosen to invest more
time and effort into their education, and generally they felt that education
would open possibilities that would otherwise be unobtainable.

In 1993 I spent graduation day at the agricultural high school in Lesko. The
students had initially started a three-year trade school program in 1987. At the
time, about forty per cent of high school students attended trade programs
that emphasized job training without granting a high school diploma. By the
time these students completed their program in 1990, state socialism had
fallen, and the agricultural sector collapsed. With no idea what else to do,
they decided to stay in school to earn a high school diploma through a three-
year technical program (one that combines academic and vocational training).
They did not expect it to improve their chances of employment, but rather
saw it as a way of postponing having to face the lack of prospects for work.

Uncertainty about the future influenced the principal's speech at their
graduation ceremony. He advised students to remember the moral lessons
they learned at school. He told them that times are hard now, but they should
go into the world with hope. He reminded them about values associated with
honor, nation and religion. They should be patriots and remember what
the country has given them – it took care of them, helped them grow and
provided them with an education. Just one year earlier, this same principal's
graduation speech had emphasized the important skills graduating seniors
had learned. By contrast, in 1993 he advised graduates to fall back on moral
lessons and hope. Notably absent was any specific reference to the viability of
the agricultural training they had received. Indeed, these graduates finished
school during the awkward period when both the educational system and
agricultural production were in the process of reform; their classes had taught
them how to manage the very state farms that were being liquidated.

After the ceremony, the graduates met one last time for a bonfire in a
neighboring village. As the evening progressed, and everyone had their fair

share of vodka, the tongues of the usually reticent boys loosened. The girls said little that night, but they had shared similar stories with me on other occasions. Notably, none of the graduates had a plan for the future. Several were going back to their villages, even though there was no way to make a profit as a small family farmer in the changing economy. None had enough money to go to college, which would have required moving to a city anyway. Some were considering going abroad to work, despite protests by others that life would be no easier in another country. One of the girls had no plans beyond caring for her newborn daughter, and perhaps applying for a job at the local prison. Marcin was the only one with concrete hopes for the future; he dreamed of becoming a musician. Still, because his girlfriend was pregnant, they were getting married right after graduation. Then they were going to live with her family since neither of them had steady jobs. The boys expressed regret that the simple carefree days were over, and they probably would not see much of each other anymore; they approached the future with reluctance and resignation. Expressing both his sense of fatalism and *beztroska młodości*, Marcin comforted his classmates: "God decides what will be, whether life or death. All we can do is accept our fate." Then, he picked up his guitar and sang a cheerful song.

The graduates' comments echo Tarkowska's characterization of a collective uncertainty about the future:

> Responses to an unclear and threatening future take the form of passivity and waiting. Today we are a society that waits. Nor are we waiting for the effects of our work. We wait for a miracle. We wait impatiently for [the time] when it will finally be Switzerland or Sweden here. No one is interested in how to act in order to create that Western affluence, people just wonder: when [will it arrive]? (Bogucka 1993, 8)

Just as this passage suggests, some graduates in 1993 were headed home to wait for better times. However, others felt pushed to seek opportunities abroad. In this, we can see one of the ways that "Western Europe" played an important role in participants' social imaginary (and for Poles generally) as a model for the kind of place in which they wanted to live. However, Tarkowska associates this longed-for future with Western levels of affluence coming to Poland, while the boys at the bonfire had little hope that their native place would resemble Western Europe anytime soon. Rather, they looked toward the West as a place of refuge – a place to find work and to gain the material well-being that was out of reach in Poland.

In fact, most of the participants in my study did not just sit around doing nothing while they waited for economic conditions in Poland to improve. Many, like Józef and his friends, enrolled in university or professional training programs. Others, like Paulina, joined the undocumented workforce in Western Europe:

> I finished technical school without any prospects for the future. We had no work, we were at a complete zero. In other words, we threw our five years of high school in the mud because we didn't have money for university. With just a technical school education, we didn't have the option of going to work because there was no work. There was no work for us. Many people like me had to go abroad, beginning with their parents, who already worked abroad. For example, my mother had to go abroad to earn money to support the family.

The way Paulina repeated "there was no work" highlights the profound shock she, and indeed many Poles, experienced when unemployment rates, which had been nonexistent during state socialism, shot up to 20 per cent in rural regions like Bieszczady and to 50 per cent for 18- to 24-year-olds entering the workforce (Czarnocka 1992; Życie Warszawy 1994). Paulina went to Italy with very little thought about the future. In 2005, she explained, "I went to see the world, to make a little money, and to have some fun. But then I met my husband. I didn't realize that when you marry a man in another country, you'll miss your own country and family. I only realized this after two or three years."

Democratic capitalism requires self-motivated citizens who actively pursue opportunities to improve their well-being. This notion is familiar to Poles, who never totally gave up free enterprise even under communism. Nevertheless, given uncertain everyday conditions, people who wait are less likely to be disappointed when conditions change; as long as they have not placed their hopes in any particular outcome, they are more likely to recognize the advantage that might be gained from unexpected circumstances. In the 1990s, clear pathways to economic security were not yet established in Poland. In 1992, a student at a semiprivate lyceum in Krakow explained, "I don't have concrete plans because I don't know what profession will be profitable. I might start in one discipline, then find that it fails [to be a good career choice]. It will be hard for us in our school year to choose." This approach resembles what de Certeau (1984) calls tactics; without institutional pathways to power, people would "make do" by using whatever means they could and by taking advantage of opportunities as they arose. Success tended to come out of idiosyncratic opportunities rather than established channels. As Kaufman (1989) noted with regard to romantic dreams of national sovereignty, in the immediate aftermath of the fall of state socialism, waiting for "miracles" often proved a more realistic way of overcoming uncertainty than working consistently toward a clearly defined goal.

The good sense of participants' "wait and see" approach to the future has been confirmed by my visits to Poland since 1997 (figure 3.3). By the late

Figure 3.3. In the late 1990s, construction of new apartments such as these in Krakow signalled economic development and growing confidence in the future

1990s, most participants had weathered the difficult challenges associated with the dismantling of state socialism. Despite varying degrees of success finding their place in the new system, they no longer had the sense that the ground was shifting under them. Urban participants in particular expressed complacency about their future, in marked contrast to the uncertainty that plagued them just a few years earlier, and even those whose prospects remained grim seemed more oriented toward coping with what was available to them. By 2008, most rural participants also said they were doing much better and expressed confidence about what the future will bring.

The Twenty-First Century: Looking toward the Future

By and large, by 2011 participants had a sense of having arrived at, or at least of being well on their way to, a better life. They had hopes and plans for the future. For example, when I met Aneta at the bar she had recently opened with some friends, I mentioned the shift I had observed toward a future orientation. She responded, "Finally." For people like her – young, urban, educated and innovative – the changes of the past twenty years have made all kinds of things possible. Overall, they are better off than their parents, free to travel where they wish, and well-positioned to take advantage of new opportunities as they arise.

Of course, the success of some makes it all the more painful for others who feel left behind by the very same historic processes. Participants in my study do not have to look far to find relatives and friends who are not doing well, and who do not look toward the future with the same degree of confidence that they do. Most of the people who expressed more grim views in 2011 were older. For example, Pan Sławek, who receives a disability subsidy for a heart condition, suggested to me that I "sit a while with the old men drinking on park benches around Lesko and ask them if things are better." Similarly, Zosia's mother, Pani Józefa, used phrases that many repeated like a mantra in the early 1990s, such as "it's worse and worse" (*jest coraz gorzej*) and "there are no possibilities" (*nie ma możliwości*).

Just a few participants still use these expressions themselves. Grzesiek has struggled to establish his own computer repair business in Krakow. It has been difficult to compete with larger companies, and the EU subsidies he has heard about are only available for new businesses, not for ones like his that have been around for a few years. Bogdan adamantly opposed Poland's accession to the EU; he called the EU another form of centralized leadership, just like communism was. He also said the EU benefits countries who started it, and each group of new member states gains progressively less from joining. Agata said she sees little hope in EU membership, and anticipates it will cause the downfall of small family farms like her own. Despite their pessimistic views of integration into the European Union, Grzesiek, Bogdan and Agata articulated their own individual hopes for a better future: Grzesiek wants his business to be successful; Bogdan criticizes his boss for instituting EU policies without considering more forward-looking, efficient and environmentally responsible practices; Agata is building a *karczma*, something like an old-fashioned inn where tourists can eat and spend the night. Notably, it is not that these individuals lack a future orientation, but rather they do not believe EU membership will help them achieve their goals.

Four practices reflect the growing future orientation among participants: pursuing higher education, obtaining mortgages, having children and planning for retirement. These practices emerge out of, and reinforce, the increased sense of security and predictability participants experience in their daily lives, despite the privatization of risk. In the next sections I link these practices to EU integration by identifying the associated policy changes that have made these kinds of projections into the future possible.

Education

"Everyone is studying now," Polish friends have told me over the past several years. For example, Czarek remarked that because it is impossible to make a living as a farmer in his village, even people in their forties or fifties have enrolled in programs in marketing or management.

During state socialism, the Polish education system favored technical and trade education, as reflected in the kinds of degrees students earned. When I began my study in 1991, 40 per cent of high school students attended three-year trade programs that provided vocational training but did not qualify them for higher education. Of those in schools that granted high school diplomas, more than half attended technical programs that taught both academic subjects and vocational skills. By 1993, the education system was shifting away from this vocational orientation toward a college preparatory emphasis. Simultaneously, the variety and number of postsecondary programs of higher education were exploding, including: private universities; new degree programs; night, weekend and part-time programs; and advanced professional training in areas like nursing, business and languages.[5]

Thus, participants in this study who chose to postpone their search for a job by continuing their studies had many educational pathways to choose from. According to the OECD (Organization for Economic Cooperation and Development) data, the percentage of Polish 25- to 64-year-olds who completed university increased from 10 per cent in 1997 to 21 per cent in 2009 (OECD 2011, 42). The growth in educational achievement among younger generations is even more marked; thirty-five per cent of 25- to 34-year-olds have completed university (OECD 2011, 40). Efforts to harmonize the Polish education system with EU standards has only strengthened the trend toward higher educational attainment by offering more degree completion programs for working adults, and by replacing five-year master's programs, which was the norm until recently, with two-step programs in which students first obtain a *licencjat* (similar to an American bachelor's degree) and then a master's degree.

Basia is a graduate of one of the first private business schools in Poland. Even though her degree helped her land a job in a multinational corporation, she has continued to further her education by earning a second degree in public relations and learning foreign languages in her free time. She says she likes to expand her knowledge of new things, but also these additional skills give her a competitive edge in her professional career. In fact, nearly all of the participants living in urban areas have pursued some sort of supplemental professional training in recent years. No doubt this inclination to learn is in part an artifact of the criteria by which I originally invited high school students to participate in individual interviews; I sought out the students who were most articulate in group interviews, and who seemed interested and willing to engage with me in conversations about national identity and social transformation. Nevertheless, the national statistics cited above confirm the general trend toward greater educational achievement since the early 1990s. I have also witnessed the growth of interest in higher education among rural participants, including some who were not academically inclined in high school. Józef and his friends, featured in the portrait at the beginning of the chapter, are representative of the way many pursued higher education because they did not know what else to do after finishing school. They have since landed in professions that require periodic training. Another trend is that participants' younger siblings are more likely to have completed university than their older ones.

Other participants' life stories also illustrate the increased relevance of higher education for job security. Agnieszka, another Bieszczady resident, only had a two-year diploma in 2005. She, like a number of participants, feared she would lose her job unless she returned to get a *licencjat* and master's degree in her profession. She had already enrolled in a weekend program when she learned she was pregnant. Initially, she thought she would have to give up on further studies, but when her baby was a few months old, she started leaving both her children in the care of her husband and father and traveling eight hours by bus on alternate weekends to take classes in Warsaw. When I visited in 2011, Agnieszka had successfully completed her *licencjat*, and had already decided on the topic of her master's thesis. She was expecting again, but was confident a third child would not stop her from completing her degree. Similarly, Ewelina, who has a good job in the legal department of a utility company, is studying for a doctorate. She says she is doing it for professional reasons: "Everyone has a master's degree now," she explained, "so you need more to advance." The greater emphasis on higher education can also be seen in participants' aspirations for their children. Marcin, who only completed technical high school himself, is proud of his daughter, who gets good grades and wants to go to university. Marcin is encouraging her to consider a profession like dentistry in which she can earn a good living.

The rise in participation in higher education is all the more striking because most students pay tuition now, particularly returning students who attend weekend, evening or part-time programs. Subsidized higher education, which under state socialism was provided to all students, is only available for high school graduates with the highest test scores who are admitted to public universities on a full-time basis. A number of participants commented in 2011 that the rate of university attendance has increased so sharply and so quickly that it is getting harder for graduates to find work, and there are fewer specialists in technical trades. For example, Marcin, despite his hopes that his daughter will continue her education, also remarked, "There are too many people today with master's degrees in Poland, but there is not enough work for them. Instead, there is a shortage of experts in the building trades; people don't want to do that work because the wages are too low. Today, everyone is going to university, even retirees, or working people who go part-time."

Mortgages

Jurek, who is an architect in Krakow, said, "Building a home marks a life stage – in Poland particularly – because it isn't like homes are commonly bought and sold, rather a home is a kind of symbol. There's a saying, 'Build a house, plant a tree, and have a son.'" Having one's own home is an important marker of adulthood, and the increased availability of mortgages and reasonable interest rates has made it easier to obtain one.

Mortgage loans only began to be common practice in Poland in the 2000s. During state socialism, much of the existing housing stock was in state-owned or cooperative apartment complexes, and chronic shortages of new housing meant that children lived with their parents long after they married and had children of their own. Through the 1990s, even as more housing was built, mortgages remained rare. In rural areas, many continued the practice of building their homes in fits and starts as they could afford to, and doing much of the labor themselves. Most homebuilding was financed by temporary employment abroad. Interest rates were high because of the instability of the Polish currency and high rates of inflation. As the financial sector stabilized, both encouraged by and encouraging foreign investment, mortgages became easier to obtain, especially when loans in more stable foreign currencies were offered to borrowers at substantially lower interest rates. By 2008, 70 per cent of Polish mortgages were in foreign currencies (Strojwas 2010; cited in Leven 2011, 184). Growth in the housing market has remained steady, contributing to the Polish economy's resilience during the economic crisis that struck the US and Europe in 2008 (Leven 2011). The stabilization of the financial sector, and the availability of credit that has resulted, has been a powerful contributor to participants' ability to plan for their future by investing in private real estate.

Indeed, during my visit in 2011, it seemed that just about everyone I knew had recently moved or renovated their homes. Józef, whose story started this chapter, provides a good example of the changes in participants' residence patterns since the early 1990s. Until the mid-2000s, he lived in the same farmhouse in which he and his three siblings had grown up. As his brothers married, various sections of the house were subdivided into semi-independent households for them. Similarly, Józef and his wife spent their first years together in the upstairs section of the house. The number of kitchens is the clearest marker of separate households within the same structure; in Józef's parents' house there are three kitchens, meaning that his parents and as many as two siblings have lived in the house with their respective spouses and children.[6] By the late 2000s, two of the siblings, including Józef, had built their own homes on land deeded to them by their parents, and a third lived with his wife's family. The fourth continued to live with their parents, and had put an addition on the house to better accommodate his growing family. Józef built his house over a number of years; he and his brothers did much of the work themselves, only calling on experts for the most specialized tasks. Józef explained that he does not like to be in debt so he relied on savings from brief periods of work in Germany, except for a small loan in Swiss francs. It was not quite enough to finish the garage, but he preferred to postpone its completion rather than get a larger loan.

Some urban participants have recently sold smaller apartments and used their profits for down payments on larger places that require bigger mortgages. The process went smoothly for Ewelina and her husband, who secured a buyer for their old apartment before buying their new house. For Basia, the transition was a bit rockier. Through a combination of savings, short-term loans from family and a new mortgage, she had calculated that she would just about be able to afford to stay in her old apartment for a couple of months while she did essential renovations on her new place. Then, the buyer she had for her old apartment was denied a loan, leaving her with two mortgage payments for a few anxious months until she found another buyer. Her new mortgage payments are about half her monthly pension. "That's a lot of money," she said, "but I remember how I managed when I got my first apartment. Then, too, much of my salary went toward the mortgage, and I had little left over for entertainment and other pleasures. But over time it got easier. My salary increased, but the payments remained the same." What is notable about Basia's calculations is that plans for the future are predicated on a stable economic system in which she expects her employment status to improve.

Not everyone is willing to go into debt like this, not because they are less certain about the future, but rather because they envision a different future for themselves and their family. Wala, a Lesko resident who runs a small business remarked, "People complain they have no money, but then on the other hand, everyone is building or renovating, and everyone is going on vacation." She criticized people who get into debt until retirement, including friends whose whole pensions go to paying the mortgage while their spouse's salary covers other essential expenses. "They never go anywhere, never have anything extra to go out to eat. What kind of a life is that?" she asked. "What are they going to do, just sit in their pretty house? What about giving their children experiences they will remember?"

Children

Participants' decisions about parenthood reflect a growing future orientation as well. Although a few participants had children right out of high school or shortly thereafter, most waited. This was common among their generation, as is reflected in the sharp decline in births after 1989. By 2003, Poland had a birthrate of 1.23, one of the lowest in Europe. The rate has since climbed a bit, and my participants' life stories suggest some reasons for this. Essentially, the reluctance to have children was for many a direct response to the uncertainty they faced in the early years of postsocialism, and consistent with the present orientation and "wait and see" attitude I have described above (see also Galbraith 2008). Most have achieved a degree of economic security in the ensuing years, which gives them confidence they will be able to provide their children with a reasonable quality of life. As a result, they have been having children at the same time as a younger generation, still in their twenties, who came of age in more secure times and so have not postponed parenthood (or at least have not done so in the same numbers for the same reasons). This increased confidence in the ability to remain economically secure even after becoming a parent is well illustrated by Wiola's life story (told in greater detail below; see also Ewelina's life story in Chapter 5). When she became pregnant the first time, she was terrified she might lose her job because of it. In 2011, she was hoping for a third child, confident her employer would accommodate her right to maternity leave and sure she would be able to find another job if she lost the one she had.

The reluctance to have children in the 1990s can also be traced, I believe, to the privatization of risk as the government rolled back provisions for childcare leave (Galbraith 2008). Even more significantly, few private sector employers considered it their responsibility to make provisions that would facilitate an employee's ability to reconcile obligations at home and work (and usually, the responsibility for home and children has fallen disproportionately on mothers). Within the framework of neoliberal capitalism, what makes companies flexible, competitive and efficient contributes to workers' insecurity; they could lose their jobs at any time should they be seen as underperforming, or should the company face economic difficulties or simply change its business strategy (Dunn 2004; Pine 1998). Some private sector firms pressured employees to agree to long hours and irregular schedules, and even in some cases had employees sign written declarations that they are not pregnant, they are not planning to become pregnant and they will not take time off if their child gets sick (Heinen 2002; Heinen and Wator 2006, 197). Even though there are laws that protect working mothers, the social climate was such that employers nevertheless felt entitled to demand women voluntarily gave up legally guaranteed maternity privileges or risk losing their jobs. The threats were real; because of high rates of unemployment, there was no shortage of candidates eager to replace women who went on temporary maternity leave. Furthermore, the logic of market capitalism is such that it requires businesses to prioritize efficiency, and in particular to minimize labor costs. By this logic, women who are entitled by law to take paid leave become less attractive for employment in the first place (see Gliniecki 2006). Thus, workers were expected to be flexible and to constantly reshape themselves to better fit company needs, without any corresponding expectation that employers provide flexible work schedules in return.

While the logic of neoliberal capitalism remains the dominant paradigm, EU integration seems, at least for now, to have helped the Polish unemployment rate decline, in part because of the mass migration of young Poles to work in other EU countries. Correspondingly, Polish workers feel less pressure to postpone parenthood to keep their jobs. Post accession, participants also expressed increasing satisfaction that the standard of living in Poland is improving. With this positive outlook on the future, more participants have chosen to invest in more children.

Retirement

Since participants in my study were still in their thirties, it surprised me how many of them were already anticipating a time in the near future when they would no longer be able to work as hard. For instance, in addition to his day job as a nurse, Darek has been in a band since high school. He told me that the late nights and long hours traveling to weddings and music festivals are getting harder to do, and it is time to think about resting. He no longer does weekday performances, and has taken on more responsibility at the hospital to help make up some lost income. It helps to consider that Poles have tended to retire at a relatively young age. Until 1998, the retirement age for men was 60 and for women it was 55. Although retirement system reforms have set out to change this, the average age at retirement in Poland remains one of the lowest in Europe, and under thirty per cent of 55- to 64-year-olds are employed, in contrast to an EU average over forty per cent (Chlon-Dominczak 2009, 2).

Planning for retirement has also become a necessity due to structural changes in the pension system. Under state socialism, retirement pensions were government funded. This was characteristic of the paternal role the state filled in citizens' lives, and also a direct outcome of the fact that most jobs were in state-run enterprises. Correspondingly, most Poles were state-sector employees who were entitled to retirement pensions from their place of employment (i.e., the state). Retirement system reform legislation was passed in 1998. Motivated by the desire to cut government expenditures, retirement pensions became linked to workers' personal contributions over the course of their working lives. In other words, there was a shift away from an egalitarian distributive system, where retirement pensions were relatively equal regardless of lifelong earnings, toward a more graduated system, where high-wage earners could look forward to larger retirement pensions than low-wage workers (Armeanu 2010; Wiktorów 2007). In addition, while part of the mandatory contributions continue to be government funded, the rest is placed in private funds that invest in the financial market. Employees can also make additional contributions to a third category of voluntary pension funds which are also invested in the market (Armeanu 2010; Wiktorów 2007; Uścińska 2010). These changes mean that Poles have to be more actively engaged in financial decisions related to retirement. It is in their interest to weigh the relative advantages of various funds, to make calculations about their financial needs now and in the future, and to decide whether they should make additional voluntary contributions. Another part of the 1998 pension system reform was increasing the retirement age to 60 for women and to 65 for men. Employees have to work the requisite number of years and reach retirement age to receive full benefits, and if they elect to work longer, they get larger monthly pensions when they eventually stop working.

Pressures are mounting in the EU to make pension funds "sustainable," meaning they should bring in as much or more money than they pay out. While asserting the rights of member states to set their own policies, the European Commission White Paper on pension reform also pushes for a "more coordinated European-wide response" that would involve uniform standards and polices across EU countries (Cicero Consulting 2012, 3). Specific policy recommendations include raising the retirement age by linking it to life expectancy, encouraging longer working lives, and insuring gender parity in retirement age and in the amount received upon retirement (7).

Like Darek, Marcin also makes good money as a musician and does not think he will be able to play for much longer. He has been saving for his retirement because he wants to stop working when he is still young enough to enjoy himself. In 2008, he told me he dreams of touring Europe on a motorcycle. By 2011, he had purchased the motorcycle but could not take the time from work to use it much. Marcin's wife Monika told me, "We work all the time, we invest, so later, after however many years, our children have it better and so that when we're old, we won't have to work so hard anymore." Marcin agreed: "We want to give our children a better start, and greater certainty."[7] Similarly, Jasia quit her job at a supermarket and got an office job, explaining that she can't imagine working in retail when she reaches her fifties; it is physically demanding work with no possibility of advance. Part of her decision was also based on the fact that retirement pensions are linked to lifelong earnings; getting a better-paying job means she is accumulating more for the future, after she stops working.

The above examples help to illustrate how it has become possible, and even necessary, for participants to project themselves into the future.

The social structural factors that contribute to this include: workplace demands for advanced training, expansion of the education system to meet those needs, availability of credit for mortgages, limited social provisions and employer programs to support work–life balance, and reorganization of social security and pensions. All of these institutional changes can be traced back to postcommunist restructuring and processes of economic liberalization. It is important to note that while these reforms were consistent with the conditions the EU set in the late 1990s as prerequisites for integration, these processes had for the most part already been set in motion before then. In other words, my observations here support those made by Knudson (2012) in her ethnography of farmers in Lithuania that the process of Europeanization is an extension of postcommunist reforms. Furthermore, as she also notes, it is often those who are "furthest from the decision making, people who might not even recognize themselves as a part of the current changes, who have to deal with the greater consequences following the long process of restructuring" (5).

"Even the Crisis Didn't Work Out"

It still remains to be explained how participants' confidence in the future and greater sense of security have emerged despite the privatization of risk in Poland. One simple explanation lies in the country's economic prosperity. For the most part, Poland has bypassed the economic crisis that struck Eurozone countries like Greece, Ireland and Spain. In fact, Poland was the only European economy that grew in 2009, and it was expected to be the fastest growing in 2012 (European Commission 2012). This has been attributed to Poland's large internal market, the continuing strength of foreign investment and the robust real estate sector. Also, significantly, Poland maintains its own currency, the zloty, which has allowed it to adjust its monetary policy in a way that faltering Eurozone countries could not. The fact that most participants in my study are doing well economically seems also to be an artifact of their generation. They experienced the country's economic liberalization at a particular point in their own personal development; they were old enough to have their own personal memories of state socialism (so they can temper nostalgia with a realistic assessment of the hardships older generations endured), but they were young enough to adjust to new expectations of persons. In high school, they feared they were the last state-socialist generation, but it turns out they were the first postcommunist one. Their "wait and see" approach proved effective. Most were able to broker that flexibility into opportunity once new structures and processes stabilized.

In addition to internal factors, Poland's recent economic success can also be attributed to the EU acting as both an engine of capitalism and a provider of social welfare. European integration has accelerated processes of market liberalization, including foreign investment in Poland, the growth of foreign markets for Polish products and easy credit at reasonable interest rates. Beyond these neoliberal measures, the EU has provided opportunities for mobility. As long as Poles can be "tourists," free to leave and return as they wish, rather than "vagabonds" compelled to abandon their native place (Bauman 1998, 92–3), mobility is likely to contribute to a general sense of security. The EU has also been an important source of subsidies for social and economic development. To the extent that funds meet their stated goals of creating lasting opportunities and decreasing inequalities between regions, the EU can gain legitimacy for realizing its ethical responsibility to its citizens.

An explanation for greater confidence in the future can also be found on the level of self-identity, in interaction with broader social and economic factors.

Figure 3.4. Poland: Here even the crisis didn't work out

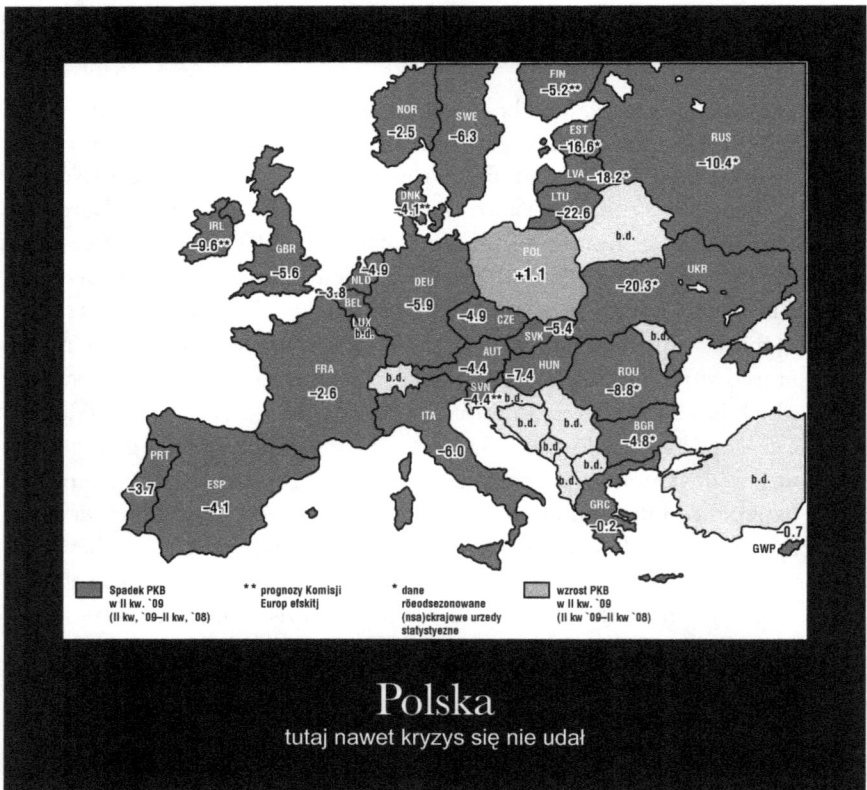

Source: www.demotywatory.pl. Text by Marcin Daniec. Used with permission from demotywatory.pl

Participants may indeed have more personal responsibility for their own well-being, but they also have more personal opportunities and thus a greater sense of personal control over their life outcomes. In 2011, my Polish friends were pleased, but also wary of Poland's economic success. Ewa, a student in Krakow, shared an Internet post that her friends had been passing around (figure 3.4) consisting of a map of Europe representing rates of economic growth. Most of the countries are red, indicating negative growth; only Poland is green, with a positive growth rate of 1.1 per cent. The caption reads, "Poland: here, even the crisis didn't work out." The humor of this comment lies in the way it marks a positive development in negative terms, simultaneously signaling and making fun of Poland's tragic history and its citizens' continued unease about celebrating success. As outlined at the beginning of the chapter, I witnessed a parallel ambivalence in participants' reluctance to acknowledge that "Poles are happy." Throughout the chapter, I have shown how a future orientation emerges from a growing sense of security and stability. Participants are pleased and even proud of their recent successes. Nevertheless, they are also sensitive to the possibility that things could change, and that new gains could be torn away from them, as they have been for so many earlier generations of Poles.

Participants associate the EU with the future. Joasia, a librarian in Lesko, said, "The EU is sold as promise for the future." Others, including Józef and Wala, said, "EU membership equals hope for the future." Similarly, Wiola explains:

> I voted in favor of the referendum to join the European Union for many reasons. I hoped that a lot would change in our country, that everything would become invigorated and that the market would change and begin to work. That people would have more of a chance to help themselves, to emigrate somewhere. I didn't expect any sort of radical change at once, but rather that with time it would slowly pay off. Otherwise we would be neither here or there, we would be just somewhere in the middle. We would stagnate in place. But as it is, there's a chance that it will be better. I know that I can't expect it to change quickly, but maybe it will be different for my son.

Wiola's refrain about a better life for her children was echoed by a number of participants. The lesson for the EU may well be that as long as membership is linked to prosperity, or at least increased opportunity and a better standard of living, Euroskepticism is likely to be muted. Poland's isolation from the Eurozone crisis supports this. But Poland's economic success should not be interpreted as a triumph of neoliberalism; I see it rather as the outcome of careful attention to the sequencing and pacing of reforms.[8] Considering populist opposition to EU integration, the biggest danger lies in the continued growth of economic inequality, where "have-nots" are chronically excluded from the benefits of membership. EU policy seeks to address this via opportunities for mobility and economic subsidies designed to reduce economic and social disparities, though it remains to be seen how effectively.

From a cultural perspective, the future orientation of European identity has often been viewed as a weakness due to the presumption that future promises are a flimsy basis for deep attachment, in contrast to national identity, which gains much deeper moral and emotional legitimacy through its connection with the past. Above, I have shown how projections into a more prosperous future, nearer the center of power in Europe, can indeed be a compelling source of validation for the EU and a united European identity, even though it engenders support in a very different way from traditional national allegiances, which are linked to the perception of a shared history. The EU is a forward-looking institution. It bases its legitimacy on promises for the future. I return to Elżbieta Tarkowska's observations from the 1990s. Perhaps Poles are becoming better able to plan their lives because they have a stable notion of what conditions will be like in the future. EU integration has become an important milestone in this process of stabilization, and of moving up in an imagined hierarchy of nations.

Wiola: Everything on Schedule

When I met Wiola during a group interview in 1992, she appeared shy and even frightened. About the future in postcommunist Poland, she said, "I don't see that it will be better. I'm afraid because I don't know what I will do in the future. I can't imagine it. The situation for my family keeps getting worse; they laid off my father, and they want to lay off my mother. I just don't know." Nevertheless, she went on to finish university, to marry her college sweetheart and to move back to Bieszczady. In 2000, she started working for a local government office, where she remains today. In the years since, she has expressed to me a growing sense of confidence in herself, and about the future. In 2005 she told me:

> After finishing lyceum and learning that I had gotten into university, the first thing I did was leave for Italy, because that's where it was easiest to find work for a short time. I really wanted to go somewhere, to see a bit more, and I wanted to test my own strength in the world without my mother or father. So I went there and it was a kind of shock, like an awakening. It was just me and unfamiliar people, a foreign language, a foreign country, a different mentality, different customs, different food. Everything was different. I took care of a 3-year-old child; he talked, but I couldn't understand what he wanted! But somehow I managed.

The time passed quickly, but after three months it was time to return to my studies. Later, when the academic year ended, something pulled me back to Italy. It wasn't even a matter of finances, but rather of testing myself in different conditions. Because I always had too little courage, I was always humble and had complexes, and going there helped me change a little. I befriended those people so that each year I returned to the same place. Still, I haven't been back since 1996. I had to stop after I got to know Tomek [her husband], during my fourth year of studies, because he didn't want to agree to it.

After I graduated, Tomek and I married. I wanted everything to be on schedule, in the proper order. My husband says that I'm not spontaneous enough. I'm not crazy enough, I do everything like it is supposed to be. I wanted to first finish university, then marry and then have a child. And that is how it happened. Because if it had happened otherwise it would have been against what I feel.

Right after graduation I registered as unemployed, and the Labor Office provided funds for me to gain practical training in an office somewhere. I chose the local government offices because they were the closest to my home. As it turned out, I liked that institution. My mother also worked for the local government, and I always liked the way she spread out her papers at home and wrote. And then I got pregnant. And that pregnancy actually helped me keep my job. Because there is a provision that if a woman is pregnant she can't be dismissed from her job. They couldn't fire me, but I had to work until I gave birth. Then came my maternity leave, and later it turned out that they needed me [to handle the paperwork associated with] reforms of education, healthcare and social security. So that's how my son helped me find work. But after he was born, my boss told me that if I wanted to keep my job I needed to get back to work, or they would find someone else. And even though my son was very sick, I had to return so I wouldn't lose my job. I had no other choice. Or rather, I had a choice, but I was afraid that if I resigned, I might not have such a chance again.

Now, I feel good at work, though at the beginning there was this pressure, because ten people were just waiting to take your place. It caused such fear that I often brought work home, and sat up at night, just to show that I'm a good worker.

From my perspective, things have definitely gotten better [in Poland]. Because I remember how it was [under communism]. Nothing was in stores, and I couldn't afford anything, and now we can afford everything we need, within certain boundaries – a car, an apartment. But I don't think everyone sees it that way. Because today is for resourceful, assertive people, who can manage in this new situation. I know a lot of people who are older than me, who grew up during communist times, and they can't find themselves in these new conditions, they are completely lost. And it's definitely hard for older people, because younger people can more easily change their work, or home, or they can move to a new place.

When I visited Wiola in 2008, she felt much more secure in her job and confident enough about the future to consider having another child. When I returned in 2011, she was thrilled to be a mother again and that her daughter was such a sweet, healthy and easy child. "Because of the trouble I had with my son, with his illnesses, going in and out of the hospital, I was afraid to have another. But finally we decided to. Pola is the kind of child you dream of having, where everything happens just as planned and on schedule. My husband always wanted more children, too. We're hoping that I'm pregnant again."

Wiola is happy. She says she is less anxious than she used to be, and she does not worry so much about what everyone is thinking or what they expect. This has served her well at work, where she has been for over eleven years now. When she became pregnant the second time, losing her job was not a concern. At her doctor's recommendation, she even took sick leave during the months before her daughter's birth to avoid traveling to work in the winter. Once her daughter was born, though, she took both paid and unpaid leave so she could stay home until Pola was a year old.

As her life story reveals, Wiola is a planner. She has a set idea of how her life should unfold, but only recently has she become less perpetually anxious about the future. Notably, this existential security has taken hold even though her personal living situation is in some ways less stable than it was a few years ago. She and her husband sold their apartment in Lesko, thinking they would move into a house she inherited in her native village. She wanted to be closer to work, and to have more living space. Instead, they had to move in with her parents because their tenant refused to leave. She was in the midst of an unpleasant legal battle with the renter, but nevertheless felt more in control of her life than in years past. She was confident they would eventually reclaim their house, and confident she could find another job if she needed to.

Broader social structural and economic changes are providing more pathways to a higher standard of living even in a remote rural area like Bieszczady, especially for people with modest needs. The shift is particularly striking in Wiola's life story because her family experienced such economic hardship in the early years of postcommunist transformation, but she nevertheless managed to finish college, get a stable job and achieve a degree of financial security. She has undergone a marked personal transformation as well, becoming more confident and secure in herself. I see the two as intertwined – she is less anxious because the behavioral environment makes it possible to achieve a predictable, stable life, which is psychologically important to her. Because the broader structural supports, like childcare provisions and employment opportunities, are relatively stable, she is better able to handle more transient insecurities like the legal battle over her house.

Chapter 4

"WE'RE EUROPEAN BECAUSE WE'RE POLISH": LOCAL, NATIONAL AND EUROPEAN IDENTITIES

Wojtek: Pole, European and Euroskeptic

Considering how studious and articulate Wojtek was in high school, it is not surprising that he is now a professor in Krakow. Nevertheless, it is an impressive achievement for the son of foresters and farmers, raised in a remote mountain village. Wojtek has always expressed a deep sense of attachment to the multiethnic region from which he comes. He says that his Polish Catholic identity means more to him because it was something he thought a lot about while growing up among ethnic Ukrainians. Although a few participants from Bieszczady attended university in Krakow, Wojtek is the only one who has stayed in the city. He lives with his wife and two children in an apartment they recently purchased. Wojtek's view of the EU is colored by his faith, his place of origin and his professional experiences. In 2005, he explained:

> I was and·to this day remain a Euroskeptic. In other words, I don't believe everything that comes from the EU is good. Rather, it's a process that will take twenty to thirty years, and our standard of living will probably never be equal [to that of other member states] because, after all, they don't stay in one place either. It's good they have aid programs [for us], but how much is it intended to improve *our* quality of life, and how much is it meant to make it better for the EU, for *them*?
>
> Of course, we had been adapting our legal system for a number of years already, so at the moment of integration there wasn't that much disharmony that still had to be addressed. And it's hard to say if we wouldn't have made those changes without the EU, perhaps under pressure from other interest groups. Therefore, for me it's a continuum of reform we had, with the goal of joining Western countries, but my feeling is nothing has changed *because* of EU integration. The country is reforming, we're moving forward, and it is costing us a great deal of sacrifice.

I voted "no" on the referendum to join the EU. I am definitely in favor of the EU, but not under the conditions they offered us. It made me sad because the Pope [John Paul II] called for Poles to support integration. I respect him, but I had to vote "no" to show my opposition to the form that the EU is taking. The ideal of the EU for me is not primarily to make money, even though the EU was conceived as an economic union, to compete against the US. The EU is just like a centralized economy because they decide how much grain we will produce, and how many liters of milk. But we've already had a centralized economy. In my opinion this system doesn't have a chance of surviving. Already people are saying something has to change.

Mainly, if we form a European constitution, we want it to say that European unity grew out of our shared Christianity. The French say no. But that's how we feel. We would definitely be a Muslim country if we hadn't fought so much with the Turks and Mongols. My point is that our past is based in Christianity, whether we like it or not. I knew it was our role to argue about this. And now everyone will say, "Poles are so argumentative." Yes, but as members of the union you can't take away our right to vote, and when you admitted us you knew very well from our history that we will fight for what we believe in. We have it in our blood.

How strong is my feeling of attachment to Poland? It's hard to measure. In fact, that feeling is dormant. I feel more Polish when I go to my family home and I see that my neighbor is not a Pole. Living here in Krakow doesn't require asserting my identity or my patriotism. It's a pretty patriotic city. There are marches and meetings. I have attended such things, but have never taken them very seriously. My feelings of attachment only awaken when something upsets me, or someone cheats us. I don't hide that I'm a Pole, or that I'm a Christian, but I don't advertise it; I don't keep a portrait of any heroes, or a flag, or a cross on my wall. Of course I try to teach my son those values. Even if he'll be a European, which I want, he should know he also has the right to decide about the fate of Europe through his country, even if that country isn't always drawn on the map in the same form as today.

How strong is my feeling of attachment to Europe? Long before we entered the EU we said that we are a part of Europe. I understand this based on the fact that we have the Roman alphabet; because it's enough to look at our historical buildings that are connected to European styles. We're not some sort of island with a different culture. We aren't the same, but we have many common elements. Due to various historical circumstances, our cultural contribution is not proportional to our potential, because we could definitely give more to Europe, and Europe could take more from us.

I'm a European like this: if someone asks me, "Where are you from?" I answer, "From Poland," or "From Europe" if they don't understand. When we're at the airport and someone arrives from France or England, we behave similarly. If I were from Bangladesh, I would have different clothes and different behavior. Because European culture may not be the peak of civilization, but it has a certain quality. I can feel it more strongly now that I have traveled more. But in Poland we still definitely have that feeling of local patriotism. It's organized like this: our little *ojczyzna* [fatherland] is very close to our big *ojczyzna*, Poland, and considerably farther from Europe. Because, as I've told you, at this time Europe doesn't represent me like I would want to be represented.

Where do my priority loyalties lie? I would say with Poland. Because I see a very dangerous trend toward local society in Poland. The EU funds the development of national minorities, and suddenly problems appear; some say they are Silesians and not Poles. They take advantage of their feeling of a little *ojczyzna* to become independent. But even though I'm from the east and they're from the west, we have common ideas and goals. We talk and write in the same language. We also have a lot in common with Slovaks and with Ukrainians, looking at language and culture. At one time, the word "Poland" didn't just mean one nation or one country. It meant a certain collection of states without designated borders, including regions with predominantly Ukrainian or Belarusian residents.

Even this brief narrative makes it clear that Wojtek has reflected more often and more deeply about ethnic and national identity than most participants. His feelings of attachment to various scales of place – local, national and European – are grounded in intimate connections with familiar landscapes and people, but he also engages on a cognitive level with issues of national history, religion, regional culture and nationalism. In recent years, the European scale has become increasingly salient to him, even though he remains highly skeptical about European integration and stresses the preeminence of the national scale.

The concept of *ojczyzna* is used in this narrative in a way that is consistent with Polish sociologist Stanisław Ossowski's (1967) distinction between the "private *ojczyzna*," which derives from direct personal experience of a locality, and the "ideological *ojczyzna*," which corresponds with the nation constructed through rhetoric and ideas. Ossowski's formulation effectively explains the way emotional attachment to region can often lend affective intimacy to broader ideological loyalty to the nation.

Imagining Territorial Scales of Social Organization

The past two chapters have considered temporal shifts in participants' perspectives. This chapter examines participants' perceptions of space and place, especially in relation to their sense of belonging to various scales of social organization. It also shows how European identity, when it is expressed at all, functions very differently from local and national identity. These matters speak to the central questions that drive this study: How does identification with various territorial scales figure in participants' evolving sense of self, and what do relationships between these identities suggest about European integration? Is it a zero-sum equation, where increased loyalty to one scale diminishes loyalty to another? Or are they cumulative and complementary, wherein those with the strongest sense of attachment at one level are also most likely to have a strong sense of attachment at others (Hooghe and Marks 2001)? Do they interact in some other way? Engaging with questions about identity and European integration at the level of individual experience provides a window into the means through which Europe comes to have "entitativity" (see Costano 2004), and helps reveal what kind of an entity Europe is seen to be. More broadly relevant for political theory, I argue that the way in which national and supranational "European" identities are reconciled (or fail to be reconciled) in citizens' minds suggests the EU constitutes a unique form of political structure, whose basis for long-term viability and legitimacy is fundamentally different from that of nation-states.

The chapter is structured around responses to specific questions I asked during life story interviews in 2005, the year after Poland became an EU member. I asked questions similar to those posed in survey-based studies about scales of identity, attachment, loyalty and belonging (especially McManus-Czubińska et al. 2003; see also Jasińska-Kania and Marody 2004; McLaren 2006; Ruiz et al. 2004), but because I used an interview format, participants' responses provide more insight into *why* they answered as they did. In other words, I took advantage of the self-reflexivity that characterizes identity in the global era (Cohen 1994; Giddens 1991); I encouraged participants to engage their "creative selves" (Cohen 1994) and contemplate the thoughts and feelings evoked by territorial scales of belonging. Participants' explanations were often surprising, and sometimes they challenge generalizations derived from questionnaires. As I have done throughout the book, I consider responses from 2005 in relation to participants' life stories before and since then, and in relation to broader influences of postsocialist reforms, EU integration and other global processes.

A rich body of interdisciplinary research explores the emergence of European identity, and proposes models for how territorial scales of identity fit together. A central debate revolves around the question of how much autonomy national governments will retain within the EU. Will federalism or pluralism prevail? Approaches that emphasize federalism focus on strong supranational institutions that provide a uniform structure and rules for member nation-states to follow. According to one model, federalism is conceived as a supranational order of social organization that is growing in significance, and replacing lower-level territorial scales. For instance, Giesen and Eder characterize European citizenship as both supranational and *post*national, and consider "strong persistent feelings of belonging to attached nations" a direct threat to the development of attachment to Europe (2001, 9). According to a second model of federalism, as European structures take shape, national identities weaken but regional identities become more salient; in this configuration, regional interests, especially those associated with ethnic minorities, are better supported by pan-European structures, leading those subgroups to identify more strongly with Europe than with the nation (Bukowski et al. 2003; Hadler et al. 2012; Wagstaff 2007).

Pluralist approaches fall along a continuum, emphasizing greater or lesser degrees of national autonomy within the EU. According to one model, pluralism is conceived in terms of the continued predominance of national-level identities within a weakly united Europe. For instance, Zielonka (2006) stresses the polycentric character of the EU, and says that, like a neomedieval empire, various cross-cutting agreements result in different rules and competing networks of clients in different places. He warns that "pan-European identity will be blurred and fragile with no truly European demos" (1). A second model of pluralism, which best matches the perspective of the participants in my study, suggests identification to various territorial scales are not mutually exclusive (Antonsich 2009; Hadler et al. 2012). In other words, European identity can grow without threatening either national or regional identity; it is a fundamentally additive model in which there is no conflict between pluralism at smaller scales and European integration. The term "nested identities" has been used to describe such affiliation to progressively wider social groups within the EU (Galbraith 2004; Herb and Kaplan 1999; Herrman et al. 2004; McManus-Czubińska et al. 2003).

Whether they emphasize federalism or pluralism, most scholars agree that institutional unification has not led to European identity with the kinds of emotional commitments that national identity often commands (Cederman 2001; Hooghe and Marks 2004; McLaren 2006; Pederson 2008; Ruiz Jimenez et al. 2004;). Some studies suggest this may not be a problem, but rather look for other bases of European identity and unity: shared culture and values (Demossier 2007; Mach and Niedźwiedzki 2002; Pederson 2008; Robyn 2005; Wintle 1996); increased mobility across borders (Bruter 2005; Wagstaff 2007); common EU citizenship (Bruter 2005; Eder and Giesen 2001); shared economic interests (Berend 2009); common institutional rules and structures (Schimmelfennig and Sedelmeier 2005); or unifying structures that simultaneously strengthen local political agency or regionalism (Bukowski et al.

2003; Kockel 2007; Wagstaff 2007). Fligstein recognizes the combined effect of mobility, economic interdependence and governmental and nongovernmental organizations in "European social fields" (2008, 6–16), where horizontal linkages become the "glue to connect people" across national borders (3). Qualitative studies such as my own are valuable because they help to reveal the constellations of debate that ordinary citizens engage in about the place of local and national identities within an integrated Europe (see also Meinhof 2004; Stacul 2006). I contribute a person-centered perspective on European identity – its cognitive, emotional and practical associations in participants' personal accounts.

I first noted evidence of nested identities while doing fieldwork in 1999 and 2000, when participants expressed their affiliation to region, nation and Europe in ways that suggested these levels of identity do not conflict (Galbraith 2004). My goal in 2005 was to ask a series of questions that would prompt participants to explicitly reflect on their loyalties to various scales of "imagined communities" in order to better understand how they think about each level individually and in relation to each other. While I recognize that such solicited reflections will not always correspond to the ways in which people operationalize constructions of identity in their day-to-day lives, allowing them to think out loud (as these prompts were designed to do) helps to reveal the cultural models that inform action.

Attachment to Place: Quality and Intensity at Different Scales

This section addresses two questions: How does attachment to place figure in self-identity? And do attachments to different territorial scales – local region, nation and Europe – have different qualities and intensities? Briefly, I found that most participants associate their place of origin with social and emotional connections to family and friends, and reference some kind of essential, "natural" bond with that place. They believe that the place in which they were born and grew up had considerable influence on the kind of person they are, though some attribute those intimate feelings of connection to their local region, while others extend them to the Polish nation. Participants from Bieszczady were more likely to prioritize their attachment to region, while those from Krakow attributed that primary sense of belonging to the nation as a whole.[1] Rural residents referred to the quality of the landscape when explaining their emotional connection to their local region, but they complained about the lack of economic opportunities that can make it hard to live there. Urban and rural residents who said they identify most strongly with the Polish nation tended to explain their attachment in terms of a shared culture and history, even as many argued that national mythological associations with historical conditions of occupation and hardship are no longer salient in politics or in everyday life. Most participants characterized affiliation with Europe as fundamentally different from lower-level attachments. For one, most reported that it is much weaker in intensity. Second, the language of sentiment and kinship was almost never used to describe it. Further, although Wojtek and a few others based their affiliation to Europe on shared history, religion, language and the like, most associated Europe with economic and symbolic preeminence within an imagined hierarchy of nations.

Talking about region

Within the category "region," participants include scales smaller than the nation – village, city or the Bieszczady Mountains. Participants most often grounded their sense of regional belonging in personal memories and aesthetics of landscape. A common refrain was "I was born here, and I grew up here." References to roots, ancestry, childhood and youth were common. Most participants who were raised in Bieszczady said their sense of belonging and solidarity is more strongly linked to locality than to nation or Europe. Notably, sentiments toward the mountain region remained strong even among those who moved to cities or abroad. Joasia, a librarian in Lesko, explained: "All of us who are born in a certain place are connected [*związani*] to that place; we have a fondness for that place and feel drawn to it. Even if someone moves – I'm thinking of friends of mine – they always look for a chance to come back and spend some time, and even built themselves a home here for their retirement." Others emphasized the importance of local social connections, especially to family. There is often a pragmatic dimension to these family ties in that many rely on parents for childcare, and rural residents often live with their parents until well into adulthood.

Some characterized their connection to place as inextricably bound with their self-identity; they understand "self" in terms of their fundamental essence, sometimes connected to the concept of "soul." Krzysiek, a Lesko native who does service-related seasonal work, told me, "I even talked with a friend about this topic yesterday. He read somewhere, maybe in the Bible, that a person's place is there where his soul is connected. I don't know – it's where you feel fantastic, you feel safe, where your soul feels the best. In fact, I feel the best here. Why? Because I was born here, and that won't change." Wala, who runs her family's store,[2] returned to Lesko after completing university in Krakow. About urban living she said, "The big city weighed me down. Somehow I couldn't find myself there." For a few years, she lived in a town just 14 kilometers from Lesko, but "even there," she said, "I couldn't acclimatize. Here, I have more friends, my parents, my sister. I wouldn't want to live anywhere else. Maybe because this is where I grew up." Paweł, a sales manager in Lesko, is one of the few who complained about "small town talk," the darker side of small, intimate communities. He cannot escape public criticism for being divorced, even though his wife left him for another man. Nevertheless, he does not consider moving because he likes the region and his job.

Bieszczady residents also identify with the distinctive landscape of the region and the qualities they associate with rural living. The mountains figure strongly in their expressions of regional attachment, and they say they value the peace and safety of life in a rural setting. Marcin, who lives in a village by Lake Solina, said, "I wouldn't want to move away from this place. It needs the kinds of tourist services I provide. Besides that, I have water, mountains, forest. Where could it be prettier?" Halina, a farmer, asserted: "I was born in Bieszczady, and I love Bieszczady. For the time being, it has clean air, lovely mountains. You can definitely live more calmly than in other places. There isn't that constant hurry like somewhere in the cities. It's hard here because conditions are difficult for work, but generally it's good for sure."

Others similarly compared Bieszczady favorably with more urban areas. Robert, a school teacher in Lesko, described the region as quiet and safe in contrast to the crime and noise of the city. He also emphasized, "If I've had enough of everything, I get into my car or onto my bike, or even on foot, and within fifteen minutes I'm in the mountains or at the lake." As participants describe it, they respond viscerally to the physical qualities of the terrain around them. Agnieszka, a librarian from Lesko, remarked, "As soon as I see the foothills, I know I'm home. Maybe it results from my character. I like nature, I like hiking. I like the quiet, the peacefulness. All I have to do is walk out of my home and there it is." Both Agata and Joasia told stories about visiting their husbands' native places in the "flatlands" and feeling that they "wouldn't last long" there. They said they feel "out of place" away from familiar mountains and valleys.

Attachment to region may also be stronger than attachment to nation in part because of the historic fluidity of political boundaries, a condition in which "region" becomes a marked category. For instance, Darek, a nurse, calls the region his "substitute *ojczyzna*." He feels alienated from Poland because of the discrimination and repression his father endured as an ethnic Ukrainian. If anything, Darek's deep loyalty to Bieszczady grows out of all that his father suffered in order to return after being forced to leave following World War II. Darek said he would not work abroad, even though he regularly hears about opportunities for nurses. Bartek traces his ancestral link to the region through his grandmother, even though she came from what is now Ukraine. When considered geographically and historically, this claim makes sense.

Geographically, Bieszczady is part of the Carpathian mountain range that extends from the Polish-Slovak border region through Ukraine to Hungary and Romania. Bartek's grandmother was a native of a village that lies within these mountains and is only about seventy kilometers from Lesko. Historically, borders have shifted, and those eastern lands (commonly called the Kresy) used to be within the boundaries of the Polish state. Bartek is one of several participants whose families have maintained connections across the Polish-Ukrainian border, and even on occasion visit relatives in their ancestral villages. Thus, regional identity can encompass multiple ethnicities and cut across state boundaries.

Feeling connected to the region and wanting to live there does not mean that participants hesitate to criticize certain aspects of life in Bieszczady. The biggest problem they identified was the difficulty of finding a job. Most have gone elsewhere at some point, either to study or to work. Nevertheless, most have returned or express a sense of longing for their native place. In other words, their sentiments of attachment are not due to limited knowledge of other places, and that connection can grow despite long periods of residence elsewhere. Marta has felt compelled to seek work abroad because, as she explained, "it's good to be home, but it is like it is; there isn't any work. And a person has to work. If people could have normal work here, they would never emigrate. Because as it is now, thousands emigrate, even married people, and then they break up because of it." Paulina, who was raised in a mountain village, but now lives in Italy with her Italian husband and two children, explained, "Bieszczady always has my priority because it connects with my psyche, with my childhood, with my world when I was young. [...] That's where I have my memories, my life and my people." Regional identity is thus in many ways a marked category for emigrants. They have thought about it while living elsewhere, and it has figured in their decisions about their future – whether to return "home" or to live as a nonlocal in a place with more opportunity.

A few have no intention of returning, except to visit. Basia, who works for a multinational company in Warsaw, has made a significant break with her native Lesko. She explained:

> I wouldn't want to live in Lesko now, definitely, because of the things I would like to do. I know myself, and I don't like it when it's quiet. I like it when there's activity, when there's a lot of noise and people and a lot is happening. I like coming here to relax. But later, I like to return and have all that commotion around me. I also think it would be hard for me to move back, even sometime in the future, because fewer and fewer of the people I like to spend time with are here. Mostly, I come because I have family, but they are all older and someday they will be gone.

Participants disparage the overall state of underdevelopment in the mountains, even for tourism, the local industry that is supposed to replace socialist-era state farms and state industries and usher the region into the global capitalist economy.

In 2005, at least, expressions of connection to region were quite different among participants who went to high school in Krakow. A number seem to have experienced a weakening of their identification with the city, especially as Poland has moved toward European integration. Most still remarked on the special "something" the city has, and the richness of its culture, history and historic monuments. Like Bieszczady residents, they also noted a sense of belonging and attachment to the place where they were born and grew up. Ewelina, a lawyer who has lived her whole life in Krakow said:

> It's very hard for me to imagine moving away from Krakow, or even living on the outskirts of Krakow. I like walking around the market square, and feeling that atmosphere. It's very specific. Maybe it's because the city doesn't have an awfully large number of residents, people know each other. It's not very formal socially, compared with Warsaw, for example where there's an unbelievable amount of competition between people. Krakow has that charm.

Marzena, a banker, said it was very hard for her to leave Krakow for a job in Warsaw. Still, banks have their central offices in Warsaw, so that is also where the high-level positions are. Marzena said she tolerates Warsaw; what she misses the most are her parents, whom she visits every other weekend. Other Krakow natives emphasized the opportunities associated with living in the city. Michał, a real estate investor, explained he has good business opportunities in Krakow; while Grzesiek, a computer repairman, prides himself in coming from a more developed urban area closer to the center of commerce and modernization.

Some participants noted that they feel "less and less" connected to Krakow, or that they "don't feel so terribly close anymore," and they attributed this change to European integration. Grzesiek has eagerly embraced the expanded opportunities to travel. Ania, an artist who in the past expressed deep attachment to Krakow and to the Polish nation, said she sees her former regional patriotism as childish; she cannot identify with local politics and so has distanced herself from it. She explained, "I have definitely opened up to Europe, and Europe has become closer to me, so I have definitely withdrawn a little from Krakow itself. But I don't think this is a negative trait; seeing your own society from above, both the good and the bad, the positive and the negative, leads to development, doesn't it? It's a creative and, I believe, positive trait." Ania's comments are interesting because they explicitly acknowledge a growing sense of European identity.

As much as regional identity emerges from embodied sentiments of attachment to one's place of birth and childhood, linked to intimate relationships, some participants' comments reveal how regional identity is also a construction of the imagination. This can be seen especially in the way several participants expressed close feelings of connection to a regional culture different from their own – that of the Górale, natives of the Tatra Mountains who speak a distinct dialect of Polish and who have retained a distinct regional identity (Pine 1993, 1996; Schneider 2006). Two participants from Krakow (Aneta and Jurek) claimed an affinity to the Tatra Mountains, noting some of their ancestors were Górale; Jurek has even made architectural styles inspired by traditional mountaineer construction his signature as an architect. Although Agata's family roots are all grounded in Bieszczady, her parents hired Górale builders to construct a home in the traditional Górale style. It evokes for her family "traditional mountain culture" better than the kinds of homes that were found historically in the Bieszczady region.

Talking about nation

Attachment to nation tends to be linked to historical consciousness, and to past events that carry meaning for the constitution and maintenance of the Polish nation. As with regional identity, participants claim a "natural" connection to the nation of their birth, upbringing and ancestry, but family history is also framed by elements of national history and culture. Participants expressed pride in their nation, but did not hesitate to criticize it, their government and the behavior of fellow Poles. For many, religion functions as a mostly unmarked element of national identity; they associate Poland with Catholicism as a matter of course, but when asked explicitly, asserted that a Pole need not be Catholic. It is just a matter of historical circumstance that most Poles are Catholic today, they explained. Almost no one made reference to the features of landscape that figure so prominently in expressions of connection to region.

I will not repeat what I have said about history in the previous two chapters, but I do want to stress a certain refrain about national identity repeated by many – that Poles only unite during times of hardship, and since the fall of communism, there have been few such pivotal moments inspiring that kind of solidarity:

I feel that national identity when something bad happens. That's when people associate themselves more with being a Pole. That's how it was after the Pope died; suddenly everyone felt unified. Poles are this way. (Agnieszka, a librarian in Lesko)

> Because of the history that Poles endured, that attachment is very strong for me. I also think that all Poles may not show it except in the case of certain problems or political situations that make them unite together. (Halina, a farmer in Bieszczady)

> Over the centuries, Poles have been a nation that becomes united only when pilloried. Then we can fight together for the good of everyone, and together oppose evil. As things are, we're a nation that doesn't live too well together. (Paweł, a sales manager in Lesko)

Participants noted a lack of unity and mutual concern at the national level during times like the present, when there is no clear outside enemy.

Echoing sentiments that have been common since the early 1990s, participants identified dimensions of everyday practice as the proper venue for the expression of patriotism during "ordinary times," as opposed to the extraordinary personal sacrifices demanded of patriots during times of crisis:

> I go to work for my own interest, but because I am a part of this country, I also work for the country. I also think that because there is no threat, our patriotism is sleeping. If a threat appears, we'll become like people from the center-right party who protest daily, who stand and carry their banner to battle. Then, of course, there will be consolidation and unification. (Wojtek, a professor in Krakow)

> I think that if something bad started to occur in my country, I would do everything to try and help. The elections are coming up. The biggest danger for Poland at this time is Poles. That's why I want to vote for what I believe will be the best. (Stasiek, a computer programmer from Bieszczady)

As the above comments show, participants consider "nation" a category that gains salience when Poland's autonomy is threatened. The pragmatic orientation expressed here was already common in the early 1990s, when participants told me there was little need for patriotic heroism and self-sacrifice, but rather "It's time to get back to work." The best way to demonstrate their patriotism, they explained, was by being good citizens and responsible workers. With few situations that inspire or demand expressions of belonging to Poland, "nation" is largely unmarked in their everyday lives. Only in relation to encounters with other ethnicities, usually when traveling abroad, nationality commonly becomes a marked category, subject to critique by others and by themselves (a point I explore in Chapter 6).

An area where perspectives *have* shifted since the early 1990s is with regard to the relation between nation and state. To review, the Polish "nation" –

the people who consider themselves to be united by common traits such as history, culture, language, religion and territory – has tended to be defined in opposition to the "state" – the institutions of government that for much of Poland's modern history have been controlled by non-Polish powers. This distinction was often conceptualized in terms of "us" (the nation) and "them" (the state) (Davies 1984; Galbraith 1997; Kaufman 1989; Kubik 1994; Wedel 1986). The Polish nation regained sovereignty – in other words control of the state – when the communist party was soundly defeated in the first free elections after the Round Table Agreement of 1989. This did not mean, however, that the Polish government immediately gained the support of citizens. On the contrary, distrust of state institutions has persisted, especially as frequent political scandals and corruption have reinforced the popular perception that politicians are more concerned with their own interests than the good of the country as a whole.

Grzesiek articulated this tension between legitimacy of democratic state institutions and the failure of politicians to fairly represent the nation's interests. He said, "Because the government system changed, I've begun to feel more connected to Poland." However, in the next breath he griped, "It would be great to have a government that reacted appropriately, that made us someone in the world." He said he welcomes the system that guarantees personal liberties and a free market economy, but criticized a whole slew of government practices, including nepotism, corruption, high taxes and the failure to improve the economy on a level equivalent to Western Europe. His enumeration of weaknesses also included what he called "the Polish psyche" (more a matter of nation than state) that makes ordinary Poles get drunk, steal and earn a bad reputation abroad. I want to emphasize how critiques like Grzesiek's do not sharply distinguish nation (the Polish people) from state (government institutions), and even sometimes conflate the two.

Frustration with an "inner enemy" in government is particularly apparent in Wala's remark: "Sometimes I'm embarrassed to be Polish. When I look at everything that goes on here, especially considering what our government, what people in high positions do, as I learn about one corruption scandal after another. I recently read that the prime minister spent millions on tablecloths, napkins and place settings. This thoughtlessness infuriates me because children are starving, hospitals are in debt."

Similarly Józef, who works in regional government, said, "Sometimes I am embarrassed of Poles – like when there is some kind of scandal – of our politicians, of government, how they act inappropriately. From this you can see that I feel like a Pole. I am not indifferent to Polish matters and how everything will work out. I feel that bond." Józef reads his discomfiture with government corruption as a sign of his attachment to nation. Participants regularly referred to their embarrassment, or conversely asserted their national pride despite embarrassing practices of politicians. Notably, they take the actions of government officials as reflective of the Polish nation as a whole. Their comments are akin to the laments Ries (1997, 83–125) identified among Russians during perestroika, because they reflect certain social expectations and moral judgments, and signal how things are not as they should be.

These examples also show how participants both reinscribe and revise distinctions between nation and state. Despite ongoing distrust of the state, the political system has gained legitimacy in the sense that elected representation and associated institutional structures are well established. Over the past two decades, these democratic reforms have withstood power shifts from post-Solidarity to neosocialist parties, and back and forth between nationalist-leaning and pro-European neoliberal parties. Correspondingly, participants sometimes used the terms "nation" and "state" interchangeably. Nevertheless, they were more likely to complain about the actions of political figures than to identify with them. Their comments suggest that the nation has lost legitimacy through its association with the state, even as the state has gained legitimacy through associations with the nation. Eglitis and Ardava describe a similar situation in contemporary Latvia, where political elites are viewed by some as an "inner enemy" that is neither fully included nor excluded from the public perception of "we" (2012, 1039).

Talking about Europe

Whereas participants talk about attachment to local region and to nation in similar ways, they tend to describe connections to Europe quite differently. This is not a particularly surprising observation; others have also noted how sentiments expressed toward Europe tend to be cooler, more distant and even more rational (McManus-Czubińska et al. 2003; Citrin and Sides 2004; Galbraith 2004; Robyn 2005; Roguska 2005; McLaren 2006). In this section, I elaborate on three patterns in participants' responses to questions about their attachment to Europe. First, only about half said they feel they have anything like a European identity, and some had trouble even grasping what it means to apply the concept of belonging to the wider European scale. Second, most participants, including a few who said they do not know if they feel any attachment to Europe, emphasized that Poland has always been in Europe. Third, despite only vague agreement about what Europe is, participants nevertheless regard Europe favorably. As an instrument, Europe is considered a means to economic opportunity, especially when conceived of in terms of EU membership. As an idea, Europe symbolizes global power and importance.

All participants found it easy to discuss their attachment to region and to Poland, but some struggled when asked about their attachment to Europe. Marta and Zosia, who live in rural Bieszczady, simply did not understand the question. Dorota and Paulina, who live elsewhere in Europe, talked instead about their attachment to two national-level scales – to Poland and to their country of destination. Notably, all four of these participants have spent time working abroad, so it is not just a matter of limited experience beyond the local or national sphere. Piotr, a Krakow resident, only said, "I never thought about it!" Darek, a nurse in Bieszczady, also said he had never thought about it, but he went on to explain why many Bieszczady residents might have trouble with this question: "Life is more down to earth here. Consciousness about being European already goes beyond the normal life of the people in Bieszczady. Here, you think about what kind of winter there will be, whether there will be enough hot weather until the fall, whether there will be work, whether you will be healthy. Such thoughts about 'being' are a luxury for people who are economically well off." Marta fits this description; she tends to think in concrete terms about the everyday practicalities of life and resists more abstract reflections about self and identity. The fact that some participants had trouble even talking about Europe as a locus for identity indicates that "Europe" does not have "entitativity" to the same degree that "nation," "Bieszczady" or "Krakow" do.

Nevertheless, for most participants, Poland's place within Europe is long-standing and unquestioned. Most explained this in terms of geography:

I feel like a Pole, therefore I feel European. [...] I am a European because I'm Polish. (Agata, a farmer)

I am a Pole, and Poland is in Europe, so I am also a European. I am in two groups. (Aneta, who works in television and film production)

If we talk about geographic borders, we are a part of Europe. (Wojtek, a professor)

Furthermore, participants commonly expressed annoyance with discourse that characterizes Poland's accession to the EU as "joining Europe," exclaiming, "Where else has Poland ever been?" Agnieszka explained, "I have always felt like a European. It didn't require entrance into the EU." Similarly, Basia, who works in public relations in Warsaw, said, "I don't know what it means to 'feel like a European' because I believe that much earlier, before we found ourselves in the EU, we were 'in Europe.'" Bogdan, a civil servant in a town near Bieszczady, expressed a similar sentiment: "What does it mean that Poland entered Europe? Does that mean that we were in Asia before?" Ewelina, a lawyer in Krakow, said, "I find it very disturbing when people come to Poland and act as if some miracle happened and we suddenly became civilized when we entered the EU on 1 May [2004]."

"Europe" usually evokes positive associations for participants (even among those critical of the EU), but it remains essentially an "empty" category (Mummendey and Waldzus 2004; Risse 2004), variously understood by different people and in different situations. Some point to common historical and cultural elements, such as Roman Catholicism and the value of freedom. In the portrait at the beginning of the chapter, Wojtek emphasized the linguistic and architectural connections between Poland and Europe. More commonly, participants imagine Europe as a global center of culture, power and economic development. Similarly, Horolets (2006) notes that discourse in the Polish press tends to equate Europe with "civilization," and to see the "return to Europe" as a way of gaining higher social and political status. Some of my participants emphasized Poland's (and especially Bieszczady's) as-yet peripheral position within such a global imaginary. Darek, explained, "I think we can be proud because Europe is the cradle of knowledge and culture. But Poland is on the edge of Europe, and we live on the edge of Poland." For some the idea of unity is itself a positive value emerging out of European integration. Basia explained, "The EU isn't there so that each of us individually lives better, but rather to build something that will be strong, that allows us to speak in a united voice; to be able to really have what's good; to have bargaining chips against other powers." Basia's words also contain a critique of the instrumentality with which Poles generally approach the EU (see Galbraith 2011a).

European Integration and Territorial Scales of Belonging

The next few sections review responses to interview questions that asked participants to further explore comparisons across territorial scales. Participants often made such comparisons without prompting; where appropriate, I include these comments, as well.

Do scales of belonging preclude each other?

I wanted to find out whether participants experience any sense of conflict between a broader European identity and smaller-scale national or regional identities. Of course, this gets at the heart of some of the most fundamental debates about European integration, and about globalization generally. Are cosmopolitan, deterritorialized identities emerging in response to increasing interconnectedness across national boundaries? Are they replacing geographically and historically bounded attachments to particular places and people? Participants' responses suggest that, even as some sense of being and becoming European is growing, it is not replacing national and regional identities, which tend to remain stronger.

All participants agreed that feelings of identity at local, national and European levels do not preclude each other (*nie wykluczają się*). On the contrary, these loyalties were most often considered complementary, as illustrated in responses such as:

> Bieszczady is contained [*się zawiera*] within Poland; Poland is contained within the European continent. Even if we've been told otherwise, that's how it is. (Agnieszka)

> It's like this: Bieszczady is in Poland, and so is a part [*część*] of Poland; at the same time, Poland lies within Europe and so is a part of Europe. So it is possible to be connected with all of them – with Europe and with Poland and with Bieszczady. (Józef)

The specific language participants used helps to illustrate how they conceptualized the relationship among scales of territorial identity: as either "connected" (fundamentally linked) or as "separate" (fundamentally distinct). Those who said such identities are connected see the various scales as either "indivisible" or "nested." Those who talked about them as separate characterized the scales of territorial identity either as "parallel" or as "divided by context, time, or subjectivity." I review each of these four models in turn.

Put simply, most participants espouse the view "We are European because we are Polish." In other words, "being European" is viewed as a fundamental characteristic of "being Polish" (see figure 4.1a). About the various levels of territorial identity, participants said, "They can all be reconciled" (*wszystko się da pogodzić*) and "You can connect them all" (*wszystko można się połączyć*). Some further expressed a sense that territorial identities are essentially indivisible; they mesh and blend into each other like a "marble cake" (see Risse 2004, 251–2). For example, Józef explained, "They don't stand one next to the other – this part Poland, this part locality, and yet another part Europe. They're all part of myself." Grzesiek pointed out a common source for all territorial attachments: "They all have a lot in common, because the same patriotism is connected to them all – attachment to place, culture, people and the like." Comments such as these emphasize connections, integration and indivisibility of territorial identities. Further, assertions like "that's how it is" point to the taken-for-granted nature of such viewpoints.

More commonly, participants talked about territorial identities in ways that suggest they are "nested" (see figure 4.1b). This is evident in the language used

Figure 4.1. Territorial identities: indivisible vs. nested

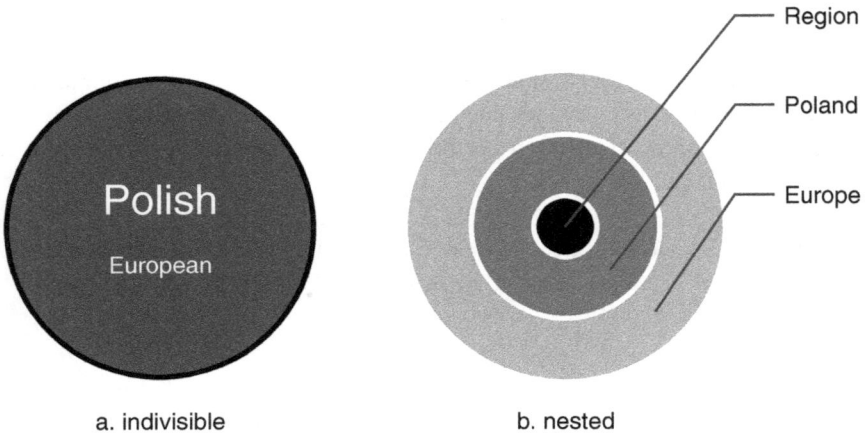

a. indivisible   b. nested

in the first two quotes in this section, that each territorial scale is a "part" (*część*) of the other or "contained within" (*zawiera się*) each other. Others used related terms like "they overlap" (*zasiębiają*) and they "lie within" (*leży w*) each other. Piotr, a salesman in Krakow, referred specifically to concentric circles: "I see it like this: the bigger circle is Europe, the smaller circle is Poland. Smaller still is Małopolska [the province], and smaller still is the heart, in the middle, which is Krakow. It's all together. They don't preclude each other." Piotr's characterization captures the way many associate smaller scales with intimacy and emotion, while wider scales are seen to be progressively farther from that "heart."

A few participants consider various levels of territorial identity to be separate rather than connected. Michał, a real estate broker in Krakow, characterized them as "parallel," while Zbysiek, a business owner in Lesko, described them as "completely disparate things that don't bother each other." Similarly, Krzysiek explained, "In my opinion, they are three completely different issues. I don't know why they would preclude each other. It's better to simply consider each one separately than to talk about them in a unifying manner. They can't be simply connected together." Others said territorial identities are divided by context, time and subjectivity. In other words, they emphasized that different scales are relevant in different situations. For example, participants might call themselves "Polish" while elsewhere in Europe, but in the US they might rather tell people they are "European." Alternatively, they pointed out that not everyone shares the same level of attachment to all places; some do not feel connected to Europe, while others may feel less intensely attached to their native place.

Whether they characterized territorial identities as connected or distinct from each other, participants agreed European identity does not displace regional or national identity. Wiola, a civil servant in Bieszczady explained, "You don't have to renounce your nationality to feel good in Europe." Similarly, Paweł, a sales manager in Bieszczady, said, "You can be connected to every one of these structures." Participants associate their regional (and in many regards national) identity with their essence. By contrast some describe European identity as "artificial."

Which do you consider your priority?

While participants unambiguously asserted it is possible, even natural, to feel attached to various territorial scales, I also wanted to know how they weigh the scales of territorial identity in relation to each other. In table 4.1, I summarize responses to the question of whether they feel one level has priority over the others. As I previously noted, rural participants were more likely to say they place priority on their region (15 out of 23). The frequency of this response follows residence patterns neatly; it was most frequent among participants who continue to live in villages (7 out of 9), followed by those in towns (6 out of 10), and 2 of the 4 raised in Bieszczady but now living in cities said they prioritize region over nation. By contrast, none of the participants from Krakow said they prioritize their attachment to the city. Rather, 6 placed priority on the nation, while 3 claimed no priority. Notably, no one said their priority loyalty is to Europe.

Table 4.1. Which do you consider your priority?

Priority	From Bieszczady (now live in village, town, city)	From Krakow	TOTALS
Region	15 (7,6,2)	0	15
Poland	6 (1,3,2)	6	12
None	2 (1 – don't know; 1 – depends on context)	3 (2 – none; 1 – all related)	5
TOTAL	23	9	32

Responses were consistent with what I have already reported above. Participants who prioritized their attachment to region referred to connections to people, landscapes and memories; some also referred to their "essential self" – their "psyche" or "character" – like Darek:

I believe it's a question of character. Because there are people like my sister, for example, but not my wife, who have no problem leaving everything and emigrating. My sister always dreamed of leaving here because there is no future, no conditions. I, by contrast, went to Spain for vacation; it was really everything you could dream of, with the beach and historic monuments. But by the end of our stay, I longed to get back home, even though it was 30 degrees [Celsius] there, and 10 degrees, foggy and cold here.

Those who said they prioritize the nation tended instead to explain their attachment in terms of culture and tradition. Marcin referenced the patriotic slogan "God, Honor and Fatherland," while Piotr referred to his "beloved fatherland." Both Wojtek and Ewelina explained their priority is the nation and pointed out the danger of regionalism, which they associate with minority movements that could provoke ethnic conflict.

The connection between nation and region reveals itself in two forms of explanation – one conceptual and one grounded in experience. Experientially, a number of participants noted that no matter where they live within the country, the culture and language are essentially the same. Marzena was the only Krakow native who deliberated whether her priority loyalty is with the nation or the city. She settled on the nation because she has moved to another city (Warsaw) where, she says, there are more or less the same customs, and where it is basically "our same internal home." Similarly, although Dorota dreams of returning from England to her native Bieszczady, she said her priority lies with the nation because if she does come back to Poland, she expects she will live in a city where there are more work opportunities. Conceptually, participants linked their regional identity to national identity by calling their region their "little fatherland" (*mała ojczyzna*), and referring to themselves as "local patriots" or "regional patriots."

Even participants who have traveled widely, including some who live in other European countries, had a hard time conceptualizing "European identity." I have already noted that Paulina, who has lived in Italy since she was twenty, and Dorota, who has lived in England since her mid-twenties, espouse what might be called dual *national* identities, or even more specific dual *regional* identities. When I asked Dorota about "Europe," she always responded with specific remarks about England. She distinguished between her primarily instrumental affiliation with England, where she can earn a decent living, and her more emotional attachment to Poland, anchored by her deep sense of connection to the familiar landscapes of the Bieszczady Mountains. Similarly, Paulina called herself an "Italian-Polish citizen" and said she loves both countries. She also said she could live anywhere: "With my character, I could adapt to every country. What's important is that I don't have to suffer, or have to do without things like I did when I was young."

Some participants identified priorities independent of territorial scales, including more individualistic values: for Aneta it was happiness; for Krzysiek,

Table 4.2. Which describes you best? Responses by residence and educational achievement

Which describes you best?	Total responses (%)	From Bieszczady (now in village, town, city)	From Krakow	Attended technical high school	Attended lyceum	Did not complete university	Completed university
Only Polish	4 (12.5)	2 (2,0,0)	2	3	1	3	1
Much more Polish	6 (18.8)	5 (3,2,0)	1	6	0	3	3
More Polish	5 (15.6)	5 (1,4,0)	0	1	4	0	5
Equally Polish	14 (43.8)	9 (2,3,4)	5	7	7	6	8
More European	0	0	0	0	0	0	0
Only European	1 (3.1)	0	1	1	0	0	1
Other	2 (6.3)	2 (0,2,0)	0	1	1	2	0
TOTAL	32	23 (8,11,4)	9	19	13	14	18

it was romantic love; for Marek and Paulina it was financial opportunity; for Stasiek it was freedom. Ania emphasized the importance of collective human rights that transcend territorial divisions. Each asserted that they could live anywhere, as long as these other values are satisfied.

Which describes you best?

Besides asking participants about their priority loyalty, I wanted to know how they weigh Polish and European identity in relation to each other. Although it was awkward to ask in an oral interview, I borrowed a multiple choice question from a survey-based study that set out to measure and explain variations in Polish national identity, especially in relation to European identity (McManus-Czubińska et al. 2003). The question is based on a scale of choices, ranging from "only Polish" to "only European," with various steps in between. I asked participants which describes them best: only Polish; much more Polish than European; more Polish than European; equally Polish and European; or only European. I also showed them a written list of the choices (see table 4.2). Since 1981, different versions of this question have been used on Eurobarometer and related surveys in numerous European countries, making it a useful source for comparative data on changes in identity across time and space (see Anderson and Kaltenthaler 1996; Antonsich 2009; Ruiz Jimenez et al. 2004). Instead of Eurobarometer's symmetrical scale, I used this asymmetrical one because, as McManus-Czubińska and her colleagues point out, "Symmetry is the product of a tidy but lazy mind, a typically bureaucratic rather than street-wise solution to an intellectual problem" (2003, 123). There is no symmetry in the way "Europe" and "nation" are commonly conceptualized in relation to each other. Since so few people claim stronger affiliation to the "European" side of the scale, it makes fine distinctions in that direction unnecessary and potentially confusing for respondents. McManus-Czubińska et al. also argue it is important to have a middle category so respondents they call "dual identifiers" can say they are "equally Polish and European." They found that dual identifiers tend to espouse a whole constellation of viewpoints that stand in contrast to so-called "exclusive identifiers," who say they are "only Polish."

Although they base their study on the premise that Poles relate national identity to European identity along a continuum, McManus-Czubińska et al. (2003) nevertheless emphasize binary distinctions between dual identifiers and exclusive identifiers, characterizing the former as "cosmopolitan" and the latter as "parochial." In other words, they distinguish between the openness and inclusiveness of dual identities in contrast to the narrow, inward-looking orientations of exclusive identities. Also, they distinguish between "progressive" dual identifiers and "traditional" exclusive identifiers (126–7). By contrast, when I asked participants in my study why they answered the way that they did, their responses were more messy; they did not conform so neatly into two dichotomous perspectives. I argue that it is valuable to examine that deeper variation to see what story it reveals about changing perceptions of Polishness, Europeanness and their relation to each other.

There was a smaller percentage of exclusive identifiers (12.5 per cent compared with 34 per cent) and a higher percentage of dual identifiers (43.8 per cent compared with 23 per cent) in my study than in McManus-Czubińska et al. (see table 4.2). My sample is too small to test these differences statistically, but I can hypothesize demographic, methodological and historical explanations for them. In terms of demography, my participants fit within a narrow age range, and younger Poles tend to identify more strongly with Europe. The group I studied also has higher-than-average levels of educational achievement, another factor that tends to correlate with stronger European identity. Methodologically, it is possible that the format of my study, in which participants were able to explain their answer, provided the opportunity for more nuanced responses, making exclusive identification less likely. With regard to historical factors, I talked with participants after Poland was already a member of the EU, making connections to Europe more salient in their everyday lives. Certain generalized demographic patterns are borne out in participants' responses. Specifically, those who live in cities (including those originally from Bieszczady), attended lyceum and completed university also tended to express stronger feelings of connection to Europe (table 4.2). Below, I consider each cluster of responses to the question "Which fits you best?" and note the patterns that reinforce particular insights about territorial scales of identity within Poland shortly after EU accession.

All four participants who described themselves as "only Polish" have spent time abroad. Marta even lived and worked in Italy for years before returning to her native village in Bieszczady.[3] She and Agata, who has occasionally done seasonal agricultural work in Germany, do not feel European because of experiences of discrimination and proscribed work opportunities in other countries. This sense of exclusion persisted for Marta even after she learned Italian and gained a legal work permit; with nothing but a high school diploma from Poland, the only jobs available to her were low-paying service positions. For years, she was a virtual captive of the household in which she cared for an elderly woman, sleeping in the same room as her, with few days off, and compelled to explain her every movement when she left the apartment. Grzesiek is a Krakow resident who has gone on a number of excursions to the Mediterranean; nevertheless, he has very little concept of what "being European" means. He says that economic interest is all that connects him to Europe. Jurek's claim to be "only Polish" is a bit more complex. The only lyceum and university graduate to answer this way, his family is part of the old Krakow elite; he explains, "In my system of values there is no other option, because I am a Pole and I can't be someone else." He sees this as both a biological and a cultural fact. Still, his views do not stem from parochialism; in fact, he deconstructed the question and concluded that separating identity into comparative scales amounts to "social engineering" on the part of politicians seeking to persuade people to feel European and support the EU. He, by contrast, considers identity indivisible, and national identity the level at which all others converge.

Evidence for changing viewpoints, in the form of growing awareness of "Europe," can be seen especially among participants who described themselves as "much more Polish than European" and "more Polish than European." Out of 11 who responded this way, 10 are from Bieszczady, 7 attended technical schools, and 3 did not complete university. Collectively, they expect a sense of "Europeanness" to grow because of Poland's accession to the EU. As Bogdan explained, he would have said he was "only Polish" a few years earlier, but "because we are connected to the EU, I can't avoid the fact that we're a part of that structure." Others referred to specific practices that have increased their awareness of "Europe." Joasia uses European subsidies for new educational programs at the school in which she works. Krzysiek, Marcin and Dorota pointed out increased opportunities to travel to other EU member states. Marcin and Józef also said they expect their children to have stronger feelings of European identity than they do. Some participants made comments showing there is still a way to go before they will feel European. Piotr and Józef pointed out there is "still no unity in Europe." Bartek and Józef observed that Poland has been in the EU too briefly for them to feel European yet, and they still associate "Europe" with "free," "democratic" Western European countries.

Although 14 out of 32 participants identified themselves as "equally Polish and European," most espoused an essentialized identity, as opposed to one that has changed with European integration. Specifically, they made assertions such as: "Poland has always been in Europe"; "I've always felt Poland is part of Europe, and it's not because of the EU"; "I always considered us in Europe. We are geographically, culturally, and psychologically in Europe"; and "Where else would Poland be but in Europe?" These claims affirm the standing of Poland within the broader global sphere, but notably do not attribute this to EU integration. Marzena, who lives in Warsaw, explained, "I have no complexes, so I feel Polish and I feel European." Wojtek said he feels equally Polish and European within a "unified" Europe, but remarkably he voted against Poland's accession to the EU. Participants' views conform to the model depicted in figure 4.1a, in which "being European" is considered a fundamental characteristic of "being Polish." A few participants provided explanations that suggest they are becoming more European, cosmopolitan and progressive. Paweł, a sales manager in Bieszczady, elaborated:

> Poland is in Europe, and maybe that's why something has changed. Maybe in the past it was hard for us to say we are European, because Europe was free, and we were not free. We were tied to the Soviet Union. It was a completely different life. Maybe we could have identified with Europe in terms of geography, but it would have been hard to identify with the people. And now we can identify with Europeans because of the region in which we live, but also because we live the same, we are free.

Paweł identified historical and political processes, as well as values like freedom, which point to the ways in which Poland's connection to Europe is strengthening. Nevertheless, selecting the middle category did not necessarily correlate with more progressive, cosmopolitan views, nor even with support for EU accession.

Marek, a Krakow native who works as a computer scientist in Prague, was the only participant who answered that he is "only European." He said his outlook is purely pragmatic: "I would say I'm only European. I would go even further and say I'm a citizen of the world. Which state I live in isn't important to me… As long as a place can guarantee me the good conditions I require, it could be anywhere." While this perspective can be called both cosmopolitan and progressive, it is worth noting that even Marek expresses minimal loyalty to "Europe." In fact, as he says in his portrait below, he feels no sense of attachment to place at any scale. Rather, he is content to live wherever best serves his own personal interests.[4]

To summarize, certain patterns emerge within participants' diverse responses. Their comments support Risse's (2004, 249) observation that attachment to various territorial scales is not a zero-sum matter. More commonly, participants conceptualize region, nation and Europe as nested, each associated with different qualities that are not seen to be in conflict. Sometimes, they can even reinforce each other, as when European identity is legitimated as a positive characteristic of being Polish. Regional and national identity are conceived as stronger, more intimate and based in more deep-seated emotions than European identity. Also, familiarity with other places in Europe and with European institutions does not necessarily correlate with dual identities, cosmopolitanism, progressive viewpoints or stronger European identity. Participants who said they feel equally Polish and European do not necessarily have a more developed sense of European identity, either. Some have rarely thought about the issue, but rather consider "European" a descriptor of the more salient category "Polish." Participants do, however, say their European identity is growing, and generally hold a positive view of "Europe."

Being and Becoming European

In this chapter, I explored the quality and intensity of territorial scales of identity, and the relationships among attachments to region, nation and Europe. I hope that careful consideration of responses to each interview question has had a layering effect, as the same patterns emerge over and over again, and reinforce particular interpretations. Just as participants' experiences and backgrounds vary, so too do their perspectives on space and place. I have argued that delving into their particular stories, and confronting the "mess," so to speak, can provide insight into what "being and becoming European" means for new citizens of the EU. Close attention to individuals' perspectives shows the inadequacy of simple dichotomies between "cosmopolitan" and "parochial," "progressive" and "traditional," or "exclusive identity" and "dual identity." As globalization scholars contend, it is important to see how local and global (or more specifically in this case regional, national and European) take shape in relation to each other (Appadurai 2008; Tsing 2000). Participants' responses show how "European" is more often understood as a characteristic of "Polish" than as a separate supranational scale of identification. This makes Europe familiar, and endows it with entitativity, but it remains conceptually undeveloped, even for many who have had frequent encounters beyond the national sphere. Although participants claim to feel much more intensely connected to their region and/or nation, most nevertheless express some degree of allegiance to Europe, and many say their sense of European identity has grown since Poland became a member of the EU.

While region and nation tend to be defined differently – region in terms of emotional connection to distinct landscapes and people, and nation in terms of historical and cultural associations – the two are often linked via the concept of *ojczyzna*, further elaborated in terms of the distinct but complementary elements defined by Ossowski (1967): the more intimate "private *ojczyzna*" associated with immediate surroundings and personal networks; and the "ideological *ojczyzna*" associated with public narratives about the broader nation. Although rural residents are more likely to say they prioritize region over other territorial attachments, this is not best explained as narrow, inward-looking parochialism because most have also traveled to other parts of Europe, and some have lived and worked abroad for extended periods time. For various reasons, they continue to hold the strongest emotional connection to their region of origin, but again, that does not mean they are closed off to Europe, or to the nation. Some acknowledged a stronger attachment to Europe since Poland became a member of the EU. Perceptions of Europe have a strong moral dimension, shaped by participants' beliefs about the way they should be treated as members. Several said negative experiences working or traveling in other parts of Europe have led them to strengthen their identification with Poland and their local region.

Determining how EU citizens perceive "Europe" has implications for the long-term viability of the EU, and in particular the question of how much legitimacy a united Europe can and will have. Participants' responses suggest that European identity is emerging from national allegiances. As such, it would seem that the EU is most likely to bolster popular support by promoting national interests.

Marek: I Can Live Anywhere

I met Marek during a group interview at a technical high school in the working-class district of Nowa Huta, a model socialist workers' community built in the 1950s to overshadow historic Krakow. Marek has an easy confidence that made him a leader in high school. A self-avowed troublemaker, he was nevertheless a good student, and passionate about computers. For fun, he taught himself to compose electronic music, and his songs have won music contests and been used as jingles for commercials. Marek studied computer science at the Jagiellonian University "*zaoczny*," which means he paid to attend classes two weekends per month. The whole time, he worked full-time, designing computer graphics for print advertisements and websites. Since graduating, he has worked as a programmer and database manager.

Until he was about eight, Marek lived in a town on the Czech border. When his parents divorced, he moved back to Krakow (where he was born) with his mother and sister. Despite the stigma he experienced growing up as the child of divorced parents, in 1993, Marek said, "My life is complicated, but not because of my family background. I am a person with a certain character; they say that I make trouble for myself, but I can't say that I have had a hard life – I'm not the poorest. My family is incomplete, but I have one. I'm not the worst student either." While still in high school, Marek called himself a patriot and said he would fight for his country, but he also said he might accept foreign domination if it did not compromise his right to identify as Polish, speak his language, and go to Polish schools. He told me he would not mind emigrating if he had more opportunities somewhere else. By the time we met again in 1999, he said, "I'm not a patriot nor even a local patriot. I can't give my life for *ojczyzna*. *Ojczyzna* doesn't exist. The country exists as a place, but I don't feel any attachment to *ojczyzna*." When we spoke in 2005, Marek had been living in Prague for about a year, and his identification with the Polish nation had weakened even more:

I moved to the Czech Republic a half year after the border opened so I was optimistic I would be able to find work. My girlfriend, who is Czech, also assured me it would be easy, and in fact it was. Her friend knew about a company that needed someone, so I went there and talked with the boss as well as I could in Czech. And he agreed to hire me. It was no problem.

I'm not the patriotic type. Like I said before, I'm not a romantic type, maybe it's related to that. I don't feel any connection at all to Poland as a country. Krakow might be the place where I was born. It isn't something I'd have a hard time leaving behind. Because I'm a practical person; I make decisions for practical reasons, if something adds up for me or not. In this regard, I didn't have a problem moving to Prague, because I moved somewhere where I had more opportunity. I found work, I earn more, and if I buy something, I know that it's good quality.

Unfortunately, even though we strive to reach Europe [*dążymy do Europy*], we've made a big mess of it. I mean, everyone who made it to the proverbial trough did whatever they could so money would fall into their own pockets, often illegally. Those people were caught and sent to jail, but what does it matter when they have so much money that their family is set for the next fifty years? And I don't have conditions at home like they have in jail, because they can afford everything. The people on the very top of the power pyramid are the same people who scam, who stole millions, and now they help each other. And the people agreed to this. What I mean is, the people elected the government, and the government supports itself. Unfortunately. That's why what's going on in Poland bothers me.

I don't know, but maybe journalists shouldn't bother to go after scandals and secrets, like for example finding out who in government cooperated with the SB [*Służba Bezpieczeństwa*; secret police] in the 1980s. That isn't important anymore. It was that kind of system, and it forced people to do certain things. Why doesn't the government pay attention to those things that influence the economy now, that slow down the economy? We have uneven roads, potholes. In fifty years, there won't be any asphalt left if it continues like this. All the money we pay goes toward filling the hole in the budget, or for retirees and pensioners, or into someone's pocket.

That's why, returning to your question, the decision to get away from Poland, and from Krakow wasn't hard. In a certain sense, it was a relief because it was a chance for me to get away from a place I have no possibility of changing. And that irritates me.

My feelings of connection or solidarity to Europe? I don't have any. Just like I don't have any for Poland. I'm incapable of connecting to a place. Europe, Asia, the US – they're just the place where you live, where you work. It doesn't change the character of your life much.

Of course, I wouldn't want to move to some worse place, for example to Siberia or somewhere. But cities that offer similar living conditions: Krakow, Prague, Warsaw. Or even New York, London or Liverpool. Wherever – Madrid. I can move anywhere where I could work for decent money and where I could live decently. Nothing holds me back.

I would say I'm "only European." I would go even further and say I'm a citizen of the world. Which state I live in isn't important to me. I also wouldn't want someone to say, "I'm a European and I don't like Australia," for example, or the United States. I'm a citizen of the world. As long as a place can guarantee me the good conditions I require, it could be anywhere.

Since emigrating, I feel really good because I have distanced myself from all of my frustrations connected with the economic situation of the country. What they say in the media, in the political realm, is one per cent of what really happens. The problem isn't that we have poor education and healthcare. I think the problem is the Polish mentality, and unfortunately the prognosis isn't good. We have a new economic system but because of the mentality of the majority of

Poles, I don't see anything changing. Maybe in fifty or a hundred years, when the generation in control now dies, youth will be at such a level that they won't want to steal everything, and there will be some kind of opportunity. But just as easily, we could become a second Argentina, and Poland will go bankrupt.

Marek's privileging of individual interest over territorial scales of belonging is notable for its rareness. He is the only Pole I have met who dissociates himself to such a degree from his nation. But even though he claims to be "only European," he does not shift his loyalty to the larger territorial scale of Europe. I emphasize this because it reveals another piece of the puzzle of "becoming European." While other participants' life stories show that strong attachment to nation and region does not necessarily interfere with growing European identity, Marek's story suggests that weak attachments to smaller territorial scales may not support stronger connections to Europe either. Rather, there may be something about the psychology of attachment that makes some people more or less prone to feelings of affiliation to place, no matter what the scale. As such, perhaps the more likely expectation is that European identity will become a wider level of affiliation that overlaps and intertwines with national and regional identity. It will not replace smaller scales.

Chapter 5

"EU MEMBERSHIP GIVES POLAND A BETTER CHANCE": PERSPECTIVES ON EUROPEAN INTEGRATION

Ewelina: Prospects for a Better Life in the European Union

Ewelina grew up in a working-class district of long, gray, socialist-period apartment blocks, but attended a college preparatory lyceum near the historic center of Krakow. The daughter of a state utility worker who had been active in the Solidarity movement, Ewelina was already a strong advocate of democratic and market reform while in high school. Now a lawyer, she remains a champion of market liberalization. She is convinced that EU membership gives Poland the best chance of developing economically, and individuals must work hard and exercise initiative to succeed. In 2005, Ewelina explained:

> Not long ago, I turned 30. I married four years ago, three years ago my son was born. In the meantime, I completed two postgraduate certificates and began my doctoral studies. I'm a director at the same company where I have been since university. I moved out of my parents' apartment and my husband and I bought our own place nearby. In other words, everything has changed. I'm a different person now.
>
> Have conditions gotten better or worse in Poland? Definitely better. Not only in terms of basic conditions, like what is available in stores, but also you live much better. Of course some people say it's gotten worse and worse, but I think those people remember how it used to be selectively. I think that if someone is resourceful, hardworking and wants to achieve something in life, it's possible because there are a lot of possibilities. You can emigrate wherever you want. We've become more normalized; we don't have to chase after anyone; we have nothing to be embarrassed about.
>
> And in my own life? Nearly everything in my life that I thought of and dreamed of has worked out. The only thing that hasn't worked out is I haven't

been able to get my certification to become an *adwokat* [a lawyer licensed to represent clients in court], but after I finish my doctoral studies, I'll have the same powers as an *adwokat*. I hope that everything I've planned for will be fulfilled; in other words I want two children, but for now I only have one. I've learned that it's very difficult to reconcile home life with a professional career. Generally, I'm very tired taking care of the home on the same level as my mother – she never worked professionally – but I think that everything in my life has worked out, and I can't complain.

I voted in favor of joining the EU. I think there are prospects for a better life, for a more open job market, more for my child, so one day he can live and work where he chooses. I also think it's a chance for Poland to move forward in those areas where we can't manage financially. I think that we have profited a lot. All of those fears that they would flood us with EU products, that Polish agriculture would be liquidated, that big EU companies would bring cheap products here – on the contrary, farmers produce not for the internal market, but rather send everything to EU countries. It worked out well; we have a big, inexpensive workforce, we also have inexpensive products that may not be as nicely packaged, but they're very good. The food we produce, because we can't afford expensive chemicals, is organic. The job market is also very open. Many acquaintances emigrated to work. They work in very bad conditions, but at the same time financially beneficial ones – it's a big life chance. None of them want to stay [abroad], but in the past they worked illegally, had to escape from the police to avoid deportation, and had trouble getting healthcare. Now they can have normal health insurance, and on top of that they work legally.

I think that in the future we'll have many more benefits. For now, we can't take advantage of all the financial help the EU offers. We don't know how to prepare all the documents. I think we'll learn just as other countries have, and I think there will be a great deal of development because of it. I think that in ten or fifteen years our infrastructure won't differ much from other EU countries. I think countries will come to the conclusion that not everyone can conform to a lot of the regulations. I think each country has such a strong feeling of distinctness, identity, connection to history, to certain cultural differences, and that they will not agree to the idea of a supranational state. I think we can establish a united neighborhood policy, but it will be hard to establish a united economic policy like the euro. I think it's the same kind of artificiality as the international language Esperanto; it's introducing certain things by force. The euro might simplify life because you can pay in every country without changing money. But it isn't a perfect system either.

Has membership brought more benefits or losses to my life? I don't think my personal situation has changed much; because every country has its own laws, it would be hard to work in my profession in any other EU country. Right now my company benefits from an ISPA [Instrument for Structural Policies for Pre-Accession] grant for environmental protection. We want to expand the plant and bring in new technology. There is a lot of bureaucracy. The system of work is a little different. Some of the grant money is designated for training programs, to improve the effectiveness of the firm, to take full advantage of the firm's resources, to manage workers correctly. This is a benefit, too; it's something new.

I'm a member of the committee that submitted two applications to ISPA, and for now we are waiting. There should be a decision by the end of the month. When you use EU money, inspectors come all the time, and each checks the exact same papers on the basis of their own criteria. We were also one of the first firms to get ISPA funds, and now everyone learns from our mistakes. I don't think it's fair that I'm judged, not on the basis of what I knew when I applied, but on the basis of what actually happened. It's very easy to look back and say how it should have been done. Now, despite various errors, we're trying to realize our project, even though we might have to return money to the EU budget.

How strongly do I feel attached to Europe? For me that's weird. I think we've always been Europeans, but they always treated us as a second- or third-class country. I think that I'm first a Pole, and only later a European. But I have a feeling of connection to cultural traditions, so that's some kind of attachment. It upsets me a lot when people come to Poland and act like we entered the EU on 1 May [2004] and by some miracle we suddenly became civilized. I was in Slovakia on 1 May, and I observed the officials at the border who didn't know what to do, whether to check documents or not, and that's symbolic to me. No one uninvited us from Europe – they invited us into the EU, not into Europe. It's a little irritating. In some areas we're more technologically advanced. At work, there was a funny situation in which representatives of a British company came to Krakow, and wanted to sell us some equipment. They were surprised when they saw what we had, and later said that they could learn from us, not the reverse. So my own life experience shows that we're not completely third world, in need of catching up with anyone, it's just that they still treat us a little like that. And we let them treat us that way.

I have always thought that when you say Poland, you're also talking about Europe. We're geographically in Europe, and culturally and psychologically we are European. I think that in all these countries, everyone looks at themselves first as someone who belongs to their country, and then later looks at themselves in the broader scale of the continent.

By exercising diligence and entrepreneurship, Ewelina and her husband, a business owner, have "made it" in the new economy. When I visited in 2011, they had recently moved from their apartment into a house on the outskirts of the city. They own two cars, have just had a third child and send their children to private school. Ewelina is committed to her job, and never even took full advantage of the maternity leave that is provided to all mothers. Even during her mandatory leave, she visited the office regularly and brought work home. She does not like to delegate the most important matters to others because she does not trust they will be done properly. Ewelina stressed that "being European" has always been a characteristic of Polishness, and thus it is something separate from integration into the EU. Nevertheless, she also sees integration as part of a process of solidifying ties with Western European institutions, and Poles are, in a sense, "becoming European" as they learn to navigate these institutions with their new status as EU citizens.

Becoming European: Overview of the Integration Process

Whereas Chapter 4 highlighted orientations toward "Europe," I shift my focus now to perceptions of the EU. Although the two are often conflated in everyday discourse, it is both analytically useful and ethnographically accurate to emphasize how they carry different meanings and serve different functions. Below, I explore the cognitive and emotional spaces the "European Union" fills for participants; they may well *be* European (see their comments in Chapter 4), but they have only recently *become* citizens of the European Union. I review their perceptions of EU institutions and policies, not to distill a fixed national disposition toward the EU but rather to reveal the constellations of debate, the range of viewpoints that emerge about EU integration. Specifically, debates tend to revolve around issues of sovereignty, advancement and security, and they substantiate the ongoing value of the national scale for most participants.

EU integration is often explained within a narrative about social advancement. As a cultural anthropologist used to approaching cultural diversity from a culturally relativistic perspective, it can be uncomfortable to hear research subjects accept as a matter of course the metanarrative of progress, which positions the most developed countries at the pinnacle and ascribes lesser value to their own culture. Numerous scholars have argued for alternative readings of global political economy, starting with the seminal works of Wolf (1982) and Said (1979), and continuing with studies comparing postcommunism with postcolonialism (see Buchowski 2006; and Verdery 2002). Gille (2010, 15–16) challenges scholars to find an alternative to modernization approaches by looking for ways in which the so-called first world (i.e., the US, the UK and Allied countries) and second world (i.e., the former state-socialist countries) have been mutually constitutive. Nevertheless, it is also important to recognize the position participants take, and try to understand it in their own terms. Delegitimizing their perspective as a product of false consciousness or hegemony is itself a kind of cultural imperialism. Follis (2008) suggests using the postcolonial lens to "draw attention to the tensions between repudiating and celebrating the past, between expectations of a better future and a sense of abandonment and powerlessness" (337) in what she calls "postcolonial ambivalence" (345).

Ambivalence is an apt term to describe the way many participants approach integration into the global capitalist economy and the EU. Expressions of ambivalence, I suggest, provide a way of bridging local and global scales wherein allegiances to familiar people and places can be affirmed even as participants engage more with transnational institutions and locales. The focus on ambivalence allows us to see beyond the common dichotomization between "global forces" that act on "local places" and instead, following Anna Tsing, helps us uncover "the ways that cultural processes of all 'place' making and all 'force' making are both local *and* global" (2000, 352). Specifically, when participants reflect upon opportunities made possible by EU membership, as well as their experiences of loss when their native place is either left behind or transformed, they conceive of mutually constitutive local and European places, shaped by forces of integration that are themselves both local and global. Ambivalence does important psychological work, helping individuals cope with, and even sometimes reconcile, contradictory impulses. These personal engagements also promote the entitativity of Europe, and make the EU socially and psychologically real.

I would argue that it is hardly surprising that most people want the material comforts that others have, even if it means comparing their own group unfavorably with others. In relation to his observations in Nepal, Liechty explains that modernism and dependence "converge to provide an 'education' for young people that is alienating to the extent that it instills a self-peripheralizing consciousness" (1995, 187). Similarly, Greenberg notes that "the internalization of civilizational tropes" leads Serbians to associate the "normal" with modernization and European integration (2012, 96). Pajo (2008) argues that Albanian migrants to Greece overlook their own social demotion, instead reproducing a global imaginary of a hierarchy of nations. These kinds of associations can even shape sociological categories, as when Mach and Niedźwiedzki label the ability to take advantage of opportunities offered by EU integration "civilizational competence" (2002, 183–4). Questions of social advancement and social demotion are elements of the constellations of debate that participants in my study articulated in relation to European integration. I consider how these debates, and the ambivalence expressed through them, are constitutive of participants' self-identity and sense of belonging.

I begin with an overview of the process by which Poland has become integrated into EU structures. Then, I distill patterns in responses to interview questions about Poland's entry into the EU. Responses show that the legitimacy of the EU is bolstered by perceived benefits for the Polish nation and, especially among Bieszczady residents, for the local region. Here, and in the next two chapters, I explore how the EU functions as an *idea*, a symbol of Poland's rightful place at the center of Europe, and as an *instrument* for achieving economic prosperity and political influence within Europe, and indeed within a global imaginary of nations.

Association

Almost as soon as the regime changed in 1989, membership in the European Community (the organization that became the EU in 1993) was touted as a goal of Poland's "return to Europe." Poland's first postcommunist prime minister, Tadeusz Mazowiecki, introduced the idea of Polish integration, and European Community countries agreed to help Poland and Hungary with economic restructuring (Bokajło and Dziubka 2003; Słomski 2001, 25).[1] My group interviews with high school students in the early 1990s became a fruitful context for constellations of debate – what Schwartz (1978) calls the "litigation of culture" – about Poland's likely place within a united Europe. Participants volunteered their thoughts about eventual European integration, even though it did not occur to me at the time to ask about it directly. For instance, some lyceum students in Lesko had the following discussion:

RAFAŁ: There's this ideal that nations [*narody*] can blend – I don't see it happening. If Poles were to emigrate and Poland became 60 per cent German, what would you become?
ELKA: A European.
MARIUSZ: The problem is rather that Poland will not be admitted [into the European Community].
MAGDA: We need to work on our economy so that we can be an equal partner.

Concerns about European integration echo dilemmas faced by other developing countries undergoing broader processes of globalization. Most participants believed membership in the European Community was as yet out of reach. They alternately described a united Europe as a source of opportunity for Poles or a threat to Polish autonomy, as something to be aspired to or avoided. They questioned how Poland could achieve the economic conditions associated with unification. They also considered political and cultural implications of membership. Some feared Poland would be "bought up" by wealthier Western neighbors, and the market for native agricultural and industrial products would be weakened. A number of students expressed concern about the kind of relationship Poland would have with other members – would Poland be a "parasite" on more powerful nations or would those more powerful economies "occupy" Poland? Some distinguished between "moving closer" (*zbliżenie*) to the West, which they wanted to do, and "mixing" (*mieszanie*) with other nations, which they did not. Many objected to anything that might compromise Polish cultural uniqueness. Still others saw Poland's entrance into the European Community as a "return to normalcy" (Galbraith 2003b) or pointed out that Poland has always been a part of Europe (Galbraith 2004). Some inverted the imagined hierarchy of nations by arguing that in Poland Christian values undergirding European culture have not been corrupted by modern influences, thus making Poland a role model for the rest of Europe. The constellations of debate and the associated ambivalence participants voiced in the early 1990s continued to shape negotiations about Poland's entrance into the EU for the next ten years.

In June 1993, the Copenhagen criteria confirmed the possibility of Central and Eastern Europe countries joining the EU after fulfilling certain political, economic and social conditions, including stable democratic institutions, human and minority rights, market economy, competitiveness and a strong internal market (Blazyca 1999; Bokajło and Dziubka 2003, 121). In 1994, the Polish foreign minister submitted the official application for membership, and later that year the EU agreed to have yearly meetings with Poland. Still, there was little clarity about the specific steps required to fully become integrated. Vachudova (2005) effectively shows how European Community members were themselves ambivalent about whether to open up to the East, and unsure how to do so. The differences in economic institutions, economic development, and per capita income seemed too great to bridge. Nevertheless, there was at the same time a strong rhetorical push for unification, fueled in part by guilt over the way the allied powers had conceded to Stalin's demand for a "sphere of influence" after World War II, and in part by triumph over the defeat of Soviet domination in Eastern Europe.

Candidacy

The disconnect within the EU between ideological support for integration and pragmatic reluctance to spell out exactly how it could be achieved was finally bridged when in 1997 the conditions for accession were more clearly defined for countries wishing to join (Vachudova 2005, 108–10). These conditions were approved by some member states who assumed setting a high bar would act as a deterrent for candidate states (110). Instead, the policy divisions in the *acquis communautaire* (the accumulated corpus of EU laws and regulations) became a roadmap to what had before been an abstract goal. Certain countries, especially the Czech Republic, Hungary, Poland and the

Baltic States, were quick to begin the process of matching their systems to EU standards, a process called "harmonization." The most important changes involved democratization of political institutions, market liberalization and institution of the "rule of law" (a legal system that is enforced uniformly).

Although critics of the EU have called this process a form of imperialism, Vachudova (2005) emphasizes some key ways in which harmonization differs from the imposition of rules by a dominant power. First, member states remained ambivalent about Eastern expansion of the EU (see also Słomski 2001). Therefore, it was up to candidate states to decide if they wanted to seek membership. Second, independent of EU pressure, candidate countries were already pursuing goals later identified as conditions for membership. Indeed, in many ways EU integration involved a continuation of the same processes of reform that began after the fall of state socialism (see also Knudsen 2012). Third, candidate states were able to choose the sequencing and pacing of reforms; as long as they made enough progress overall, they could postpone some reforms until after their accession to the EU. Economist Joseph Stiglitz notes that "the rules of the game that govern globalization are [...] designed to benefit the advanced industrialized countries" and "the way globalization has been managed has taken away much of the developing countries' sovereignty" (2006, 9). He argues that a central way of "making globalization work" – of ensuring that developing countries have a better chance of benefiting from participation in global structures – is by letting local experts with in-depth knowledge of local conditions determine the sequence and pacing of reforms (2002, 73–8). According to Vachudova, this is exactly what happened with the process of European integration; candidate states were allowed to decide the order and the speed at which they would implement reforms. In other words, even though the process of integration required conformity with externally mandated standards, many associated reforms had already been deemed legitimate and desirable by the governments of candidate states (Vachudova 2005, 109, 228).

By the late 1990s, with the road map before them, Poland was well on the way to EU integration, though a great deal of uncertainty remained. Koczanowicz calls the simultaneous fear and sense of belonging with Western Europe that characterized political identity and public discourse a "paradox of temporalities" (2008, 78). These dilemmas were played out in the Polish media. Would Poland be one of the first postcommunist countries admitted? Would the expansion occur in three years, in five years, or at some later date? Would Poland enter as a full member with all the same rights and responsibilities as existing members, or would some sort of alternative status be established? In a radio interview on 2 July 2000, President Aleksander Kwaśniewski outlined his position on these issues. He said that the idea of the expansion of the EU had already been agreed upon, but negotiations remained about just how and when it will occur. He also expressed concern about the establishment of two-tiered membership, where new members would be admitted but granted a different, lesser status from long-standing members. This decision, he emphasized, has implications for the kind of Europe people will live in. He pointed out the danger of institutionalizing divisions rather than promoting unity, making it harder for poorer countries to ever reach the level of wealthier countries. Participants in my study echoed Kwaśniewski's concerns, particularly with regard to EU conditions that would hamper Poland's ability to overcome economic disparities.

By 2000, experts generally agreed that the Polish political system had successfully established democratic institutions, and the legal system was well on its way to insuring the rule of law, thus meeting EU conditions. The stumbling block remained the Polish economic system: the average annual income was one third that of Portugal and Greece, the countries with the lowest averages of all EU members, and domestic businesses struggled to be competitive in the global market (Słomski 2001, 23). While the Polish government pushed for full membership as soon as possible, I heard expressions of caution in everyday conversations. Is Poland really ready to join Europe? Is the economy strong enough to benefit from membership, or will Poland just become a market for foreign firms? How much autonomy will be lost, and is it worth the extra security gained via stronger alliances with the West? EU member states had their own concerns about the level of investment required to reduce economic disparities, about economic migrants from Poland flooding into the stronger economies of Western Europe, and about the size and inefficiency of Poland's agricultural sphere. Nevertheless, by the end of 2002 the EU had agreed to admit Poland among ten new members, with a target date of 2004.[2]

Accession

In June 2003, after five years of negotiation and even longer speculation, the Polish people voted in a referendum on EU membership. To be valid, over fifty per cent of the eligible public had to cast their vote, a majority of whom had to support unification. Despite a tense first day in which only 17.6 per cent of eligible voters went to the polls, by the second day 59 per cent had voted, 77 per cent of whom favored Poland's entrance to the EU (Kublik and Pacewicz 2003). Expressions of triumph dominated in the Polish press (BBC News 2003) and President Kwaśniewski proclaimed "We are back! Back to the great European Family. We are back to the place Poland and Poles deserve after their 1,000 year history and the great courage Poles have shown over the past several years" (Gazeta.pl 2003). This statement is notable for the way it merged national mythological elements with expressions of connection to Europe. Despite this show of support for unification, a great deal of ambivalence was expressed about entrance into the EU by participants in my study and in surveys conducted in Poland by the CBOS. On 1 May 2004, Poland officially joined the EU.

Since 1993, surveys have consistently shown that the majority of Poles support EU membership. Nevertheless, this trend obscures variation across occupational and regional categories, and during various historical periods. Nor does it capture the widespread ambivalence about the effects of integration on Poland expressed by both supporters and opponents of accession. Change over time can be seen in figure 5.1; whereas 70–80 per cent of those surveyed favored integration before 1997, when membership remained an abstract goal, support waned during what Vachudova calls the period of "active leverage," when the EU clearly defined the conditions for membership and candidate countries began to meet those conditions in earnest. Subsequently, support rose after the referendum on membership passed, dropped around the time of Poland's accession, and then rose steadily until leveling off around 2008. Since the middle of 2006, over eighty per cent of the surveyed population has supported integration (Hipsz 2011). This support tends to be stronger among professionals and businesspeople, urban residents, younger generations and the more educated; it tends to be weakest among farmers, rural residents, retirees and those with lower levels of education. Also, supporters of some

Figure 5.1. Support and opposition to European integration

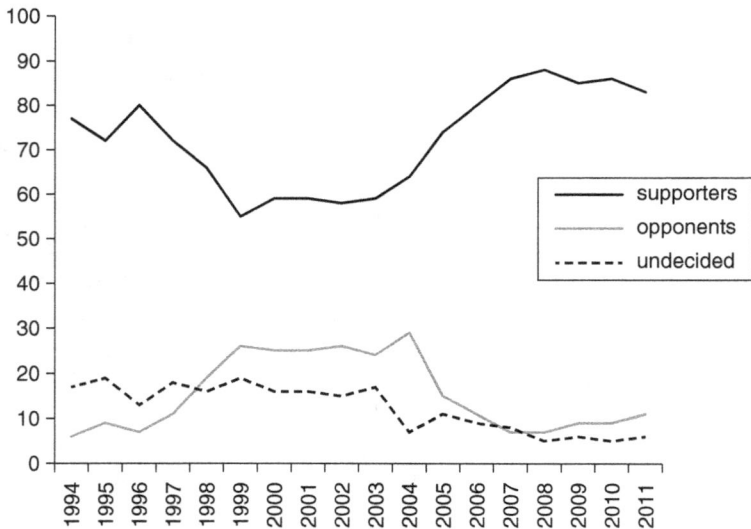

Sources: Roguska 2000; 2002; 2004b; Hipsz 2011

political parties, such as the Civic Platform (PO), tend to view the EU more favorably than do supporters of other parties, such as Law and Justice (PiS). My qualitative data help to reveal the reasons supporters and opponents alike express ambivalence about integration.

Perspectives on the European Union

When I visited participants in 2005, Poland had been a member of the EU for just over a year. Most explained to me that not enough time had passed for much to change as a result of Poland's accession. Rather, integration was more often described as an important symbolic marker of progress in the transformation that began with the fall of state socialism, ideally leading to a more central place for Poland among the most developed and powerful countries in the world. While participants overwhelmingly supported EU integration (in numbers consistent with national survey results), even supporters voiced ambivalence about the actual effects of membership. I bring to focus in this section a snapshot of participants' perceptions of the EU and its likely impact on Poland, as reported in interviews in 2005. Notably, already in 2008, and very markedly in 2011, they viewed the EU more favorably. But in 2005, participants articulated uncertainty about the economic, political and cultural influence of EU integration. Specifically, I asked why participants voted for or against Poland's accession, what influence they thought membership would have on Poland and on their personal lives, and who they believed benefits more from membership: Poland or other member states. Responses are perhaps better read as statements about values rather than reasoned assessments of objective conditions. They reflect the value participants place on the nation, whether they believe European cohesion is possible, and even fundamental assumptions about human nature. Commonly, participants said "nothing has changed," and EU integration was the "only path" open to Poland. Two constellations of debate came into focus in their discussions about integration: in terms of economics, whether membership brings opportunity to Poland or serves the interests of established member states; and in terms of governance, whether the EU promotes order and equality or is just a new form of imperialism challenging Polish autonomy.

In 2005, most participants claimed that little or nothing had changed since Poland became a member of the EU. They explained the event was too recent to have much effect. I suspect other factors came into play as well. First, it is not easy to step back far enough from everyday experiences to bring into focus how things used to be and to assess the incremental changes that have occurred. Similarly, in the early 1990s, participants had difficulty articulating a coherent story about the transition from state socialism; it took several more years before they were comfortable reflecting about how different their lives had been before and after 1989. In 2005, EU membership was too new for participants to have settled on a developed narrative about it. Second, EU membership tends to be experienced as a step in a more extended transition from state socialism (see Knudsen 2012). As such, it is hard to isolate which changes result from EU membership and which ones are a product of more general processes of globalization and neoliberal reform. Third, the claim that "nothing has changed" has a rhetorical function independent of European integration; it is a common mode of critique of the political authorities in Poland, who are seen as ineffectual and self-interested. I develop this third point in my discussion of governance below.

Frequently, participants described EU integration as "the only path" open to the country, though they variously characterized the process as unavoidable, as a source of hope or as a matter of destiny. Each of these characterizations is indicative of very different orientations toward the EU, even though some participants expressed their ambivalence about membership by alternating among explanations. Language emphasizing the unavoidability of joining the EU includes phrases such as "only way," "no choice" and "it would make no sense not to." Those who responded this way do not necessarily trust nor like the EU; rather, they consider EU membership unavoidable because they question the viability of Poland without strong allies. Some referred to Poland's history of domination by aggressive neighbors, while others cited the realities of globalization, especially competition in the global capitalist economy. Some asked who else Poland could unite with – if not Europe, they're left with Russia. In short, they emphasized the opportunities that would be missed and dangers that might await if Poland did not join. Others used the language of hope: they called membership a "chance for Poland," a source of "hope for a better life" and for "new opportunities." Those who used the language of destiny emphasized that Poland's rightful place is and always has been within Europe, and the EU is the mechanism by which Poland will regain its social position nearer the top of an imagined hierarchy of nations. For them, gaining an equal position in Europe was "meant to be" and is a "return to normality."

These different ways of talking about EU integration reflect different ways of thinking about membership and varying levels of support for EU institutions. They also indicate conflicting values emerging from contrasting perceptions of transnational relations. I suggest ambivalence marks a field in which participants seek to reconcile ideals of European culture and the actual opportunities and challenges EU integration offers Poland. I explore these ambivalences as they manifested in reflections about economic factors and governance.

Economic opportunity vs. consumer market

Participants talked about EU integration in terms of economic factors far more than anything else. "Prospects for a better life," as Ewelina characterized it, come from two avenues: opportunities for mobility, particularly to work legally in other EU countries, and direct subsidies from EU structural funds for economic development *within* Poland. In brief, participants enumerated benefits in the form of open borders with other EU countries, opportunities to travel without a passport or visa, and official channels for employment abroad (see Chapter 6). They further identified financial support for farm subsidies, infrastructural projects such as roads and sewer systems, and educational and cultural programs, as well as increased employment at foreign companies and in Poland's tourism sector (see Chapter 7). As Zosia, who lives in Bieszczady, put it, "Poland isn't such a rich country, and we get a good amount of money from their till. So it's to our benefit." Similarly, Ewelina said, "It's a chance for Poland to move forward in those areas where we can't manage financially."

Despite their hope for prosperity, participants debated whether EU membership would fulfill that promise. A common concern they raised was that the established EU countries were really just looking out for their own economic welfare. Participants expressed this in a number of ways, including statements such as: "They would not admit us if it were not in their interest." Some identified skilled workers and professionals who were trained at Poland's expense (for the most high-achieving students, university remains free in Poland) but now contribute to another country's economy. Joasia, a librarian in Bieszczady, further explained, "We have very many intelligent people, scientists, who emigrate, because no one can sponsor their research here; they sell their patents, or someone else underwrites them, because no one here in Poland can afford to sponsor them. It's a shame, and I hope it changes." Participants also talked about other Europeans gaining access to high-quality, low-price Polish products. Frequently, the demand for Polish food was highlighted, because it is grown without chemical additives. Conversely, other participants emphasized that Poland provides investment opportunities for wealthy foreigners who have bought up Polish companies, land and real estate. Ania remarked that her family stands to benefit because they expect to get a premium price when they sell a house they own in Zakopane (a tourist center in the Tatra Mountains). Michał makes a good living in Krakow handling the real estate interests of foreign companies. These same forces, however, made it very difficult for Grzesiek, who struggles to keep his computer business afloat, and had to borrow money from his in-laws to buy an apartment. Commonly, participants said their most direct experience of integration into the global economy was in the form of rising prices, leading them to lament, "We have Western prices, but Eastern salaries."

Some remarked upon the EU priority to balance economic inequality by providing subsidies for underdeveloped regions, as in Robert's comment: "The main goal, as I understand it, is to equalize the level [of development] in all member states. Those at the higher level pay more than they receive; those on a lower level get more than they receive." But, as Paweł said, "Nothing is for free." Despite economic benefits coming from EU integration, participants emphasized that Poland is the weaker partner in the union. Several expressed concern that Poland would just become a consumer market (*rynek zbytu*) for Western Europe's surplus merchandise. *Rynek zbytu* can be translated simply as "market," as in an arena for the sale of products, but it more commonly carries a negative connotation, as for example, when Grzesiek explained: "The EU wanted to connect more countries to themselves because it opened a *rynek zbytu*. Because they have already saturated their own. And this is the next problem [with EU integration]. There are many [Polish] firms that lacked the proper infrastructure or finances to improve their company so it would meet EU requirements. And essentially this squeezed our work places, squeezed our industry."

Bogdan, a government employee, expressed it even more strongly: "Germany, Brussels, France and Spain, too, have taken advantage of our *rynek zbytu*. They dumped old lines of production. The ones who benefited were the first ones to form the EU. There is no equality. The rich always look out for themselves. After all, no one will give 100 million unless they were going to get 200 million back." Serving as the *rynek zbytu* of established EU countries implies a weaker position in the balance of trade, and correspondingly, in a global imaginary in which nations are hierarchically organized around powerful centers that dictate the criteria for participation within the global sphere. Bogdan and Grzesiek give voice to a deep and widespread ambivalence toward EU integration (and globalization generally), as indicated by their expression of concern about Poland being taken advantage of, or being used for the enrichment of stronger partners. Paulina expressed this same concern when discussing a proposal to build a waste dump in Bieszczady. She fears the natural beauty of the region will be polluted, literally, by Western European trash.

Governance: Transnational order vs. external control

Ambivalence about the overall effect of membership on Poland's sovereignty, advancement and stability emerged most clearly in reflections about governance. Participants alternated between praise for the order and equality promoted by EU standards, and criticism of the rigidity of those same standards. As Zbysiek, a business owner in Lesko, put it:

> It would be foolish to not enter such a structure, which is a kind of insurance of stability of certain processes. Few can afford to be completely independent states. Exceptions such as Switzerland or Norway haven't, for either economic or historical reasons, been involved in such things. However, I believe that all of the effort, the transformation so to speak, the changed regulations that were forced on us so that Poland could enter the EU, made it possible to organize many things that lay fallow, were not done at all, or were done poorly over those fifty years in the Eastern Bloc. That's why I think it was the only way, a reasonable solution; it was a "marriage of convenience." But it wasn't an accident, or blind reverie. We always wanted to be in the West.

Zbysiek described the necessity of integration, and even the benefits of harmonization; his lack of enthusiasm derives from a sense of being forced into the EU and the corresponding loss of national autonomy. Despite his ambivalence, Zbysiek suggested that, on balance, the trade-off of some sovereignty for greater stability and social advancement is worth it; the EU promises to finally repair the infrastructural neglect that characterized governance during late socialism.

Robert and Stasiek posed another contrast, specifically between leadership styles common in Poland and in the EU:

> I am in favor of Poland's integration in the EU because, despite the obligations, it brings many benefits. One thing in which I place hope is that the laws that are established will not be something that one [government] minister, together with another minister, just thinks up. Or that a majority in parliament just votes for something. Even if those things happen, it will have to be in agreement with EU law, and if not it will have to be judged and changed. (Robert, a teacher in Lesko)

> It definitely puts the breaks on the silly ideas of our politicians. Because EU law doesn't allow this and that. So that is a positive influence. The negative is the pervasive bureaucracy. We barely were liberated from the communist bureaucracy. And now bureaucracy comes from Brussels and it's even more powerful. (Stasiek, a computer programmer)

In other words, the EU was seen as a kind of civilizing force, counteracting the fractiousness and corruption that characterized post-1989 politics in Poland, but it also signaled a new era of external controls on the Polish nation. Stasiek raised another common criticism of EU governance: the rigid and pervasive bureaucracy.

Aneta's perspective on EU bureaucracy is shaped by her experiences pursuing EU support for projects such as international film festivals:

> It's not democracy, but rather bureaucracy. It's true that new opportunities have appeared [following EU integration], but no one knows about those opportunities. It's like a situation in *Hitchhiker's Guide to the Galaxy*, where a notice is posted about demolishing a house:
> How can that be?
> – A notice was posted.
> Where?
> – Well, in our office.
> Where?
> – In the basement.
> What do you mean in the basement? But I didn't see it!
> – In fact, the light was out.[3]
> It's a big thing that we can try for subsidies for various projects. But it's very difficult to find information about these grants. We send applications, and sometimes we get funding, but sometimes we don't. When you look on the Internet, there is such a mass of information, you get lost. Or sometimes it turns out that some rule you didn't know about makes you ineligible and you have to withdraw your application. There is an awful lot of paperwork, and that's not good.

Aneta uses humor to make the point that although agencies publicize funding programs, it can still be hard to locate essential facts about them. As she also stated, applications require a lot of work, and there is no guarantee that worthwhile projects will be supported. In other words, EU subsidies offer new forms of opportunity, but also new forms of uncertainty.

Despite frustration with the rigidity and scope of EU bureaucracy, participants expressed respect for a system that actually makes it possible to get things done. This must be understood against the backdrop of the inefficiencies of state socialism, when government reports of progress were contradicted by daily struggles to accommodate systemic shortages, followed by the uncertain 1990s when official channels continued to provide unreliable or poorly defined pathways to opportunities. By contrast, the EU delivers a clear and stable structure for individual and national social advancement, even though outcomes remain uncertain. Information about subsidies may be readily available for those who know where to look, but there are no guarantees that funds will be granted. Open borders provide the freedom to travel and seek employment abroad, but they do not guarantee good pay, or even decent working conditions. Participants explain their growing sense of security in terms of stable EU-supported structures. Nevertheless, they remain subject to the uncertainties emerging from the privatization of risk, where opportunities are open to those in positions of privilege, or for those who exercise characteristics valued by neoliberal ideology, such as initiative, flexibility and entrepreneurship.

Rather than criticizing the EU bureaucracy, some participants blamed the country's failure to take full advantage of EU funding opportunities on the continued inadequacies of Polish leadership. They condemned the "stupidity" with which Polish authorities make funding decisions and the lack of qualified people to propose and carry out projects successfully. Krzysiek castigated those in power for failing to support young entrepreneurs:

> Our system is sick because rather than give young people a chance to open their own firms, for example by giving them a tax break, it's more comfortable for Poland to lose these experts, and give them to the Germans, French or British. If they [young people] just had that tax break for two or three years, they would have that base, and the whole economy would grow. All the wheels would turn – blocks, wire, steel, cement – they would build their homes and everyone would have a job.

Krzysiek spoke from experience (see his portrait below). He has met official roadblocks in his efforts to run a small business in Lesko. Notably, this viewpoint embraces neoliberal values, but condemns Polish power holders for failing to insure conditions for people seeking to exercise those values. It suggests ways in which the system fails to function as it should not because the system is wrong, but rather because of poor execution of its standards.

Marzena has had a very different experience of work; she makes a good living and has a secure position at a bank in Warsaw. Nevertheless, she shares Krzysiek's opinion that the weaknesses of the Polish economy stem from internal shortcomings: "I think that whether or not Poland will develop depends on good management. That's why I say membership isn't thought through completely. The same with all of those regulations. I don't know why; maybe it's because of undereducated people, too little knowledge, too little strategy. Definitely, what limits Poland doesn't depend on EU entry." Marzena does not think the EU has had much of an influence on Poland. She said the country was developing before integration and would have continued to do so at about the same rate even without entering the EU. The stumbling blocks remain incompetent Polish governance and the deficiencies of the Polish workforce.

Ambivalence extends, as well, to comparisons between Soviet influence before 1989 and the more recent influence of the EU. On the one hand, there is a sharp contrast between characterizations of the contemporary alliance with the EU and perceptions of past affiliation with the Soviet Union. Rothschild and Wingfield note that in response to Soviet hegemony Central and Eastern European "publics remained nationalist, often religious, self-consciously 'European' and culturally 'Western' in the sense of anti-Soviet" (2008, 117). By contrast, the EU does not face the same problems of legitimacy because membership is more often viewed as a *chosen* allegiance, and integration is associated with social advancement. As Basia explained, "If we hadn't [voted for EU membership] where would we find ourselves? Would we be in the same bag as Russia? For me, it was natural that we're going in a certain direction."

Nevertheless, others pointed out uncomfortable similarities between EU and Soviet management styles. Bogdan complained about the lack of sovereignty in the EU, in which member states are compelled to follow the dictates of Brussels without any effective voice in the European parliament. Wojtek, a professor, argued, "The EU is just like a centralized economy. Because they decide: how many tons of grain to produce, how many liters of milk. After all, we already had that. I don't believe that kind of system has a chance of surviving." Agata, a farmer, gave a specific example of this kind of top-down regulation: all their livestock must be tagged and they are required to document every birth, death, sickness and sale. They must be prepared at any time to show detailed records to inspectors, who visit without warning. Her husband added it is worse than it was during state socialism because then they were able to slaughter and sell their livestock as they wished, to local distributers for example, but now if they want to participate in the European market, they can only sell their products through certified channels. Again, the EU is associated with loss of autonomy.

Another source of ambivalence about EU membership is uncertainty about the long-term viability of the EU itself. Marzena, a banker in Warsaw, said, "The EU is not entirely stable and I'm not entirely convinced it will continue in the form it has now, even though I don't think it brings either great losses or benefits." Similarly, Joasia said, "Honestly, I don't trust it. For now I'm suspending judgment. I believe it's difficult to support so many countries, to handle policy, to distribute funding to everyone, to more or less stabilize the legal system so it will be more or less the same everywhere. It's too much. How can they succeed?" Bogdan also agreed: "Sooner or later, it will all fall apart. You can already see divisions in the EU. There isn't that cohesion anymore." Some participants suggested that Poland has entered the EU too late, and much like a pyramid scheme, only the countries that joined early stand to profit before the whole thing crumbles.

To summarize, participants gave voice to a number of ambivalences about the EU's likely impact on economic factors and governance. They cited economic benefits from increased public and private investment in Polish infrastructure and commerce, and benefits for individuals who find more lucrative and legal employment in other member states. They also noted possible downsides of these same factors. Poland might become a consumer market enriching foreign companies, and Poland's best talent might leave and never return. Concerns about governance were more multifaceted. With regard to national autonomy, the EU was alternately viewed as a source of protection against potential threats and as a compromise of sovereignty uncomfortably similar to Soviet control. The similarities to Soviet influence were most commonly related to the EU bureaucracy and its exacting regulations and standards. However, those very same controls were alternatively praised for bringing order and reigning in Polish patterns of governance dominated by unruly managers and corrupt politicians. Concerns remained that the EU has become a new gatekeeper, with the power to set the conditions for prosperity, and to decide who measures up to those standards. And finally, not everyone was convinced that the EU experiment would succeed.

Implications for the European Union

Talk about *Europe*, and Poland's place within it, tends to be different from reflections about the *European Union* and Poland. Some participants who claim Poland's place within Europe is long-standing and unquestioned express opposition or ambivalence toward EU membership. "Europe" is held out as an ideal – something to be aspired to, perhaps even what Geertz (1973) would call a "model for" Poland. Most see the EU as a mechanism for obtaining *porządek* (order), a term they use to describe societies that function "as they should," where it does not take extraordinary measures to achieve a reasonable standard of living, and where politicians and ordinary citizens generally follow fair and just laws and social rules. Support for EU integration is bolstered by the promise membership offers for the future. As an idea, membership is considered an important marker of Poland's successful emergence from Soviet domination and state socialism, and integration into the neoliberal world system. Nevertheless, this process also stirs anxieties about the loss of national distinctiveness and about the institutionalization of inequality relative to other European states, leading some to wonder if subordination to one transnational system (the Soviet Union) is just being replaced by subordination to another (the European Union).

Attention to these constellations of debate within self-reflections constitutes an import avenue through which person-centered ethnography can contribute to globalization theory. The ambivalences expressed in negotiations about EU integration reveal simultaneously globalizing and localizing processes.

Cognitively and emotionally, the EU fills a place of promise for a better future, where the injustices of the past will be put right. It is much harder for integration to measure up to these ideals and values in actuality, when the global capitalist market can put people out of work instead of providing new economic opportunities, and EU policies can institutionalize power hierarchies instead of equalizing chances. Through their ambivalence, participants hold these opposite poles of possibility in their minds at the same time, leaving open the chance that they may eventually be reconciled. As such, it is a particularly active site for the production of lasting ties with Europe, but, significantly, one that does not require severing emotional or material ties with one's nation or region of origin.

It is striking to me how many of the hopes and concerns articulated in 2005 (when participants were in their thirties and most had a range of encounters with EU policies, institutions and citizens) are the same as the hopes and concerns expressed in 1992 (when participants were still in high school and had minimal experience with Western European institutions and citizens). I suggest that this continuity stems from the fact that views of the EU (and of Europe) emerge from values that have also been relatively stable. Deeply engrained sentiments of affiliation with the nation have serious implications for the kind of collective, centralized entity the EU is and can become. Europe as a symbol lends legitimacy to the EU, but it does so in a particular way: not *at the expense* of national allegiance, but *through* national allegiance (see Ruane 1994; Shore and Black 1994).

State socialism ultimately failed in large part because it was unable to deliver on it its promise of a prosperous future; economic stagnation in the 1970s exposed the weaknesses of centralized management and further eroded the limited legitimacy the government had garnered. Correspondingly, the contemporary crisis in the Eurozone is particularly troubling because it threatens the ability of the EU to make good on its promises to new members such as Poland. My data support Mach and Niedźwiedzki's (2002) claim that it is too simple to argue that familiarity and exposure will strengthen support for the EU. However, "civilizational competence," which they characterize as the correspondence between personal values and democratic and free market values, as well as the ability to benefit from associated reforms, does not necessarily correlate with support for the EU either. I am thinking for example of Marzena, who is well integrated into the capitalist world of global banking but who nevertheless voted against EU integration, and Aneta, who remains skeptical about the viability of the EU *because* of what she has experienced while traveling and working abroad. Clearly, the *quality* of interactions with EU institutions, policies and citizens of other member states must also be taken into account. I explore these issues further in the next two chapters.

Krzysiek: Let Someone Else Govern Us

Krzysiek is a thoughtful, sociable and sensitive person. He knows everybody in Lesko, and likes to engage in deep conversations about religion, politics, history and relationships. It can be hard to schedule a meeting with him, but we have great conversations when I meet him by chance around the town center. Since graduating from the agricultural high school, Krzysiek has struggled to find his place. Over the years, he has had a number of temporary jobs, but the only one he liked was managing a parking lot. On several occasions, he has worked abroad for a few weeks. Krzysiek displays few of the characteristics associated with neoliberal personhood. He prefers not to project himself too far into the future, he tends to work only as much as required to pay his basic expenses, and he operates in a world structured by personal social ties rather than government or commercial institutions. He told his story as follows:

> After school, I didn't go to college. I thought about going, because I passed my final exams [*matura*]. But, you remember, I was going out with that girl and she broke up with me. It affected me so much that it took a long time to recover. I went to Spain in 1994 – to escape, you could say, because I associate Spain with a colorful life, sun and the like. But it didn't work out for me. They had a lot of unemployment there, too – 20 per cent. There were other reasons I don't want to talk about. I had to return after about a month and a half. It turned out I couldn't escape from those feelings. You can say I fell apart. But slowly, I began to think in a positive manner, and I had to somehow get back to my life. I began to work out at the gym, and that gave me satisfaction. I filled out, built up my muscles and my character changed. I learned to not give up so easily.
>
> Afterward, I worked as a bartender, but then the restaurant closed. Then another job ended, and I began working for a guy in a parking lot. I collected fees, and I saw it was an okay business. My boss wanted to retire, so I asked him if I could take over. I had to put in a bid [to the city who gave management rights to the highest bidder], and my friend and I won the contract. That led to a complete change in my life. I began to earn more money than I could have dreamed of here in Poland. I could afford everything. It came to me like grain to a blind chicken, as we say in Poland – completely by chance. Imagine being supported by your parents at the age of 27, and then suddenly earning 450 zloty [about 150 dollars] a day doing work I liked. I liked the contact with people, foreigners and locals, everyone was friendly. I saved money, and bought myself an apartment and a car. I separated myself from my parents; my mother only helps me by cooking me dinner every day.
>
> After three years, I lost the bid for the parking lot because of the incompetence and corruption of people I thought were my friends. You remember the time you

came and I was so anxious I didn't even want to talk with you? Even today, I take medication for anxiety; a minimal dose, but it helps me. Though now that I am supposed to go to Germany, I feel more stress and had to increase my dose. I would prefer not to go to Germany, but what can I do? I can't get a job in Poland unless I would be willing to work for 600 zloty [per month; about 200 dollars], which is something I won't do. I live on what I earn driving people in my car. I've gained a reputation because I don't drink and I'm always agreeable. At any time I'm available, and it's much cheaper than a taxi. Granted it's illegal [without a taxi license], but at least it's something. Somehow I manage, but it's not a life. It's vegetation.

That's why I want to go to Germany. A friend arranged the paperwork for me; in other words I'll work legally picking apples for about two months. And maybe that way I'll earn enough to save some of it.

What I like about the EU is that its money goes toward concrete goals. I've heard that in order to get money from the EU, you have to fill out specific papers so precisely that you can't even imagine. Also, the work gets done quickly. Before, there was no saying where the money would go. I think there's order [*porządek*], and I like that. Looking at our history, Poles could never govern themselves. Let someone else govern us, damn it. I think the EU is good. For example, many of my buddies went to Ireland. They work there with papers [i.e., legally]. They're paid decently; they can afford everything. They stay for a year. They don't even want to come back. I go around town and sometimes there's no one to visit.

Poland has probably never been in a situation like it is now, with regard to geopolitical matters. Essentially, we have no enemy. We're actually in NATO. That means if they attack you, everyone has to help. And now entry into the EU. The EU has always been the elite. And belonging to the elite states is nice for me. Still, if only our wages were in any way similar to Germans'. A German earns about ten times what a Pole does. But still, belonging to something like this is great. For instance, sometimes I hear that Poland is a developed country, and that raises your spirits.

But besides that, Poland isn't famous for anything. We destroyed everything here. We don't produce anything – no cars, no ships, no planes. We used to, but not anymore.

I'll tell you what the EU has already brought me. I have the possibility to work abroad legally. For strong, persistent, hardworking people, that's fantastic. But not everyone is that way. Not everyone is born a businessman. Although I once operated a business, and it gave me pleasure. There are, after all, ordinary people who want to work normally, to be normally paid and nothing more. I think that's what I want Poland to achieve so I wouldn't have to go to Germany.

And what do I see in the future? Will it be better for us in the EU? That's a really hard question. I can't answer that. If people of the same caliber as now will lead, I don't think it will get better. The EU won't give us everything. They will help us rebuild, but the mentality of Poles themselves has to change. If employers don't respect their own employees, and employers their work, it'll never change. Here in Poland, it's a free-for-all [*wolna amerykanka*]; if you have connections, you're on top; if not, you have nothing.

Who profits from this? I think both sides. I just wish I knew what happens behind the scenes. Other member states get a consumer market, so they can make money. But they had that without the EU, and unloaded whatever they wanted here. I don't think they would have admitted us if they didn't get something from it.

I know that when the EU emerged, it was after the war and they had truly high aspirations. They wanted to equalize countries economically so that it would never come to war again in Europe. And now it's changed a little because nationalism has returned and disrupts everything. Germans guard their affairs, French theirs and British theirs. No one wants to help anyone else anymore. Especially us, because we got so far behind over those fifty years [of state socialism], and they have an image of us as totally wild. And that's probably the biggest problem. If they really wanted to help us, we would have entered long ago.

But who profits more, I can't say. I would have to know more. There is order in the country, which is a lot. There are benefits like subsidies, as long as people finally spend money on what it was intended for, and don't put it in their own pocket. But there's still a lot missing in Poles themselves, like respect for others, and the EU alone can't change that. Although maybe? I don't know enough to tell you.

At best, Krzysiek is getting by. At times, he has demonstrated the very characteristics of personhood encouraged by neoliberal reforms, like initiative and entrepreneurship, but for various reasons nothing has worked out for very long. Both structural and personal challenges have proven to be stumbling blocks to realizing stable employment and long-term relationships. Krzysiek's narrative includes discursive styles and themes that were more characteristic of narratives during the 1990s. He expressed nostalgia about the existential security of the state-socialist past when everyone had a job. Indeed, he might well have had more security under state socialism, when he would have had a guaranteed job and would not have had to compare his own material status to those of others who have much more than him. Despite the challenges he has confronted, he maintains hope for a better future within the EU. He welcomes opportunities to travel and work abroad, and he recognizes the order, peace, global standing and infrastructural investment that accompany membership. In fact, he is most critical of Polish leaders for mismanaging the opportunities emerging from EU membership.

Chapter 6

"NOW WE CAN TRAVEL WITHOUT A PASSPORT": MOBILITY IN THE EUROPEAN UNION

Dorota: Opportunity and Loss in England

I met Dorota when she signed up for an after-school English language course I was teaching. She already had a decent grasp of English, and took the class seriously. Dorota grew up in Lesko, where she attended lyceum. Her father died when she was a child, leaving her mother to raise and support three children. They lived with Dorota's grandmother in a small apartment within a neighborhood of unadorned buildings surrounded by weedy lawns. Dorota eventually got a degree in economics from the agricultural university, but she was neither able to find a job in her profession, nor any other steady, reasonably paid employment in Poland. As a student, she spent her summers doing agricultural work in England, often in the company of her boyfriend. After graduation, she continued to visit and work there intermittently, without legal status. When Dorota and I spoke in the summer of 2005 she was home in Bieszczady for a short visit before returning to what, since Poland joined the EU in 2004, was legal employment in England. She was several months pregnant, and anxious about having her first child in a foreign country. She told her story as follows:

> I went [to England] the first time when I was still a student, through this student agency that organizes work there over the summer. These are real agencies that bring people not just from Poland but also from Ukraine and Bulgaria. They help students … educate themselves, you can say, during summer vacation. And it's fine work because everything is legal; we didn't pay taxes because we were never there long enough to have to. [I went that way] maybe three times.
>
> Then, I finished studying. I worked for a year at a travel agency, but my pay was so low I spent half of what I earned on the commute to and from work. And because it wasn't so … easy here, I went there [to England] with my husband, only then he wasn't my husband yet [laugh], and we tried to find work, this time

illegally. We worked on farms. Later, we managed to find work via an agency in this factory where we still work. However, because we came by ourselves this time, these were not real agencies. These were people who took advantage of us, you can say, because they did everything illegally. They call themselves an agency, like normal, but we call them "gangs" [Dorota used the English word]. Because the factory can't hire people without legal papers, the agency claims that we have papers. They made me papers "on the black [market]" [*na czarno*] – they wrote something and made up signatures that they pay taxes for us. But in fact, they only pretended to pay our taxes, and they paid us less, too. This was the only option for people without legal work papers.

Twice we were caught because we were there illegally. The first time, I was working on a farm. But there it was easier, because it was a big farm and it was possible to find a place to hide [laugh]. The other time, they came to the factory – representatives of the Home Office together with the police.[1] I had been working there only one or two weeks – I don't remember exactly. The police surrounded the factory so there was no chance of escape, though three or four people managed to hide. We didn't know what to do, especially because the director [of the factory] called me because I know English. She was sure we had legal papers, just like our boss from the agency had told her. So of course, they took us to the police station. They held us there for a day. They told us this is normal and we shouldn't worry. They told us it is their obligation to catch us, but we could return; we weren't being deported, just "removed." Because, as they explained, deportation is when someone does something bad, something against the law. But we didn't do anything bad; we just ... well a little bad, but we didn't kill or steal so it's something completely different. Since this was just removal, there's nothing written that I can't return the next day, though perhaps they might question me at the border.

So then, when they removed us, we came back [to Poland] for a while. I think we were here for three months, and then returned to the same factory. Our boss now knew [we were not legal], but she didn't have to check us; all she needed was a paper from our boss at the supposed agency that everything is okay. I don't know how they could behave that way, but for us it was a way out. They exploited people horribly. Just as they did Poles in the past, they now do Ukrainians, Russians and even Brazilians. Really ... it's unpleasant.

It was hard to get through the border in the past, too, whether you'd been removed or not. If the inspectors didn't like something, they would just tell you, "You have to return to your country." People sometimes went to visit family, they had all their papers, and the inspector told them, "I don't believe you because you don't look good; I don't believe you because you have worker's hands." Whatever. It was very unpleasant sometimes, and we didn't succeed. Even though it can be hard to travel to America, you arrange everything in Poland. But when you go to England, everything was arranged on the border. You go, but you don't know; you might land in France and wait a day on the bus before they send you back to Poland. That's what it was like before the EU. Now, of course, that doesn't happen. Now when you arrive, they might not even check your passport. That's a tremendous difference. Once we entered the EU, everything changed in that we don't work for any agency any longer but are hired directly by the factory, and they helped us arrange all legal matters with the Home Office and National Insurance.

We would like so much to return to Bieszczady, but we don't know … when. It's a problem. It's beautiful here [in Bieszczady]. We love this landscape; we love the mountains. But, like I said, it's very difficult [to find] work; we couldn't afford anything. There [in England] it really is … isn't interesting. Except that there we have a car, we earn money. We don't lack for anything; if we want a small treat we can buy it. Now, my mother and brothers live there, too. We helped them get work in the same factory where we work.

I didn't vote in the referendum about Poland's membership in the EU, but I believe I'd have voted in favor of it because I've seen from my own point of view that life in England is easier. Even in terms of work. I'm not interested in politics, but I don't see any disadvantages for Poland [to join the EU], at least in terms of incomes. With regard to prices, I do see losses. I believe it would be different if the government managed things differently. One practical advantage [of membership] is that people can travel abroad easily. But does this help Poland really? Everyone, even young children in high school or primary school, is already thinking about learning English, German or French, and they're all planning to go abroad and work. Who will stay here? I think this will bring the state to ruin. But what else can we do, really? A great number of people would rather live here, and not everyone wants to earn a fortune.

To be perfectly honest, the only thing that connects me to England is work, and that's why I live there: because I can live and … not worry about the next day. However, I believe that in my heart I'm more connected to Poland. I feel good here. And if I could, if I had work and I could make a living, an average living, then I would definitely prefer to live in Poland. I have to think of my husband, too. He doesn't want to be there at all.

One thing that I must say I prefer in Poland is healthcare, even though we complain a lot about it. If I can, I wait until I'm visiting Poland to go to the doctor or to the dentist. In Britain, you have to wait too long for everything, there are too few doctors, and everything is done too officially [without the personal attention she is used to getting from Polish doctors]. It's horrible. And the hospitals are very dirty. I mean, they have a big problem with bacteria. They even prefer for women who give birth to go home after one day because they believe that there's more danger of getting sick in the hospital than at home.

Like I said, this frightens me perhaps more than anything. We'll see. If I don't like the care I'm getting, I might decide to come back to Poland to give birth.

I feel more Polish than European. Not a lot more, because as I've said, I have a lot of roots there [in England] – the mere fact that I have family in England, that I can work. Also, there are really many things I like: I love their nature, I love their monuments, because they really have a lot of them and it's wonderful. A lot of the time I'm fine there, a lot of the time I miss Poland, I miss it very much and think that I would really like to someday – I'm not saying now, but maybe in several years – be here, live here and travel [to England] only to visit friends. But like I've said, life is hard and I don't know how it will all turn out. In any case, we're going to try, to aspire to that, to finish our road, our path, this homelessness, right here in Poland.[2]

When Dorota told me her story in 2005, she was acutely aware of the trade-offs involved in her decision to settle abroad, especially as she contemplated having her first child in a foreign country with an alien healthcare system. It is particularly striking how she acknowledged the exploitation she and other undocumented workers endured, but that she nevertheless saw unofficial employment in England as "a way out." Raised in relative poverty, she characterized the unpleasantness of border crossings and uncertainty of police raids as preferable to stagnation in Poland. For her the most notable results of EU membership were the easing of restrictions against travel to wealthier EU countries, and especially gaining legal working status in England. As a long-term undocumented worker before Poland joined the EU, these changes marked a significant improvement in her life, but she nevertheless voiced regret and longing for comparable opportunities to work and earn a decent living in her native Bieszczady. In this we see some of the central contours of participants' experiences of and attitudes toward EU membership. On the one hand, new opportunities emerged, marking a path to social advancement; but on the other, these very opportunities also served to highlight and potentially deepen longstanding divisions between the "advanced" West and "backwards" East.

Mobility in the European Union

In this chapter, I probe the significance of migration and travel within the EU – what impact it has on participants' lives, and on their perceptions of and dispositions toward the EU. I also reflect upon the implications of such personal assessments for the continued formation and scope of the EU. I consider new transnational patterns of migration and identification in relation to their historical corollaries that also involved periodic cultural, political and economic engagement with, or even cyclical return to, the country of origin. Participants' personal assessments support three claims. First, the ease of travel to wealthier EU countries for work or pleasure is on the top of most participants' lists of effects of EU membership, whether they themselves have taken advantage of these new options or not. Second, membership in the EU is seen by most as social advancement. Intertwined with declarations about material and economic benefits are assertions about the symbolic promotion of Poland and of themselves as citizens of a united Europe. However, as a symbol, the quality of interactions while abroad shapes overall dispositions toward the EU. To the extent such experiences reinscribe inequalities relative to other nations (via continued legal restrictions on mobility, limited opportunity or ethnic bias) positive inclinations toward the EU suffer. Which leads me to my third claim: even though the freedom to move across borders and obtain legitimate positions in other places is highly valued, more meaningful for most is the freedom to return to, or to stay, in their native place. Life stories reveal that for many, the highest level of social advancement would involve equal opportunities for a reasonable standard of living and secure employment at home, so crossing borders would truly be a matter of choice as opposed to economic necessity. These claims help to illustrate how transnational life becomes a realm for experiencing Europeanness *as Poles*. Put another way, local and national identities are not displaced or weakened by European identity, but rather "being European" grows increasingly salient as a characteristic of Polishness. Further, this association is viewed favorably, to the extent that Europe is linked with economic opportunity and social advancement.

In his essay on the social consequences of globalization, Bauman (1998, 69–72) emphasizes a "global hierarchy of mobility" where power is increasingly mobile, and contributes to deeper stratification as some places and the people bound to them are excluded and lose control of resource allocation. In other words, degrees of mobility define a "process of world-wide *restratification*, in the course of which a new socio-cultural hierarchy, a world-wide scale, is put together" (70; emphasis original). Polarities emerge between some who are emancipated from territorial constraints and others held back in localities denuded of meaning and identity-endowing capacities (18). Bauman further distinguishes between tourists, those with the resources to be good consumers, and vagabonds, flawed consumers with more limited resources: "The tourists move because they find the world within their (global) reach irresistibly *attractive*— the vagabonds move because they find the world within their (local) reach unbearably *inhospitable*. The tourists travel because *they want to*; the vagabonds because *they have no other bearable choice*" (92–3; emphasis original). Bauman constructs a model of polarization based on the opposition between mobility and immobility, and emphasizes that the resulting stratification is an effect of globalization. He describes powerless people as mostly immobile within localities that are changed by global forces beyond their control. If they travel, they do so as vagabonds, surreptitiously and illegally (89).

Erind Pajo (2008) also examines mobility in what he calls a "social imaginary of the world as a hierarchy of countries." Focusing on the experiences of Albanian migrants, he asks why most imagine their move to Greece in terms of social advancement, and yet accept social demotion in their adopted home. At the core of the paradox is the fact that in Albania their higher education and professional experience gained them positions of authority and respect, whereas in Greece they tend to have low-skill, low-status service jobs. Pajo proposes: "Contemporary international migration might be driven by the social desire to advance from a location envisioned as low in the international hierarchy towards one envisioned as higher. Social status is at the same time a matter of territorial belonging, and that typically makes international advancement impossible." In other words, places themselves are conceptualized according to an imagined global hierarchy of relative development, wealth and power, and very often migrants base their perceptions of social advancement on this rather than on the facts of their daily lives. Furthermore, their possibilities for real advancement are hampered by the relative rigidity of ethnic and national categories; to the extent that "people irredeemably belong to countries," migrants are often relegated to lower-status positions regardless of the global status of their adopted country (2008, 10).

Both Bauman and Pajo characterize the world system in terms of the social hierarchies it entrenches. The stories participants in my study tell about their lives show that they too think of the world in terms of an imagined hierarchy of nations. Their stories also reveal, however, a wider range of mobility, and consequent possibilities for social advancement within the transnational realm. The conceptual poles between mobility and immobility, tourists and vagabonds, are difficult to map onto real people and their complex lives.[3] Correspondingly, it is not as clear as Pajo suggests that migration leads to social demotion. Some, like Marta and Krzysiek, who have limited education or skills and few opportunities for work in their native Bieszczady, feel empowered by their ability to navigate within a foreign country and earn a decent wage. Robert, a teacher who talked bitterly about his social demotion when he worked summers at a gas station in Germany, anticipated social advancement within his local community when he finally earned enough to build his own home in Bieszczady, something he would never be able to afford on his teaching salary alone. Others, like Stasiek, define social advancement in terms of the freedom to cross borders and participate as equals in professional jobs within a foreign country. For him, the ultimate evidence of that advancement is his ability to maintain social ties, and even his home, within Poland – he can commute from southeast Poland to work in England. Similarly, Marek does the same kind of computer work he did in Poland, only he earns a better wage and finds a more hospitable social environment in Prague.

Life stories also reveal for many a very different perspective on locality and staying in place than that outlined by Bauman. For them, living in Poland is not a sign of their irrelevance or lack of standing in the global imaginary, but rather shows their (and Poland's) advancement in the world hierarchy. Ewelina, a lawyer, and Aneta, a television producer, note with satisfaction that they can work in their profession and make a decent wage in Poland; emigration is unnecessary. As I discussed in Chapter 4, for most, attachment to place is very real. Life stories show that even as notions of progress and global hierarchy are reproduced, they can also be altered and sometimes inverted. Historical patterns of Polish migration show mobility has been a longstanding avenue used by Poles to "get a start in life" and to improve their standing in an imagined global hierarchy.

History of Polish Migration

Amid public discourse that emphasizes the newness of EU integration, globalization and associated migration flows, it can be easy to lose sight of historical patterns of Polish mobility and cultural orientations toward migration. Participants all have family members, friends and neighbors who have spent time abroad. For some, this mobility goes back generations to, for example, grandfathers who worked for a time in the US or Canada before returning to their family in Poland. Thus, it is not migration that is new so much as the increased opportunities for documented work abroad along particular routes that were in the past less open. Most significant has been the rapid outflow of young Poles to the UK and Ireland, two of the three EU countries that allowed migrants from new EU member states immediate unrestricted access to employment. This most recent wave of migration should be viewed in the context of earlier flows of people from Poland.

Polish discourse on mobility has tended to reinscribe two narratives, one political and the other economic, each associated with different time periods and varied demographic groups. Politically motivated migration has tended to be imagined as a response to oppression by foreign occupiers, including the Polish state-socialist regime during the last half of the twentieth century. Political narratives usually describe an intellectual and professional elite who felt compelled to move but who nevertheless maintained strong emotional ties with their homeland. Outflows of ethnic and religious minorities, often due to persecution, tend to be excluded from the standard political narrative, which emphasizes Polish patriotic themes and sentiments. Economic narratives, by contrast, usually feature the rural poor who went abroad in search of "bread." During some periods political and economic narratives have overlapped, sometimes when different groups migrated simultaneously but for different reasons and sometimes when a single group had dual motivations.

The experiences of prominent exiles in the nineteenth century, such as the poet Adam Mickiewicz and military leader Tadeusz Kościuszko, came to represent a nationalist response to the Partitions of Poland by the Russian, Prussian and Austrian empires. Polish migrants were imagined as patriots fighting from beyond Poland's borders to help the nation regain its autonomy. From the latter part of the nineteenth century through World War I, there was a corresponding outflow of landless peasants pushed out of overpopulated villages by a social structure that supported the consolidation of landholdings by gentry, a corresponding lack of political support for peasant landholders, and processes of industrialization that provided too few jobs in factories or urban centers (Reczyńska 1996; Thomas and Znaniecki 1984; Zubricki 1988). Most migrants sought employment in Europe, but as many as one quarter traveled overseas. Some joined Polish legions in foreign armies and fought in independence movements under the slogan "Za naszą i waszą wolność" (For our liberty and yours). Other poor peasants characterized their migration in exclusively economic terms, as reflected in the saying "Gdzie chleb, to ojczyzna" (Wherever there is bread, that's the fatherland). As Thomas and Znaniecki (1984) reported in their classic study of Polish peasants at home and abroad during the early twentieth century, family and religious ties dominated social life, and the social organizations Poles formed in the US tended to center around economic interests rather than political or national solidarity.

Following mass displacements during World War I, economically motivated migration patterns resumed between the world wars because the nation-state failed to address ongoing economic conditions pushing landless rural Poles to seek employment and a better life elsewhere (Reczyńska 1996). Polish policies tended to view emigration as the "natural" response to limited economic opportunities, so little effort was put into controlling outflows. Rather, restrictions in receiving countries determined shifts in the direction and volume of flows. Most migrants took short seasonal trips to Germany, France or elsewhere in Europe. The substantial minority that traveled overseas tended to be a bit more affluent, probably because it cost more to travel farther. Overseas migrants were also more likely to view their resettlement as permanent; typically, men went first and would pay for the passage of their wives and children once they established themselves. Throughout this early period, it is difficult to determine the exact volume of flow because sending and receiving countries did not use political, legal or ethnic labels uniformly (Bijak and Koryś 2009). For instance, during the interwar period, émigrés from the new Polish state included ethnic Poles, Ukrainians and Jews. By some standards, all were categorized as Polish, while by others only the ethnic Poles were (Reczyńska 1996). Nevertheless, an estimated 3.5 million Poles emigrated between 1870 and 1914, followed by another 2 million before World War II (Bijak and Koryś 2009, 195).

World War II caused massive population shifts that continued in the years following the war as ethnic and religious minorities were forced or pressured to resettle. International agreements tried to sort East-Central Europe's ethnically diverse population into monoethnic nation-states, and domestic leaders sought to solidify claims to the territory within redrawn state borders. Additionally, as the Soviet-influenced state-socialist system took shape in Poland, there was a mass exodus of educated professionals, many of whom had been active in the fight for independence during the war and became subjects of persecution for supposed anti-Soviet and anticommunist offenses. The Bieszczady region was virtually depopulated by the annihilation of Jews in the Holocaust and the dislocation of ethnic minorities during and after the war.

State-socialist policies restricted migration by limiting access to passports and controlling communication with outside countries. Also, the cost of international travel was prohibitive, especially since the Polish currency was not freely convertible. Migrants took advantage of formal and informal means to obtain work or travel visas. The bulk of foreign travel (often undocumented) was to Germany, and tended to involve outflows from regions of Poland close to the German border. Economic pressures lead many Polish households to rely on remittances from relatives abroad. The 1980s saw another wave of migration dominated by the educated elite, many of whom had visiting positions in other countries when martial law was declared, and elected not to return. When I was a graduate student in San Diego, I got to know a group of Polish professionals and academics who had immigrated around this time. They humorously named themselves the Wolni Najmici (literally, Free Mercenaries, but better translated as Free Travelers). I joined them for several trips to Death Valley where they recreated their own "little Polish homeland," complete with Polish flag atop a hill, Polish songs around the campfire and generous quantities of alcohol. A number of participants from Krakow had fathers who spent months or even years abroad during this period, while others have aunts and uncles who settled permanently in Canada, Australia and the US. These professionals found lucrative employment, often in their area of specialization.

Starting around 1981, families in Bieszczady participated in a new trajectory of immigration to Southern Europe, particularly Italy. Initially, it was seen as an intermediate step to places farther west, but the volume of movement increased when in 1987 Italy introduced camping permits that could be purchased in zloty (Iglicka 2001, 49). Immigration to Italy gained popularity due to an economic downturn in Northern and Western Europe, as well as shifts in the Italian labor market that increased the availability of low-paying service jobs for migrants. The election of a Pole as pope also contributed to an elevated interest in Italy, and new travel networks were established via Polish clergy (Iglicka 2001). Migration to Italy and other destinations in Southern Europe was dominated by rural Poles with low levels of education; they usually traveled seasonally or cyclically and worked as domestic laborers or construction workers (Triandafyllidou and Kosic 2006). Among my acquaintances, more women than men went, usually to provide domestic elder care. They established networks of what has been called "chain migration" in which relatives share a job, taking turns working abroad and returning to Poland. This was particularly attractive for adult women with spouses and children because they were able to contribute to the family economy while still fulfilling their nurturing roles, at least some of the time. These migration networks have continued through to the present.

With the liberalization that followed the fall of state socialism in 1989, Polish restrictions on emigration were lifted. This did not, however, result in a significant outflow from Poland. On the contrary, official numbers of migrants dropped in the 1990s compared with flows in the 1980s. This was due largely to restrictions in receiving countries. Iglicka (2000) reports an increase in short-term migration, and although 18- to 24-year-olds comprised the largest proportion of migrants, the overall average age increased because more 35- to 44-year-olds also went. Legal entry to the US, for example, was limited mostly to family reunification and professional employment, though some Poles "won" the right to resettle in the annual green card lottery.[4] Throughout the 1990s and into the 2000s, it was even difficult for Poles to obtain US tourist visas. Long lines of applicants became commonplace at the US embassy and consulates, where prospective visitors were interviewed to assess whether they were likely overstay their visas or seek undocumented work.[5]

EU accession in 2004 led to profound shifts in migration patterns and in Poles' perceptions of mobility. Two key developments have emerged from the recent outpouring of research on Polish mobility. First, flows of people vary a great deal, from areas with little history of outflow to regions with an established "culture of migration" that is both a product of and a rationale for ongoing and extensive mobility. Second, discourses surrounding mobility reveal changes in the length of time migrants plan to stay and in the way they employ concepts of normalcy, social advancement and social demotion.

Flows to different countries tend to vary in relation to migrants' age, education levels, gender and district of origin. Case studies highlight longstanding links between residents of particular districts and domestic, construction or healthcare jobs in Germany, Italy or elsewhere (see White 2010); some researchers contrast districts that have established channels of mobility with others where migration has increased along newly legal, "visible" pathways to destinations like the UK (see Elrick 2008). Of particular note, migrants to Germany and Italy tend to be older (averaging 36 and 33 respectively) and less well educated (six to eight per cent with a university degree) than migrants to the UK, whose average age is 25, and twenty-four per cent have finished university (Fihel and Kaczmarczyk 2009). Studies also show the continued importance of community and family networks to help migrants in their destination country (see Ryan et al 2009; White and Ryan 2008), though some have noted the growth in some places of a migration industry, where professional agents provide economic, emotional and social support to those who need it (Elrick and Lewandowska 2008; Garapich 2008).

The "culture of migration" concept, developed to describe mobility patterns from Mexico to the US (see Cohen 2004; Smith 2006), also applies to Polish communities in which migration has become a "routine and normative" part of behaving like a local person because it is increasingly difficult to move up the social ladder without spending time abroad (White 2009, 69; White 2010; Elrick 2008). Let me stress again that the culture of migration has its roots in earlier periods; Zubricki describes the late nineteenth and early twentieth centuries in terms of the "multitude of social interactions among potential emigrants leading to the rise of a *collective impulse* to leave" (1988, 14, emphasis original). Social pressure to work abroad as a means of demonstrating one's competence and fulfilling one's duty to family is not new.

A second development has been the changing discourse about migration, especially in relation to the rapid and massive flow to the UK. Several studies have noted that migrants to England tend to articulate open-ended plans, breaking away from older patterns of long-term or permanent relocation overseas or short-term, cyclical migration to other European countries (Galasińska and Kozłowska 2009; Ryan et al. 2009; White 2010). Perhaps because they are young, just beginning their working lives and see their time abroad as an opportunity for independence, migrants to England are more inclined to just see where the adventure takes them. White and Ryan (2008) also emphasize that life stage matters; parents make different choices about staying or leaving than do people who are as yet childless.

Other studies identify discourses of social advancement, social demotion and the quest for "normalcy." Migrants continue to invoke "the myth of the West" to explain their motivation to seek a better life in another country (Galasińska 2009, 2010; Rodriguez 2010), even though many actually experience social demotion in low-status, low-salary jobs and only partial and ambivalent inclusion in their destination countries (Drinkwater et al. 2009;

Fihel and Kaczmarczyk 2009; Rodriguez 2010; van Riemsdijk 2010). Fihel and Kaczmarczyk (2009, 44) call the low return that Polish migrants in England get from their university education a "brain waste" – a play on the common phrase "brain drain." Others describe how Poles discursively characterize life abroad as "normal," "ordinary" and "natural" in contrast to "abnormal" and "extraordinary" life in Poland (Galasińska 2009, 2010; Galasińska and Kozłowska 2009), and challenge the counterdiscourse of social demotion by telling their personal "small stories" about getting a good job in England solely on the basis of their merit and personal effort (Galasińska 2009). Rodriguez (2010) further notes that Polish migrant mothers invoke normalcy to describe the future they desire for their children in England.

To summarize, migration has long been a factor in Polish social life. Contemporary orientations toward migration echo in some ways historical narratives of an imagined global hierarchy of nations where the means to achieve a better life can be found outside of Poland. Especially in some places, a culture of migration goes back generations. Indeed, nearly one hundred years ago, Thomas and Znaniecki observed among Polish immigrants in America: "A general tendency to advance, of which land hunger, social climbing, and emigration to cities or abroad, are partial manifestations. This tendency is not a matter of personal, temperamental disposition, but a social current spread by imitation and fed by the popularized information about new possibilities of advance. (1984, 203)"

Since emerging from state socialism and becoming citizens of the EU, Poles continue to follow opportunities for work and financial gain – but it is also important to note how channels have been opened and closed by political divisions and economic divides. Channels have also been established and maintained independent of state regulations, via social networks through which friends, family and neighbors travel to the same places, share resources and information, and sometimes even share jobs. In this way, even in places where a culture of migration is deeply entrenched, connections to the homeland, defined by familiar landscapes and people, have been maintained as well.

In the following section, I examine more closely the ways in which participants engage with the prospect of migration and travel as EU citizens. While Thomas and Znaniecki took a sociological approach, a person-centered approach helps to show the convergence between "personal, temperamental dispositions" and the contemporary "social current" about social advancement via cross-border mobility. I explore how EU membership has influenced experiences of and associations with migration, and correspondingly, what this reveals about national and local identity within the EU.

"I Can Go Abroad with just My ID Card, and I Can Work Legally"

To the extent that Polish mobility has historically been constrained by legal restrictions, it would be hard to overestimate the significance of EU membership for easing those limits. This is particularly apparent in Dorota's account of the uncertainty she faced as an undocumented worker in England, never sure if she would be turned back at the border or "removed" for working without papers, in contrast to her present security as a legal employee with benefits and the right to cross borders freely. Nevertheless, it would also be negligent to ignore the social imbalances that continue to structure cross-border movements. For Dorota, this means that as much as she and her husband dream of returning to Poland, she nevertheless feels she cannot move back because they would not be able to find work that would pay them enough to live on.

I return now to my ethnographic data, and show how accounts of migration and travel figure in individuals' reflections about EU membership. First, participants tend to express an instrumental orientation toward EU membership; as EU citizens, it has become easier for them to cross borders and for many it has provided more work opportunities. Second, in addition to these pragmatic benefits, greater mobility symbolically marks Poland's advancement within an imagined world hierarchy of nations. However, the inequalities that nevertheless persist contribute to ongoing experiences of social demotion that challenge the idea that European integration means social advancement. Third, improved opportunities *within* Poland represent for many the pinnacle of social advancement within that global imaginary. While material benefit is a central factor that motivates participants to go abroad, they also feel pulled back to Poland by varying degrees of commitment to family, to their native place and to their identity as Poles.

Eased restrictions on mobility

In 2005, most participants said they hadn't yet felt any significant impact of Poland's entrance into the EU. However, most also said that the opening of borders throughout the EU was the most notable change for them. They described three positive outcomes: the ease of crossing borders; the increased possibilities to visit Western European countries as tourists; and the comfort of being able to work abroad legally. They associated these changes with a normalization of relations with Western Europe, whereby Poles and Poland have more opportunity to be included on an equal level with other EU citizens and countries.

While many called it a minor change, they welcomed the freedom to cross borders within the EU using nothing but their identity cards. Bartek, a school teacher in Lesko said, "Now you can boldly travel, boldly bring things [across the border], you don't have those nerves when you cross the border." Michał, a real estate broker and frequent vacation traveler, said a small thing that makes him happy is walking through the gate for "EU Citizens" at the airport. Ania, an artist in Krakow, remarked on the "psychological comfort" that comes with the fact that "you can cross the German border and they don't even look at your passport. It's so easy to go and so easy to return." She and others also noted the ease and relative affordability of travel now that inexpensive airlines fly to Krakow and even to smaller cities like Rzeszów near Bieszczady. Some recalled the uncertainty and prejudice they faced when seeking to cross these same borders before Poland entered the EU:

> They always treated us so poorly on those borders, they always checked [our papers]. When I went to Italy, especially on the Austrian and German borders, they always treated us like second-class citizens and there was always a feeling of inferiority, and I always wanted to show them somehow that it isn't like that in reality. I wanted us to have a chance to show them that we're the same as them and not worse. (Wiola, a civil servant in Bieszczady)

The ease of crossing borders is part of what makes participants feel included as equals in the EU.

Participants' tendency to minimize the significance of eased restrictions may well be associated with their sense that greater mobility is "normal." Discourse about what is "normal" has been used in particular ways in Poland to denote what *should* be, in contrast to everyday customary circumstances that are deemed "abnormal" (see Galbraith 2003b). EU membership is seen to promote normal relationships with other countries; what is more remarkable, and remarked upon, is the abnormal, unequal relationships that existed under state socialism and before EU integration. Dorota and other participants consider it normal to be able to travel freely, to work legally in other countries and receive benefits like health insurance and retirement pensions. In short, they consider Poland's membership in the EU a return to the country's normal, rightful place in Europe.

Another way in which some participants feel EU membership helps their status rise in the world hierarchy is via travel abroad as tourists. These trips act as a marker of freedom, and also of rising incomes. Ewelina, a lawyer from Krakow said, "I like to travel abroad to rest and to see something new." For her, the ability to travel like this reflects the good standard of living she has achieved within Poland. Joasia, a school librarian in Lesko remarked, "It's possible to visit England, or Italy, and it's right at hand. They aren't so far away as they used to be."

Others emphasized that they would gladly visit other countries to sightsee, but they do not want to work abroad. Whereas during my previous visits, they were more likely to talk about their *desire* to be tourists, by 2005 more had actually been on international excursions, and it was becoming more common to travel by airplane than by bus. Those who can afford to travel without having to seek work talked about it as a marker of growing equality with the West.

Aneta, a Krakow native, spent a number of years working in the US as both a nanny and a promoter of Polish cultural events. She no longer dreams of living abroad, though, because she finds it more meaningful to bring international culture to Poland than vice versa. Nevertheless, she travels frequently for both pleasure and work, and appreciates that short-term mobility to EU countries has become much easier: "I think the EU provides greater life comfort. In Poland, more than anything, you don't have that feeling of isolation that you're from Poland. At the same time, traveling to Germany, or to France, is devalued – it isn't a trip abroad anymore. We go so often that … it isn't anything special. It isn't so terribly different there anymore. And also, a lot of people from there have appeared here."

The experience of increased mobility from Western Europe to Poland was felt especially in Krakow, which became flooded with weekend visitors, mostly from England and Ireland, who took advantage of cheap airfares and gained a reputation for getting drunk and causing trouble. In the summer of 2008, this traffic had moderated somewhat because the strong zloty made it less of a bargain for visitors from Great Britain and the Eurozone.

Although tourism has increased, most Polish travel abroad continues to be for the purpose of work. Temporary economic migration has long been used as a strategy for "getting a better start in life," as participants call it. When they were younger, that usually meant earning enough to buy a car, to help pay for college or for other living expenses. Now that they have families of their own, the most common reason they seek temporary employment abroad is to help pay for a house or an apartment, though some low-wage earners still rely on work abroad to cover basic living expenses. Participants do not necessarily work abroad more now than before, but they emphasize the comfort that comes with working legally, whether they do temporary farm labor or business travel for their company. They also note that Polish professionals are in demand in Western European countries.

Social advancement and social demotion in an imagined world hierarchy

The discussion above, about eased restrictions on mobility, already alludes to changes in Poland's symbolic standing relative to other European countries.

In this section, I look more closely at examples of imagined social advancement or demotion via migration within the EU. Some, like Bieszczady residents Marta and Krzysiek, feel empowered by opportunities for legal work abroad in other EU countries. Marta has done domestic labor in Italy and Denmark, while Krzysiek has worked on farms in Germany. Both have high school degrees from an agricultural high school, and have found few prospects for employment in their home communities. They consider seasonal work abroad an opportunity for social advancement because they earn higher wages than they could in Poland. The *kind* of work does not matter because they would be unlikely to find higher-status work in Poland either.

Marcin, who created a successful tourist business in a mountain village, celebrates new opportunities which give Poles a chance to live on an equal level with other Europeans: "For many years, Poland was cut off from Europe. It was possible to go on a trip to East Germany, or maybe somewhere in the West, but it was not possible to work legally. And at this time, there are opportunities to work there normally, to live normally, to bring cars from there, which is why Europe has gained such a greater significance for Poles. Only now are there equal opportunities for Poles." Marcin is a lifelong Bieszczady resident and a strong supporter of EU membership, but it is worth noting he has no intention of living or working abroad himself, and only limited personal experience with foreigners and foreign places.

Despite the optimism expressed in the quote above, Marcin also articulated a clear sense of a hierarchy of countries distinguished by degrees of economic opportunity. He said it is "normal" for residents of less developed Eastern countries to go west in search of a better life. Just as Poles go to Germany and England, Ukrainians come to Poland. About the possibility of gaining equity with wealthier EU members, he explained:

> It takes time for everything to change, to fall into a rhythm [...] I count on it, that maybe not we but our children will have equal opportunities finally, like all of those rich countries that have been in the EU for a long time. We are far behind them. I still feel the baggage from all those communist experiences: I stood in line for toilet paper; I used ration cards for chocolates and cigarettes. And essentially, they have had luxury for a long time. It will take a long time to catch up. And so I don't know if we ever will ... we probably will never reach the level that is in the West. Just like when one car chases another, you have to drive faster. Poland will never catch up. But things are better, and they will become better still in another ten, fifteen, twenty years. In the meantime, we're learning. We're learning Europe, and what the EU looks like.

Like Marcin, other participants expressed dissatisfaction about ongoing inequality and exclusion that nevertheless persists, and can even in some instances be accentuated by the less restricted flow of people across borders. Robert is a teacher in Lesko who has traveled periodically to Germany to earn extra money as a clerk in his brother-in-law's gas station. He explained:

> All the teachers complain because we're paid so little. Compared with wages in the West, the difference is colossal. For example, in Germany – it's a small town like Lesko with seven or eight thousand residents – people ask me what I do in Poland. I tell them that I work at a school. "But what do you do there, clean or something?" "No, I'm a teacher." "How can that be? You finished university? "Of course I finished." "How can it be that you are a teacher and you must come here to work?" They didn't believe me. They scratched their heads and didn't want to talk to me because they thought I was kidding them.

Robert accepted this situation because, for one, it was easy enough to visit his sister for a couple of months in the summer and earn the extra money. Second, he traded short-term social demotion in Germany for long-term social advancement in Poland; he built a house with his summer earnings so his family could move out of their one-room apartment.

Continued prejudice and unequal treatment of Poles despite membership in the EU (another dimension of social demotion) were topics of discussion both during and outside of formal interviews. Participants were critical of countries that restricted employment opportunities for citizens of new member states. Stasiek, a computer programmer who commutes to England one week per month (I share his life story in more detail below), said he refuses to work in Germany because "I don't feel at home where they require special authorization for me to be there, because I'm not treated equally." Agata, a farmer from Bieszczady, says of her experience gathering produce in Germany, "I was there and I felt bad. Because people make you feel that you're different, lower, poorer. We're already in the EU, we should be treated the same as the French, as every person in the EU." Participants also talked about the exploitation of migrants. Some cited media reports about Polish farm workers in Italy who were promised good jobs but instead were housed in crude barracks and paid nearly nothing. Familiarity and exposure do not necessarily lead to greater connection with Europe and other Europeans, especially in such conditions of continued inequality. Furthermore, evaluations of social standing extend beyond material calculations, and also take into account issues of equality, fairness and dignity.

The controversy that emerged in France about "Polish plumbers," itself part of France's internal debate about ratifying the EU constitution, brought problems of instrumentality, inclusion and exclusion, and social advancement into public discourse. During the summer of 2005, the "Polish plumber" was used as a symbol of cheap labor from new member states that threatened to flood into France and compete with native workers. The incident exposed France's own unease about EU expansion, and fear that new members might compromise French citizens' economic interests and global standing. The discourse about Polish plumbers attempted to reassert the East–West divide in Europe, and to reinscribe social status based on territorial belonging. Poles responded in a variety of ways, but for the most part they resisted the reinscription of a subordinate position in an imagined global hierarchy of nations. Instead, they evoked the European value of equality to condemn restrictions on mobility.

In a compelling advertising campaign, the Polish Tourist Agency helped to reframe, even invert, the power dynamic by featuring a handsome, muscular man holding a large wrench and pipe before a backdrop of tourist sites in Poland. The words "Je reste en Pologne, venez nombreux" can be translated as "I'm staying in Poland, come one and all."[6] Thus, the Polish plumber was used to represent the nation as powerful, desirable and inviting for French citizens who were urged to visit Poland. Though intended for a French audience, the ad was widely reproduced and discussed in the Polish media. My conversations with participants suggest that the ad also put forward the promise of an alternative trajectory for Poles at a time when many had joined the mass exodus to jobs abroad, or were contemplating doing so. It portrayed renewed confidence in the possibility of making a decent living in Poland, and thus reversing the movement of people. Notably, by the summer of 2008, migrants were in fact returning to Poland, perhaps because the Polish economy remained strong even as the global recession reduced opportunities elsewhere. Since 2011, the number of Poles living abroad for extended periods of time has been increasing again (GUS 2013), suggesting that the pull of opportunities abroad continues to influence life choices. Some participants maintain a pattern of pendulum migration, returning at periodic, short-term intervals.

Participants' comments show that ethnicity and Europeanness became marked categories as they assessed the controversy about the Polish plumber in terms of an imagined global hierarchy of nations. For some it illustrated the inequality and even prejudice that persists despite their membership in the EU. Józef, a local government official in Bieszczady, called France's concern that native citizens would lose their jobs "propaganda," and the general reluctance to hire foreigners throughout Europe "extreme nationalism." Others were proud that Poles were singled out, saying it shows that Poles are competitive for jobs because they are hard workers and well trained. As Grażyna, a primary school director in Bieszczady, noted, "Poles are highly regarded as workers – not just the plumbers made famous in the ad campaign, but also nurses, doctors, computer scientists and other professionals." What is expressed here is an opposing narrative about Poles working abroad, one that celebrates their reputation as "hard workers." This more positive narrative does not, however, erase social hierarchy. The same point is made by Gomberg-Muñoz (2010) in her ethnography of Mexican busboys, another category of migrants who use their reputation as hard workers to access jobs and even middle-class salaries in the US. She shows how the busboys still have limited mobility and low social status due to their lack of legal papers, and stereotypes close them off from obtaining higher-status positions and better wages. The Polish plumber tourism campaign asserted another pathway to equality, by encouraging the movement of people *to* Poland *from* France, thus reversing the perceived imbalance.

Global mobility and the choice to stay home

The flip side of "getting a start in life" by working abroad (a benefit of EU membership) is that it is also a reminder of Poland's unequal economic status relative to richer Western European countries. As long as economic migration flows outward, it signals that Poland still offers fewer opportunities than wealthier countries; more pointedly, Poland is seen to be the loser when its best talent takes their skills elsewhere. Participants pointed out that Poles, whether they are professionals or service workers, only choose to work abroad because of the low wages in Poland. Most said that they would like to work for a while abroad (and most in fact have), but they want to earn some money and then return to Poland. This is what Dorota said she wishes for, but with each passing year, it is less likely she will ever return. Participants lamented that so many of their friends have emigrated. Krzysiek, for example, told me there is no one left in Lesko to talk to; he doesn't bump into anyone he knows because all his friends have moved.

The other issue raised by Dorota and others is the loss to Poland when the country's most ambitious and industrious citizens choose to settle abroad because Poland cannot offer them competitive wages. Poland is thus further impoverished, and its lower position in the hierarchy of nations is further perpetuated. Artur, a border guard in Bieszczady, expressed his distaste for Poles who get an education in Poland and then go abroad: "Everyone pays for that education with their taxes [university is free for the highest-achieving students]. We pay the cost and someone else will drink the cream. The most educated will make someone else's economy turn, while no one is left in Poland to pay for my retirement." Maciek, a nurse in Bieszczady, remarked on the shortage of doctors and nurses because so many, even from the hospital where he works, have migrated to the West. Some positions have been filled by Ukrainians who left still worse conditions farther east to work in Poland. Krzysiek, who has periodically been unemployed, evoked the discourse of normalcy when he lamented, "Not everyone was instantly born a businessman. There are, after all, regular people who want to work normally, to be normally paid, and that's all. That's what I want Poland to measure up to, so I wouldn't have to migrate to Germany [to find work]."

Much anxiety was also expressed about social problems that result when families are divided by emigration. Residents of Bieszczady in particular often talked among themselves about spouses who drifted apart after one spent long periods abroad, and children who got into trouble when their parents left them with relatives so they could earn enough to support the family. Both Beata and Agnieszka were teenagers when their mothers went to work in another country. Again, these trade-offs highlight the inequality that nevertheless persists despite inclusion in the EU. When they were in their mid-30s, participants were at a point in their life course when family obligations constrained mobility. Some explained their reluctance to travel because it required negotiating with a spouse who neither wanted to go, nor to be left alone. Others pointed out the challenge of leaving young children. This was particularly difficult for the single mothers I know. Marta and Zosia have both left their children in the care of their mothers and gone to work for several weeks or months. Even though they waited until their children were in school, they felt guilty about leaving them, and were concerned about their children's misbehavior while they were gone. Although the culture of migration is longstanding in Bieszczady, there is a general sense that these problems of divided families have gotten worse. This may in part be because since the 1980s, changes in social welfare in Western European countries created opportunities for immigrant women to work as cleaners and caregivers, just the kind of work that rural Polish women without a higher education have tended to do.

The culture of migration pressures anyone who has initiative to go abroad and prove their competence. While participants who have chosen to remain in Poland or to return after spending time abroad said they feel this pressure, they also argued that there are ways of realizing their potential in Poland. Perhaps they will not get rich, but they do meaningful work as teachers, farmers, nurses and public servants, and earn enough to support themselves and their families. Some said they would only go abroad if they had to. Most participants would agree that real equality will only be attained when Poles no longer have to travel abroad to attain their desired standard of living. While some, like Michał and Marcin, have succeeded in doing so already, others, like Dorota, feel compelled to work elsewhere in Europe. Although some migrants gain valuable professional experience, most see their time abroad as temporary, until they have made enough money to have a better start in Poland. Many say that, all things being equal, they would rather stay in Poland. The need to work abroad is an unwelcome reminder of the unequal position of Poland within the EU. Most see membership in the EU as a step toward closing that gap, but fears remain that the system just institutionalizes the existing hierarchy, making them struggle towards a constantly retreating goal.

Traveling without a Passport

In this chapter, I have explored not only what participants said about migration and travel, but also how they relate opportunities for mobility to their own sense of what it means to be a new citizen of the EU. In other words, I have deployed the "personal, temperamental disposition[s]" Thomas and Znaniecki (1984) exclude from sociological analysis. Person-centered inquiry shows how mobility in the EU can be a marker of social advancement, or social demotion. Traveling without a passport, as much as it represents for many the realization of a dream, also brings with it certain risks. It can mean the separation from familiar people and places, with no guarantee of return. It potentially leads to the loss of identity, of the sense of uniqueness and belonging that defines the self in relation to categories of people and places. So if there is a collective impulse to leave, there is also an equally forceful impulse to return. Life stories reveal a range of experiences and various ways of grappling with these common issues and challenges.

The impulse to return is worth reflecting upon for what it shows generally about social advancement and social demotion within an imagined world hierarchy of nations, and also for what it suggests specifically about the influence EU membership has had on Poles and their various social identities. On the one hand, the impulse to return points to the recognition of what is lost via the practice of certain kinds of mobility. Better paying work and greater material comforts abroad can mask social demotion via lower social status, isolation and dislocation from cultural practices, places and people that are highly valued. These insights parallel those noted in other geographic regions (see Gomberg-Munoz 2010; Pajo 2008; Smith 2006) and suggest patterns that shape migration experiences globally. I suggest that for Poles, the impulse to return is particularly strong, and that this is an important component of the distinct culture of migration that has emerged in Poland. This chapter has shown how this impulse to return figures in narratives of social equality within the EU, and frames the view that the most meaningful realization of EU membership would involve sufficient opportunities to work and earn a decent living *within* Poland, so that travel abroad, whether for work or pleasure, would truly be a matter of choice.

Ambivalence about mobility, and by extension ambivalence about the EU, can be traced to the sense that migration is often forced by economic circumstances rather than chosen. Accessing opportunities in other EU countries marks social advancement, but it comes at the expense of the cohesion of families, and perhaps also the long-term prosperity of the nation. In other words, it is not just *degrees* of mobility that contribute to a restratification of countries, as Bauman (1998) claims, but also *kinds* of mobility. Significantly, at least as of yet, local communities in Bieszczady and Krakow have not been denuded of meaning and identity-endowing capacities (Bauman 1998, 18). Attachments to local places remain strong, and continue to motivate individuals' actions within the global sphere.

To conclude, the complexities of particular lives provide a more nuanced view of the interplay of factors that shape attitudes toward the EU. Travel and migration experiences, and reflections about mobility within the EU, show intertwined motivations, grounded especially in self-interest, attachment and identity. Sometimes cognitive and moral motivations also come into play, as we have seen when participants invoked ideals of freedom and equality, and how "normal life" *should* be organized. Participant's comments also suggest that perceptions of and responses to inclusion within the EU also depend on the degree to which EU membership contributes to the respect and authority they gain *as Poles* in an imagined world hierarchy of countries. Participants' words and actions help to show how the EU gains legitimacy as a symbol of Poland's advancement, but it does so *through* national allegiance, not at the expense of it.

Stasiek: Transnational Entrepreneur

Stasiek was Dorota's classmate in high school, and yet his life story presents a fitting contrast to hers, especially with regard to the issues raised here about mobility within an imagined hierarchy of nations. He studied computer science in Krakow, where he married and had a child before graduating. Stasiek's situation is different from Dorota's in that he never had trouble finding work in Poland; nevertheless, shortly after European integration, he decided to seek employment in England. Not only does Stasiek work in his profession, but he also commutes to England from his home in a city near Bieszczady. Always confident of his abilities and the possibilities the future would bring, Stasiek enjoys the best of both worlds, so to speak. He maintains his ties with family and place in Poland, while also earning a much better income in England. In 2005, he worked as a computer specialist for a firm that allowed him to do much of his work remotely, from Poland. He explained:

> I didn't want to go to the West to work "on the black [market]," meaning not having any rights. Why do I need to feel like a second-class citizen? I didn't

see any justification [for that] after Poland entered the EU as a more normal country, of the type that isn't afraid, that doesn't have phobias – like Norway, Great Britain, Ireland – and all kinds of associated restrictions were abolished. But it's like this: We entered the EU, which is fine. But we can't work in every country. We entered the EU – in effect we fell on our knees – but in France I can't work, in Germany I can't work. I'm not really their citizen. Countries in which I can work, in which I can live and earn money, they accepted me like a citizen. So, I was interested in those countries. I considered Norway, but there is a problem with the language – I don't know it at all. So the decision fell on England. I had a friend there. He told me, "Come try it. If you don't succeed, you can return." So I went. It turned out to be easier than I thought. I was prepared for much larger problems.

Everyday life in Poland, working for a firm, I met with so many problems, but then I went to England, where everyone wants to help me, I felt like someone took me by the hand. In Poland it's harder to live day to day. I'm basically a stranger there [in England], but with an EU passport, so basically [it's] the same country. In England, I'm treated like an equal. Now, like normal, I have all my English papers. The only thing that makes me different is my accent. But there are so many nationalities there, no one pays any attention. I have work that I like. I decide when I want to work. I vowed to myself that I'll never work for less than a certain amount per hour. I like the city, the atmosphere; I have my favorite restaurant, my favorite store. I get on an airplane and I'm here [in Poland] in an hour and a half, and it costs no more than one day's work. I feel completely free. I have a restless disposition, and that's the reason why I'm here and I'm there – I live everywhere.

Looking at the cost of food and gas here, they're similar to European prices. It's minimally cheaper [in Poland]. However, salaries haven't changed, or have even fallen. Relative to the rise in prices, it's a tremendous decline. So the standard of living has dramatically worsened. As a society, we work more and more, but earn less. Working in England, I don't even feel it when I pay for food, but here … All the time I tell my colleagues in England how much they would have to pay for food if they had to live like Poles. It would lead to a revolution.

At this moment, we are too weak a country to feel so strongly Polish. Our national pride has been completely stepped on. Because our nation joined the EU and became a cheap workforce. First came the unemployed, and now the brain drain. That means that everything that is the best is taken abroad. But Poles have a strong national identity and a Pole will never become British or French. He'll just go, earn money, open a firm and be a Pole still. He'll return here, invest, build himself a home or open a second company. People will return because our roots are here. At the same time, what does it matter that I travel there, I earn some money and I return? For me it's a plus. And it probably helps

Poland, because people like me have new ideas. I have more money, I buy more than others; I try to buy Polish products, and in this way everything grows.

How does this help Poland? As long as we unite as partners, it helps Poland a lot. But if Poland had to unite with some other collective under unequal conditions, that would not help. Give us a chance and we will become equal [to the rest of Europe] ourselves.

By 2008, Stasiek's life had completely changed in some ways, but he still maintained his transnational life. He had divorced, remarried, had another child with his new wife and moved out of the city into an old wooden farmhouse on a small plot of land. He also opened up to me about his personal life in a way he never had before. When he was in high school, even when we went on long bike rides together, he projected to me an idealized image of himself as someone in control of his future. Once he moved to the city, he never invited me to his home, but rather met me in parks, cafes and restaurants. In fact, I never met his first wife. By contrast, in 2008, we met at his home, where he introduced me to his new family. Our children played together as we chatted over tea in the kitchen and around the swing set in the yard. Stasiek still worked in both England and Poland, but rather than working for a company, he had his own web design business in England, as well as some Poland-based retail interests. He traveled to England for two months in the summer and one month in the winter to take care of business matters he could not handle remotely.

About this arrangement, he said:

I have the kind of profession and the possibility to find work that gives me satisfaction. The trips to England are problematic, though. Then, my children don't see me for two months. My wife has to manage – she's a very strong person. We could give up on my work in England, but then if we did, there wouldn't be that progress. We couldn't dream of something better. I have the kind of work that allows me to develop, that insures our children's future. [We can] build a house, or change our home.

Stasiek's way of thinking about his situation changed from 2005 to 2008, though he remains motivated by economic self-interest, family attachments and the desire for freedom. In 2005, he celebrated the freedom he experienced once EU membership opened avenues to legal employment in England. In 2008, he was arguably freer, to the extent that he was now self-employed, and his trips to England had grown less frequent (though for longer periods of time). Nevertheless, he voiced some disinclination toward his transnational life. Clearly, the changes in his personal circumstances made him look at things differently. He sounded resigned to the necessity of extended periods away from his new family, though, because his business in England guarantees his children material advantages they would not otherwise have.

Stasiek's life story speaks to all three of the themes of this chapter. He describes how EU membership has made travel and work abroad easier. This has contributed to his sense of personal social advancement – he does work he finds interesting and that pays much better than he would earn in Poland. In his own words, greater mobility within the EU offers the promise of a better life. What sets him apart from past generations of circular migrants is that he has legal status, professional employment and, more recently, he established his own business. Despite his personal advancement via opportunities made possible by EU integration, he seems to go back and forth between confidence that conditions in Poland will eventually become equal to more affluent countries and frustration that boundaries nevertheless remain. He has worked out a kind of compromise in his own life, taking advantage of relatively easy access to employment in England so that he can live comfortably in Poland; but he is adamant about staying out of countries that put up stronger restrictions against Polish travelers and workers. He does not want to bother with visas or special paperwork, nor does he think he should have to. Thus, these simple institutional requirements take on symbolic force that influences personal actions and corresponding attitudes toward the EU. Personal opportunities for advancement are conceptually linked to an imagined hierarchy of nations in which Poland has been welcomed into the top, so to speak, but on unequal terms. All things being equal, Stasiek, like Dorota, would just as soon stay home.

Chapter 7

"THIS REGION IS OUR PRIORITY": EU SUBSIDIES AND THE DEVELOPMENT OF A TRANSNATIONAL REGIONAL COMMUNITY

Joasia: Social Entrepreneur

Joasia says she became a school librarian by accident. The daughter of teachers, she had absolutely no interest in working in a school herself. Rather than going to a college-track lyceum, she decided to learn a trade at a technical high school. After graduation, though, with no chance of finding a job as a woodworker, she settled on a two-year program in library science. Through personal connections, she was hired by her former high school in the late 1990s, and she was still there when I visited in 2011. By then she had earned a master's degree by studying on weekends. A perpetual student, Joasia has received additional certificates in subjects like counseling and pedagogy. She regularly attends training sessions about various EU-sponsored programs, and has had some success applying for and receiving grants for her school. When we talked in 2005, Joasia and her husband had recently purchased a partially built home in her native village, and they were finishing it room by room, as funds and time allowed:

> I still work in the school library in Lesko. And that's about it, though I also work on these EU-funded projects, which is interesting because I meet interesting people and develop my abilities. As my acquaintances expand, I have more possibilities to arrange all kinds of things. I even managed to find a job for my sister-in-law.
>
> I think that what's improved is that people have become more resilient, more capable; maybe they know it's up to them to look after their own fate. That passage from one period to another was devastating for people who always felt the state took care of them. Suddenly there was unemployment, suddenly people had to knock on doors, do something by themselves, open their own business. There's a group of people who still can't deal with the fact that they have to

manage on their own. They often fall into pathologies like alcoholism, because they have nothing to do.

And in our region? Maybe something is beginning to change. Maybe people are learning to get grants from the EU, and they're doing better. I see that farmers get subsidies for mowing their fields. But it's very hard to apply for anything, because obviously many farmers don't even have a secondary education, and often they're older. It's hard for them to understand so they close themselves off from it. And those funds are not taken advantage of, from what I hear.

Besides that, life keeps getting more expensive. Everything is going up in price and salaries stay the same. When the price of gas keeps going up, so does everything else. People say our prices have risen so much that essentially there's no difference from those in Italy or Germany.

So I don't know if things are better.

You can say they're better if you're talking about younger people. It's reaching them that it's worth studying and broadening their qualifications, so because of that, sooner or later they'll find work. Maybe not right away, or maybe not in their profession. But looking at my friends, sooner or later they found work. And once they've found a job, it's easier to have something of your own. Because the banking system has changed a lot; banks compete, and it's easier to get a loan. Honestly, it's good there are so many foreign banks in our market. For example, when we bought our house, we got a loan from PKO [the Polish state bank], but others appeared with better deals so I moved my loan to a Swiss bank.

Even before accession I found out about a center in Warsaw that sponsors EU clubs in schools. So I registered our school and received materials of all kinds about the EU, so I could find out with those students what awaits us. And then, when there was the referendum, of course I took part. Because nothing much was happening with our democracy, I thought that maybe integration with other states would help – even though my husband worked in Italy, and said that as soon as Italy entered the EU, living standards dropped. Still, I thought to myself, our standard of living is already so low, nothing could dig it deeper, so I voted to give EU integration a try. I wanted to see what would happen, even though my husband was opposed.

How would I evaluate the influence of the EU on Poland so far? I'll tell you something, Marysia, that for gray[1] citizens like me and other people in this region, we can't really feel it. It's great that there are subsidies for farming, because I can see how fields don't lie fallow, and people earn a few pennies – it motivates them to work. But the moment we entered the EU, the bureaucracy doubled. There are numerous forms to fill out, statements and confirmations. And all the time we're told that highly developed democratic countries don't have any such bureaucracy. Honestly, I don't like it.

So have there been benefits or costs? I don't know, Marysia. If the EU survives a while longer … because when I voted in the referendum, I said this: "I will vote 'yes' but I know that as soon as they admit Poland, the EU will collapse" [laugh]. It won't survive because of it. After a while, the next poor country, then the next [will join]. Honestly, when I write those applications, money isn't always rationally distributed. This is a shortcoming of the EU. Sometimes they can't find someone capable of making use of their funds where they are really needed, so they put it in another area that's in better shape, but has good people who know how to request the funds. So I don't know. For me personally, I'll tell you that nothing has changed, and probably nothing will change. Except that now at any moment I can get in my car and go to Slovakia without a passport.

Everything depends on whether EU countries will want to help us. Poland will benefit if foreign companies come into the market and we gain places of employment. Maybe that will give young people a chance; maybe we will develop scientifically and culturally. But that's also associated with how well the [Polish] state functions; without jobs, everything will crumble. We have very many intelligent people, scientists, who emigrate, because no one can sponsor their research here. It's a shame and I hope it changes. But, frankly, I don't trust the EU. For now, I'm just watching. I know it's hard with so many countries to take care of, to handle the politics, to divide funds among everyone, so that they're more or less stable, and more or less the same. How can they manage?

Before the accession, nothing was happening in this region; unfortunately there was no money for after-school activities. But then a chance appeared to get money for something, to give young people something, so they wouldn't just end up in the streets doing who knows what – theft or robbery. We decided that it's important to do something from time to time, to do something for young people.

The concept of "social entrepreneur" has been popularized in recent years by the work of organizations such as the Grameen Bank[2] and by books such as David Bornstein's *How to Change the World* (2004). A social entrepreneur is someone who makes use of market values such as innovation, efficiency and entrepreneurialism to address social problems.[3] Joasia has taken the initiative to use resources provided by the EU for regional development. Her biggest success has been to obtain funds for computerized drafting and fabrication equipment with which students learn to reproduce traditional furniture and architecture. The idea is to teach skills that will contribute to the promotion of heritage tourism in Bieszczady. Joasia has not profited personally from such efforts; her primary motivation has been to give young people reasons to stay in Bieszczady rather than being forced to leave to earn a living. In 2008, she lived alone in her unfinished house while her husband worked abroad. She told me she could not even think about having a child until their financial situation stabilized. By 2011, Joasia was doing better; she had a two-year-old son, the whole ground floor of the house was finished, and her husband was employed in Poland. Still, Joasia remained a skeptic about the benefits of EU integration. Notably, she still referred to the EU as "they" even after Poland became a member state. Nor did her social entrepreneurialism protect her school; in 2011 the local government elected to sell the school property to private developers and to merge the woodworking program into the agricultural high school next door. It was not clear whether she would have a job at the reconstituted school.

Using EU Subsidies: Social Entrepreneurs, Public Servants and Flexible Farmers

Joasia's life story illustrates how EU membership has influenced participants' lives, not only by providing opportunities for mobility as outlined in Chapter 6, but also through subsidies for economic and cultural development that provide opportunities *within* Poland. What emerges from engagements with EU programs is a hybrid form of place, what I call a "transnational regional community," because the concept of the local is fundamentally reconceived in relation to broader frames of reference. Even as these encounters with the EU make real the idea of Europe, social entrepreneurs, public servants and farmers display a hybrid form of person, simultaneously motivated by community loyalties and exercising entrepreneurial self-reliance within the wider geopolitical scale. The efforts of residents who seek EU funding offer a view into the process of Europeanization and the contemporary construction of regional identities within Europe.

I focus on the Bieszczady region for three reasons. First, its rural, agricultural character makes it eligible for EU structural funds that target underdeveloped areas. Second, border regions have long been recognized in anthropology as an important site for identity studies because implicit categories often become marked through contestation across political boundaries (see Asher 2005, 2011; Barth 1969; Berdahl 1999; Meinhof 2002; Wilson and Donnan 1998). Third, as classic anthropological studies have shown, many questions are easier to identify and to examine within clearly defined small-scale communities. The challenge, of course, is defining a meaningful, and manageable, category of place and people within which to explore *global* issues. The population of Bieszczady is relatively small, and the people I already knew helped me identify key actors and gain access to them. Through them, I learned about multiple, overlapping and contradictory convergences (see Tsing 2000) between EU priorities and local interests.

Within the Bieszczady region, I talked not only with participants in my longitudinal study, but also with other social actors who have sought funding for cultural, educational, economic and environmental projects. Several of

Figure 7.1. Rural farmers are investing in tourist facilities to encourage "agritourism"

them specified that they aspire to provide opportunities so that residents will have a reason to stay in Bieszczady rather than seeking employment elsewhere. They generally agree that the future of the region depends on the expansion of tourism, and that becomes part of the rationale for infrastructural improvements, educational programs, cultural promotion and environmental protection (figure 7.1). Participants' social positions shape their specific goals. Social entrepreneurs address social issues by means of business principles like innovation, efficiency and entrepreneurship (see Bornstein 2004). Government employees engage in public service as a condition of their employment. Some describe themselves as a *wieczny wolontariat* (eternal volunteer) because they feel a deep sense of mission about helping their communities but engage in activities intermittently, outside of their usual employment, and with no expectation of material compensation. Farmers act in the interest of preserving their own family farms, though some also volunteer to help the broader community of farmers. These categories of people can overlap, as when Joasia works in her spare time to obtain funding for an enrichment program at her school; her job does not require it, but she feels compelled to do what she can to provide opportunities for others.

Social entrepreneurs, public servants and eternal volunteers were easy to identify because they acted publicly and were well known in the community.

Some, like Joasia, were already participants in my longitudinal study. They, in turn, referred me to others whom they knew, or in some cases, with whom they had worked on projects. I made particular effort to contact individuals who were recommended to me by more than one source. Of the eighteen who participated in taped, semistructured interviews about their pursuit of EU funding, five worked for nongovernmental organizations, three had positions in local government, five were educators, one was a priest and four were farmers. All but three had been Bieszczady residents since childhood.

In this chapter, I identify the EU-funded programs that target underdeveloped rural border regions, and describe local projects involving agriculture, infrastructure and regional culture. I further consider the ways in which conforming to EU standards requires a corresponding transformation of personhood for the local agents who seek funding (see Lampland and Star [2009] on standards). I explore the emergence of a transnational regional community – one defined by its regional distinctness, but also by its connections to broader social groups, including "Europe" and neighboring ethnicities.

EU Programs and Local Projects

A priority of EU policy has been financial assistance in the form of "structural funds" and "cohesion funds" aimed at reducing economic and social disparities among regions of Europe. Earlier programs provided support to the regions within countries that had an average income below 75 per cent of the national average, declining industry, high unemployment and rural populations coping with a declining agricultural sector (Słomski 2001, 26–7; Bokajło and Dziubka 2003).[4] In the early 1990s, despite expressions of commitment to the *idea* of unification, EU member states were hesitant to take on the financial burden associated with expansion into Central and Eastern Europe. Richer member states knew they would have to cover most of the cost of economic restructuring, and poorer member states feared they would lose the subsidies that they had been receiving for their own development projects (Vachudova 2005). However, even before East-Central European countries became members, subsidies were extended to candidate states through programs such as PHARE (economic restructuring), SAPARD (agriculture and rural development) and INTERREG (cross-border cooperation).[5] All of these programs advance the fundamental EU goal to "equalize chances" for all Europeans, which in turn is seen as an important component of "cohesion" within Europe. By 2005, the positive influence of EU subsidies could be seen in Bieszczady in the form of revitalization of regional agriculture, infrastructure development projects, and cultural and environmental programs.

Agriculture

Agriculture defines the characteristic landscapes of the Bieszczady region. Meadows rise up to woodlands on rolling hills surrounding villages. Because of the steep, rocky ground and short growing season, farms have remained small with low levels of mechanization. The few state farms in the region were liquidated in the early 1990s, and these larger tracts of land have since been privatized. Participants told me the land was bought by wealthy outsiders (alternately identified as corrupt politicians, rich Varsovians or foreigners), most of whom are not farmers. Most small landholders gave up farming as centralized collection systems for farm products collapsed, and the cost of production increased relative to prices for agricultural products.[6] By the late 1990s, these economic shifts were becoming inscribed on the landscape; shrubs and trees were overtaking hillsides formerly covered with checkerboard fields in various stages of cultivation. Even though there has been a sharp decline in the number of Bieszczady residents who rely on agriculture for their livelihood, certain financial incentives have contributed to a renewed interest in preserving the agricultural landscape. As participants explained, direct payments from the EU and lower social security taxes for farmers have led many to keep their pastures mowed. Subsidies have made it possible for some young farmers to maintain viable operations, but rural policy may be more effective at preserving the *image* of the agricultural countryside than actual farms and farming communities.

The Common Agricultural Policy (CAP) remains the EU's largest expenditure, although it has decreased from over seventy-five per cent of the EU budget in the 1960s to about forty-five per cent in the 2000s (Gorton et al. 2009). The CAP bolsters certain fundamental values; it prioritizes the preservation of each member state's domestic farm production while also seeking to apply global market principals to the agricultural sector. These goals can be difficult to reconcile. Policies designed to increase global competitiveness involve lowering market prices for agricultural products, removing tariffs and dismantling other market protections between member states. All this resulted in a decrease in profits for farmers, which was initially offset by guaranteeing farmers set prices for their products. Since 1992, the CAP has shifted to direct payments linked to specific kinds of agricultural land (pasturage, arable land, food crops, etc.) in an effort to decrease surplus production but still support domestic producers. The Agenda 2000 project also outlined goals and regulations linked to broader EU aims including environmental protection, animal welfare and food safety. As Gorton et al. (2009) note, the CAP developed in response to conditions in Western Europe; even though the Agenda 2000 reforms anticipated enlargement of the EU, they failed to adequately address the development needs of rural areas in the new member states, characterized by smaller farms with lower levels of mechanization.

I have seen firsthand how, since the early 1990s, small landholders in Bieszczady have found it impossible to support themselves by farming. Still, this was due to postcommunist processes of deregulation and market liberalization that predated EU integration. In fact, even though farmers were consistently the occupational group that showed the least support for EU membership (see Roguska 2004a, 2004b), they have actually profited from direct payments, new markets and infrastructural improvements that have accompanied EU enlargement. Most of the farmers I spoke with in Bieszczady have positive views of EU integration because, as they explained, it provides them with more opportunities to make a living through agriculture. This reflects what I believe is a process of attrition, in which many who were more skeptical about EU integration already gave up farming; older farmers retired and younger ones emigrated. I report here the experiences of participants who told me they want to remain farmers, and have successfully (at least so far) exercised entrepreneurship, in the traditional sense of business acumen, and social entrepreneurship, in the form of helping others negotiate the EU bureaucracy.

Contrary to stereotypes about the traditional conservatism of agricultural communities, the farmers I interviewed are not resistant to change as long as they see benefits derived from it. Rather, they are fundamentally pragmatic. They take advantage of new markets throughout Europe and direct subsidies for productive agricultural land. For example, Zosia's family had raised sheep for 20 years when they decided to shift their operation to milk and veal production. A local dairy collects their milk daily and pays them weekly, which they prefer to the single annual payment they receive when their sheep are ready for slaughter. They have also increased their cattle production because they found that they can sell calves to a company in Italy for as much as they would get for a full-grown steer in Poland. The family got an EU loan to buy a tractor, and used other subsidies to bring their farm up to EU standards. Specifically, they installed a refrigerated storage room for their milk and a paved pathway for the cows to use when they enter the barn. They said they do not mind the new standards because they decrease spoilage and thus improve productivity.

Another way farmer participants have been better able to earn a living has been by becoming certified organic producers. This makes them eligible for additional EU subsidies and has opened up markets in other member states eager for organic food. The farmers told me organic certification is no problem for them; they have always used organic methods because they were too poor to do anything else. They compost their own manure instead of using expensive chemical fertilizers, let animals graze rather than giving them processed feed, and keep their animals healthy without antibiotics. In other contexts, some of the same farmers expressed more doubts, saying their yields are lower because they cannot use chemical additives. Also, they do not necessarily get better prices for organic products. As Halina and her husband Zygmunt explained in 2011, they sell their milk to a local dairy that does not market specifically organic products, and so pays them the same prices it would for conventionally produced milk. Halina said, "People from the city might think we are profiting the most from these subsidies, but in fact we can barely stay in place because all of our expenses have also gone up." Zygmunt added that they have taken advantage of subsidized loans to purchase equipment like a baler and a tractor, but in the past they did not need their own machinery because everyone worked together. "Farms need to be bigger to make a profit," Zygmunt explained. "And still, we just come out even."

Some farmers are also looking for ways to profit from increased tourism, most directly by developing "agritourism," wherein they offer lodging and meals for visitors who want a taste of the pastoral lifestyle. Structural funds provide farmers with opportunities for various improvements, such as updating plumbing, adding guestrooms to farmhouses or building small rental cottages. In 2005 and again in 2008, Agata told me about her plan to build a *karczma* (roadside inn), and in 2011 construction finally began. However, she received no EU funds for her project. Agata explained it was because local officials who administer the program claimed they ran out of funds, but then gave money to people with connections. When she inquired again sometime later, she was told she was ineligible because construction had already begun on her project. These kinds of situations reinforce feelings that government officials, and the EU, protect their own interests over those of regular citizens. Though frustrated, Agata said she will apply again, this time for funds earmarked for room furnishings.

In another regard as well, Agata was disappointed by the local Chamber of Agriculture's management of EU-funded programs. She attended a training scheme offered by the Agencja Restrukturyzacji i Modernizacji Rolnictwa (ARiMR; Agency for Restructuring and Modernizing Agriculture) so she could help her father apply for EU direct payments. In 2004 and 2005, she also helped other farmers, most of whom were older and found the forms confusing. Agata even traveled to their homes if they did not have their own means of transportation. "I felt sorry for those farmers," she explained, although she also felt taken advantage of when she learned the Chamber of Agriculture had received funds from the ARiMR to help farmers with their forms, but instead spent it on other things. Agata criticized the agency for misusing funds in ways that are of no help to farmers, but rather enrich people with connections. She gave the example of a conference her husband and she were invited to attend as token compensation for the work she did with older farmers. The conference was in Zakopane (a resort town in the Tatra Mountains), and she was one of just two farmers who attended. She described the other participants as "students and children of government officials," who used the opportunity as a free vacation.

These three farming families manage to support themselves through agricultural production, but the viability of their farms is tenuous. They live in multigenerational households in which some members work in local businesses, or travel seasonally to service or agricultural employment in other countries. Structural funds only return a portion of their investment in farm improvements, leaving them with debts that challenge their flexibility and autonomy. The economy of Bieszczady has changed, and with it so has village culture. Gone are the days when every household had livestock and gardens. Zygmunt remarked that the number of farmers in their village has decreased from 40 to just 10. Halina added that she does not understand her neighbors, who prefer to buy milk and eggs from the store rather than get them directly from local farmers. Zygmunt further lamented:

> [The government] did it wrong and wasted a lot of money. Because everyone claimed they had agricultural land, even city folk who bought state farms, and hired others to mow the fields for them. In fact, they get more than real farmers like us because the pay structure is based on land in agricultural production, not on the produce itself. That means people cut hay, harvest it and leave it to rot in the corner of their fields. They comply with the letter but not the spirit of the law. For us, it's worse and worse[7] because the price for milk hasn't changed since 1996, but the cost of gas and equipment has gone up a lot. Fake farmers don't have those production expenses. Now, the criteria for receiving funds have changed somewhat, but it's too late. A lot of money has already been lost.

Farmers noted the uncertainty of continued farm subsidies; they blamed it, in part, on the fact that much of the available funds were given to the wrong people.

Although organic production provided Bieszczady farmers with additional funding sources that helped make their small farms viable, in 2011 they were feeling the squeeze of higher operating costs without comparable increases in the prices they received for their products. Offermann et al. (2009) demonstrate that direct payments comprise a larger proportion of organic producers' income than that of other kinds of farmers. They argue this makes organic farmers more dependent on less stable sources of income and thus less flexible when reacting to market fluctuations. Correspondingly, the adaptations Bieszczady farmers have made may well leave them worse off if the European economic crisis continues and farm subsidies are cut in the 2014–20 EU budget.

Infrastructure

By the time Poland entered the EU, signs of EU-funded development could be seen throughout Bieszczady, including new bridges, repaved roads, pedestrian plazas and tourist amenities. These projects were marked, literally, with the EU symbol, a circle of gold stars on a blue background, on signs that also identified the EU funding agency, the regional partner and even the amount funded (see figure 7.2). Participants referred to infrastructural improvements as benefits of EU membership. However, as with the agricultural sector, it remains unclear how effectively the local economy can integrate with global market forces. Specifically, continued infrastructural weaknesses challenge the viability of the emerging tourist sector in Bieszczady.

Although creating alternative employment and sources of income for rural residents are included among the main goals of Agenda 2000, most

Figure 7.2. Sign marking EU funding: "Project co-financed with EU funds from the European Fund for Regional Development [...] We invest in the development of the Podkarpacki Voivodship"

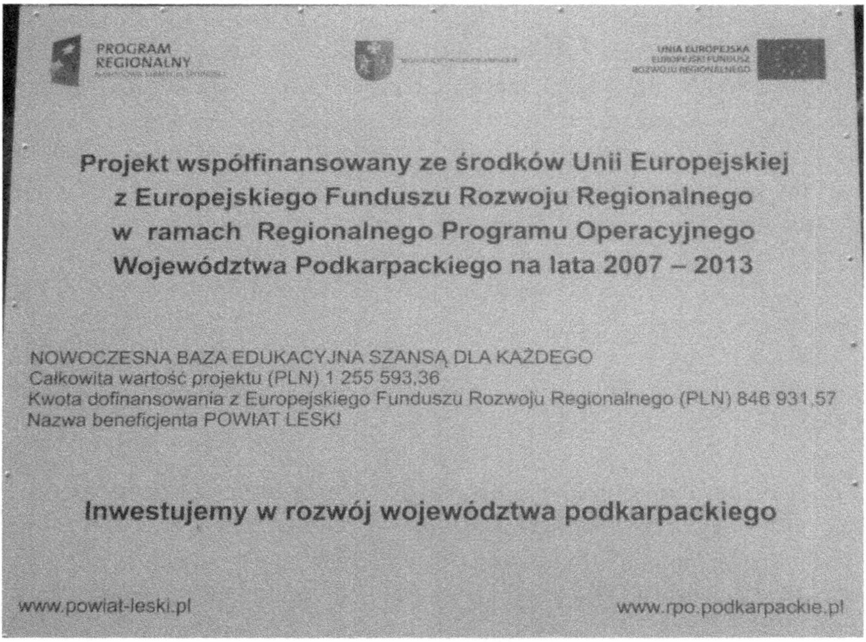

CAP funds go toward direct payments to farmers (Kutkowska 2003, 520; Gorton et al. 2009). A much smaller proportion of CAP funds, along with other structural funds for border regions and underdeveloped regions, target economic development projects. Local governments in Bieszczady obtained such funds for improvements like water works, sewage systems and roads. As one local official explained, it may not be the most glamorous project, but:

> Sewer lines are the foundation. The idea was to begin rebuilding the town from there. [...] Because if we want to improve the infrastructure of roads, sidewalks or the quality of surface features, we first have to dig those pipes. Because the pipes are deep down and they can't be redirected. While gas and water are under pressure and can be directed, sewage lines must be concretely planned and then worked around.

In this and other districts throughout the mountain region, crews were out from summer into the winter installing sewer systems that were then overlain with newly paved roads or sidewalks. Local government representatives highlighted the regional goal of economic development, including incentives for new business investment and increased employment opportunities.

One county's applications for structural funds help to illustrate how local leaders tailor regional interests to the priorities identified by EU funding instruments. The first application was for modernization of sewage lines and water supply facilities, submitted to the Zintegrowany Program Operacyjny Rozwoju Regionalnego (ZPORR; Integrated Operational Program for Regional Development).[8] This project was linked to two priorities for such structural funds: the development and modernization of infrastructure to strengthen the competitiveness of regions; and local development, specifically in the interest of rural areas and small businesses. The application also noted that the project was in agreement with the county's development plan, and identified specific goals using language closely akin to EU-identified goals:

Goal 1: To create conditions for economic activities other than farming, clean water is essential.

Goal 3.1: Counteract social and economic marginalization of villages and small towns through diversified economy, improve conditions in areas with the fewest development opportunities.

The proposal emphasized the economic benefits of the project, although the positive environmental influence of the sewage system was also noted. Additional sections of the application identified projects that had received funding previously (in this case, pipelines, sewage treatment, road construction and tourist infrastructure), projects planned for the future and a detailed budget. The application ended with a statement that EU co-funding will be recognized on a commemorative tablet at the site and on the district website.[9]

A second application was submitted to another structural fund with a different set of priorities. Funds were sought for tennis courts with support facilities and a parking lot from INTERREG, which targets projects that encourage cross-border cooperation. This application identified the goal to "increase active tourism from Poland and neighboring countries and all of Europe" as a means of promoting economic growth, and named a specific Slovakian partner with whom at least five cultural events would be organized. Calling tourism "the best chance" for the transborder region, the proposal also stated, "Very often friendly connections form through this [kind of activity]." The application included a list of previously funded projects and a detailed budget. To summarize, these cases demonstrate the importance of fitting local development plans into EU priorities and showing evidence of good management and planning.

While encouraged by these opportunities to make things happen in Bieszczady, officials emphasized that much remains to be done. Józef explained, "The truth is, there is never enough money; the needs are too large. [...] When I look from the perspective of a county worker, I see it's possible to do things. But unemployment has definitely gotten worse. Before [1989] people worked everywhere, there was no unemployment. They could even support themselves as farmers." Although structural funds have also subsidized private development of tourist infrastructure, particularly near scenic places like Lake Solina and Bieszczady National Park, more fundamental obstacles remain. In particular, Bieszczady remains relatively difficult to get to; there are no highways, and the buses and trains that service the area are slow and antiquated. Buses travel infrequently to the more remote villages, and there has periodically been talk about discontinuing the train service from Zagórz to Komańcza. Nor is there enough money to maintain the roads, let alone improve them. For example, by 2005, the pavement on the road to Zawóz had disintegrated to dirt, gravel and potholes. Although that road had been repaved by 2008, sections of the main loop through the mountains had been washed away in mudslides over the winter. In fact, bad roads and crumbling bridges made it impossible to complete either of the two primary mountain circuits. In 2011, some sections of road had been rebuilt, but then another bridge washed out, again making one of the mountain routes impassable.

Regional culture

You cannot go very far in Bieszczady without coming across traces of formerly thriving multicultural communities, and the transnational forces that destroyed them. Some are as dramatic as the synagogue in Lesko – its size

Figure 7.3. The Historic Architecture Museum (Skansen) in Sanok recently received EU funds to build a model town center

a reminder that before the Holocaust the town's Jewish population was larger than the Catholic one. Other traces are only visible to those who know what to look for, such as the fruit trees and foundation stones overgrown by forest where prewar villagers were displaced by World War II or forcibly resettled after the war ended. Over the years, efforts to preserve what remains have been undertaken by state and local governments, NGOs, UNESCO and Jewish heritage organizations. With increasing frequency, the EU logo marks EU involvement in cultural heritage and cultural revitalization projects throughout Bieszczady, including "soft projects" promoting education, cultural events and community initiatives. These projects privilege multicultural values of cross-border cooperation and multinational cohesion, but although local agents cater to this vision, they do so in pursuit of regional goals. Specifically, they want to increase local pride in Bieszczady and promote development of the local tourist sector so that residents will have reasons to stay, rather than seeking employment elsewhere.

Since World War II, Bieszczady has been characterized as "wild" (*dzikie*) and "empty" (*puste*). The postwar socialist state viewed Bieszczady as a blank slate, and sought to remake it in keeping with the "high modernist socialist order" they wanted to realize throughout Poland (Lehman 2009, 425).

In contrast to the socialist vision which favored modernization of agriculture and industrial development, the mountains also gained a reputation for attracting "restless souls" (*niespokojne duchy*) – artists, criminals and others – escaping the company of people and seeking adventure in Poland's "Wild East." Neither of these portraits recognized prewar multicultural communities that were wiped out by the Holocaust and mass resettlement as states sought to engineer ethnic homogeneity within new borders. Contemporary regional development plans promote the natural beauty of the region as well as its rich history in an effort to encourage tourism, which is seen as the most promising means of stimulating the local economy (figure 7.3). Strategies for development also champion potentially contradictory goals. Adventure tourism is encouraged in land portrayed as "wilderness" at the same time that traces of abandoned villages are recovered and preserved for heritage tourists. Farmers receive subsidies for organic production, but can do little to protect their livestock from a growing wolf population that has protected status. Logging for the local timber industry scars the view along hiking trails. Competing visions for the area correspond to contradictory EU fund priorities including agriculture, economic development, environmentalism and multiculturalism.

EU funds for regional development such as INTERREG, PHARE and EQUAL[10] promote the value of multiculturalism, which has been interpreted in a number of ways: cross-border cooperation, tolerance for diversity within an increasingly cohesive Europe, and celebration of the distinctiveness of regional cultures and ethnic minorities. Some initiatives in Bieszczady have been branded as engines for cross-border tourism. For instance, Zielony Rower (Green Bicycle; an affiliate of the international organization Greenways) creates and publicizes bicycle routes that cross national borders. The director of the NGO who helped realize this project emphasized its success at bringing Slovak bicycle tourists into the region; he said he hopes being part of a wider network of bike routes will attract bicycle enthusiasts from even farther afield. Another successfully funded project is a zoo and retreat center run by the Catholic charity organization Caritas. Its manager Father Mirek explained that Slovak, and occasionally Ukrainian, school groups visit the zoo. Although signs at the site advertise that PHARE funds for cross-border cooperation made the project possible, the priest did not express any strong feelings about the EU or Poland's membership. Rather, he said he made use of EU funds because they provide him with a means of expanding and improving the facilities, and making them more attractive to tourists. These examples (as well as Józef's application for a tennis facility described above) illustrate how local social entrepreneurs make claims about encouraging cross-border cooperation less out of a commitment to multiculturalism than a desire for economic resources for tourism development.

Moreover, cross-border collaboration with Ukraine has become more difficult as a consequence of standards regulating movement across the EU border. It has become harder and more costly for Ukrainians to obtain a visa for an EU member state, even for events designed to promote multicultural cooperation. As a result, Ukrainian school groups have had to cancel trips to Bieszczady, and few Ukrainians participate when Carpathian regional meetings take place outside of Ukraine. Thus, the increased permeability of some political borders has contributed to the rigidity of others (see also Follis 2008), potentially leading to more oppositional identities between EU member and nonmember nations.

Multiculturalism also provides the rationale for a different constellation of cultural development projects that promote Bieszczady's multicultural heritage. Whereas in the past, most towns had significant Jewish populations and many village residents had regional identities associated with Ukrainian culture (see Falkowski and Pasznycki 1935; Fastnacht 1988), the vast majority of the roughly 70,000 Bieszczady residents today consider themselves Polish.[11] Since 1989, the small community of Ukrainians has become more public about its distinctive cultural practices and Greek Catholic or Orthodox faith. By 2005, the architectural styles, religious practices and cultural traditions of prewar residents were not only publicly acknowledged by regional leaders and the Polish majority, but also celebrated in cultural festivals and on historical markers. The ethnic diversity of the region also tends to be highlighted in cultural projects that seek EU sponsorship. Indeed, educators and employees of nonprofit organizations actively construct a story about the region that they teach other residents in order to build in them a sense of pride and connection to place. As one school principal explained, "We are reaching for our roots, putting great effort into building in children that identity and attachment to this land, but also to give them an equal chance."

Locality is in many ways in the process of construction, so it is not surprising that there is some disagreement among participants about the history and culture that should comprise the basis for local identity. One participant, a teacher with deep connections in Bieszczady who has engaged in a variety of EU-funded cultural heritage projects, complained that some people are remaking the region into a historically Ukrainian territory and disregarding its Polish roots. She discussed this in terms of prewar ethnic groups, some of whose language, religion and customs were more akin to Polish, and others to Ukrainian (Falkowski and Pasznycki 1935):

Poles also lived in this region, darn it, and I don't understand how suddenly a tradition appeared connecting our territory with the tradition of Łemko and Bojko – [ethnic groups that were] Ukrainian, kind of, but their own separate ethnicities. Everyone wants to make this into Ukrainian territory. So regional dishes become Ukrainian, and the Polish culture is lost. I've also seen this fashion for preserving so-called Łemko cottages, when they are definitely Polish cottages – of the "Valley People."[12] I'm telling you, Valley People lived in cottages like that, don't upset me. Just go and look. … I'm a tolerant person, but I've noticed that some people at all costs want to identify with some different nation than Poland. Because that way it's easier for them to attract tourists.

Even as the region has become increasingly associated with the heritage of Ukrainian villagers, the history of the former Jewish population is for the most part ignored. Historic relics such as Lesko's synagogue and cemetery have been the focus of international Jewish preservation organizations rather than locally driven, EU-funded projects. This reflects what Irwin-Zarecka (1994, 116–18) calls a "memory void" – Jews are simply absent from Polish collective memory.[13]

Despite the priority placed on multiculturalism by EU structural and social funds, the historical ethnic and religious diversity of Poland stands in stark contrast to the contemporary population, which is 95 per cent Roman Catholic and Polish. Instead, invented traditions (Hobsbawm [1983] 1992) are enacted by local (and national) interests trying to capitalize on historical diversity and advance regional development schemes. As Buzalka (2007) notes, even though they are based on contemporary values of tolerance and diversity, such practices fix Ukrainian and Polish identities in ways that inscribe the contrast between them. This "artificial tolerance" replaces the "ordinary tolerance" of the past, when Greek Catholics were more likely to accept a variety of Roman Catholic symbols and rites, and mixed marriages contributed to more fluid identifications within families, and even across the life course (Buzalka 2007, 208–9). This is not to say that relations in the past were always peaceful (they were not). Rather, ethnic distinctions are being reified by the very policies designed to promote cohesion among ethnically diverse populations.

The main goal of another category of funding, the European Social Fund, is to fight unemployment. Associated programs encourage opportunities for mobility (within or between EU countries) and job retraining, especially for the most vulnerable groups. They emphasize marketable skills, innovation, adaptability and access to education and employment opportunities (Pudlak 2003). The Szkoła Marzeń (School of Dreams) program targeted rural youth, in recognition of the shortage of jobs in rural areas and among recent graduates.[14] It identified four priorities: insure equality of educational opportunities; help students choose educational and career paths; shape active attitudes toward social change; and mobilize local communities around common activities for education and upbringing. Schools were encouraged to partner with local government, businesses and other cultural organizations. In practice, the program funded extracurricular activities, many of which promoted regional history and culture. The efforts of two schools to get funding through the "Szkoła Marzeń" program illustrate how local needs are adapted to the priorities of the funding agency. I suggest that just one school was funded because it promoted regional economic development in a way that more closely fit the EU paradigm of multiculturalism, even though the second school better met the fund's main priority of "increasing educational opportunities for students from rural communities."

I spoke with officials at a college-track lyceum that received funding and a village middle school that did not. The differences between the schools reflect structural distinctions that reproduced occupational classes even during state socialism. Lycea emphasize academic subjects and admit the most gifted students; children of elite families are more likely to attend. Village children more commonly select technical or trade schools that emphasize occupational skills. Starting in the 1990s, in response to the transformation of work opportunities within a neoliberal economy, national education reforms encouraged more students to complete general academic tracks at the high school level, and then go on to higher education. The middle school serves more rural, less affluent students who have not yet been tracked into college-preparatory or vocational programs – the very population Szkoła Marzeń was designed to reach. By contrast, although the lyceum meets the program threshold of at least 35 per cent of students from rural counties, it is located in a town and tends to serve the children of teachers, business owners, doctors and the like. Nevertheless, the lyceum received funding, while the other school did not.

The lyceum's proposal emphasized extracurricular activities designed to help students develop skills and gain knowledge that would be useful in Bieszczady's growing tourism industry. Opportunities included: classes in photography, art and journalism; art exhibitions; a traditional dance group; outings into the mountains; and fieldtrips to regional historical sites. Activities emphasized regional cultural heritage and natural history; for example, there were competitions for the best photographs of local flora and fauna, and journalism students wrote articles about Bieszczady history for a local newspaper. Students were also offered career counseling to help them identify the profession best suited to their abilities and interests. Although the middle school's proposal included elements intended to strengthen local identity, it tried to meet the program's first priority, to equalize chances, by providing opportunities for students to learn about the places that are most significant for *national* culture and history. To that end, fieldtrips to Krakow, Warsaw and Gdansk were included. The school principal explained how important it is for rural children to have some familiarity with city life, including things as basic as public transportation, so they will be comfortable venturing out of their village.

In short, the rejected proposal was founded on a more antiquated notion of center–periphery, where citizens of peripheral regions must look to the economic and cultural core of the nation for resources and opportunities. As such, it reinforced the primacy of the nation over EU-friendly ideas of multiculturalism. The funded proposal, by contrast, packaged multicultural heritage as a key distinguishing feature of the Bieszczady region, and promised to teach children to use this regional distinctiveness as a tool for stimulating tourism and creating employment opportunities in Bieszczady. It is also important to note that both schools have remarkably competent and committed employees who have successfully pursued EU-sponsored funding for other projects. The lyceum has received a number of grants for school upgrades, and the middle school has received funds to establish a "green classroom" that features the unique geography of the mountains. As is typical of social entrepreneurs, the principal of the middle school was not discouraged by failure. "We feel a little satisfaction that we tried and more than anything some knowledge has been gained," she said. "So we have to be optimists."

EU Standards and New Ways of Being

Only particular kinds of persons would want to be a social entrepreneur, and they must undergo a process of socialization to successfully tap resources made available by EU integration. I now explore the rationale they offer for undertaking such efforts. I also consider how the standards imposed by EU cohesion policies compel them to adopt certain ways of doing, and indeed ways of being, in order to access funding. Through this process, I argue, the EU becomes "real" – it gains entitativity, not only through the physical markers built into the landscape (as I have described above), but also by fostering certain qualities of personhood. Applying for EU subsidies requires precision, accountability and planning, all of which participants regard as fundamental to the process of "becoming European."

As Star and Lampland point out, standard forms, technologies, and conventions are built into infrastructure and embedded in everyday use such that they become effectively invisible. Because standards "appear fixed and neutral" they obscure "the enormous amount of work needed to stabilize knowledge" (2009, 13). In 2005, the process of EU standardization had not yet stabilized, so new standards were clearly apparent, or what Brubaker et al. (2006) would call "marked." In effect, the application procedures and criteria for realizing EU-funded programs require adopting EU-sanctioned ethics and values that often clash with local infrastructures and conventions. Such challenges can keep rural and impoverished localities out of the running for funding, and thus suggest how EU cohesion policies designed to reduce economic and social disparities may in fact "shunt some people to the margin and make them invisible to the world market" (Dunn 2009, 121).[15]

Why do participants expend their own time and energy writing proposals for EU funding? For most, it arises out of a sense of attachment to the region and a desire for conditions to improve there. As they describe it, they see a local need, and recognize they have the personal ability to do something about it. This is particularly true for those who work on projects supplementary to their employment, or who have started foundations or businesses with the specific intent of promoting Bieszczady. As one teacher explained, "There's nothing happening here; there are no afterschool opportunities for students. [...] One should do something from time to time to engage those youth." The director of a nonprofit organization called it "a way of life" to encourage people to realize their aspirations.

Put simply, participants expressed a deep sense of social mission. One teacher called herself a *społecznik* (a "worker for society" or someone who does unpaid community service). She explained, "Most teachers can't or simply don't want to get involved in this kind of additional activity. Because of course it is a matter of having to stay after work hours, you have to devote your free time, and that doesn't suit everyone." Another participant called himself a *wieczny wolontariat* (eternal volunteer). He explained that the Internet service he established, while being a money-making enterprise, also includes a great deal of information that has little direct commercial value, including photo essays and articles he composes about cultural and environmental issues. "There's also a sentimental thread to what I do," he continued, "in that I want to promote this region, to show what's here, because I know that in this way people who try to advertise their businesses in Lesko will improve their economic situation." Agata told me she helped other farmers fill out their applications for EU subsidies because "you have to help people." Some participants noted that there is nothing new about working for the good of the community; during state socialism, participation in public work projects was even at times required. Social entrepreneurship emerges from participants' commitment to social justice. They define themselves as the kind of person who does not remain passive, but rather seeks to make the local community into what it should be.

Participants said they are motivated by the personal satisfaction they derive from participation in service activities. One woman explained: "I certainly don't write proposals for money, because there really isn't any institution here that would pay for writing proposals. It is more a matter of self-realization.

[We say,] 'Listen, let's do something, let's write something.' Entirely for the community [*społecznie*], like that. Because what I do professionally is completely different; this is more in keeping with my personal interests." Another participant explained, "I've set for myself as a point of honor fighting with windmills – in other words, living in a place where doing this type of thing is very difficult, but brings much satisfaction." There is a strong social aspect to their involvement, as well; they work together, share ideas and build on each other's enthusiasm. Some find that their whole social life revolves around others who are equally committed to social service. A director of a nonprofit organization explained, "Thanks to this work I have come to know thousands of people, and I have numerous friends. It turns out that there is a large number of these kinds of people, who think in a similar manner." Thus, participants express a range of motivations for participating in funding initiatives, not necessarily the self-interest presumed to be the dominant characteristic of individuals in neoliberal ideology. Still, they view EU subsidies instrumentally, as the avenue through which greater opportunities will come to the region. Participants feel a sense of social mission about what they do, and some also fuse that with an entrepreneurial sense and a willingness to seek new ways of enhancing the quality of life in Bieszczady.

Participants must master new ways of being in order to conform to EU standards and engage successfully with EU structural funds. Specifically, they have to demonstrate accountability (see Dunn 2004), resilience and planning. Participants shared with me the difficulties they had filling out the extensive and exacting applications, having their projects accepted and executing projects according to plan. Most have spent day and night, sometimes for weeks, to make sure their applications conform to very specific guidelines. They have learned that any error can be grounds for disqualification, regardless of how worthwhile the project may be. An assistant at a nonprofit organization explained: "Opportunities for applying for funds undoubtedly exist, but they often remain theoretical because of the challenge of completing the proposal. An idea alone is not enough; you can have an excellent idea, but if there is one formal error [in the proposal], the whole project is rejected. And there is no opportunity to correct it. There are very strict rules." Some participants had proposals rejected because there was a mathematical error in a budget, or the significance of the project was explained in too technical a manner.

Others described how every detail of the project must be sketched out in advance. For example, the proposal for an after-school program had to include the names of all students who would participate, a weekly calendar of lessons and events, the credentials of all those who would provide instruction, and a detailed budget for all activities, supplies and instructors. It also required letters of support from affiliated agencies and local government officials. Finally, it had to outline a plan for documenting activities and evaluating outcomes. The teachers coordinating the program stressed that projects must be realized exactly as outlined in the proposal. They had to account for every expense over ten zloty (about three dollars), and they were expected to spend exactly what they had outlined on their original budget; it was even viewed negatively to spend less. In addition, grantees had to be prepared for surprise inspections from program representatives. Local government officials explained that proposals for infrastructural improvements are subject to similarly rigid standards; prior to sending their applications, they must obtain signed budgets from subcontractors, and once funded, the project must proceed exactly as proposed. One district had to decline a grant because, by the time their proposal was approved, the subcontractor's budget estimates had expired. They were not allowed to proceed on the basis of the expired estimates, nor were they allowed to obtain new ones.

Program standards call for "ways of doing" (see de Certeau 1984) that stand in stark contrast to tactics deployed under state socialism and during the uncertain 1990s, when there were often no clear pathways to opportunities. Whereas in the past, Poles (and others within the socialist and postsocialist world) would make do with whatever resources they could obtain via social networks, informal exchange and chance encounters (Galbraith 2003a; Ledeneva 1998, 2006; Sampson 1985–86; Wedel 1986, 1992), EU funds require projects to systematically outline how they will address predetermined priorities and identify the steps they will take to achieve clearly defined goals. In other words, applicants are being socialized to abandon the black-box approach of "finagling" (*kombinowanie*) or "arranging" (*załatwianie się*), in which it is never spelled out exactly how one goes about accomplishing something (Galbraith 2003a; Wedel 1986, 1992). Instead, they are rewarded for being organized and precise in ways akin to the orderliness (*porządek*) Poles have in the past associated with Germany (Galbraith 2004). Europe is being remade in the image of certain key member states, which is not necessarily compatible with historic styles of other member states.

Participants respond to this different approach in a variety of ways. Some find clear standards a big relief because, by spelling out concrete steps to their goals, they make possible the kind of future orientation I discussed in Chapter 3. Despite the burden of the exacting application process and oversight of funded projects, they like it because it guards against what one called "a national tendency to see what we can get away with." Others resort to finagling in spite of the clear procedures dictated by EU standards. For example, one mayor explained:

> We know how everything works and who makes decisions, so it's easier for us to reach those people and persuade them. Our ad hoc trip to Brussels

shows this. It was informal. You really shouldn't arrange things [*załatwić się*] this way. The [usual] procedure is like this: there's a beneficiary like us and there are progressive levels [an application must pass through]: the province administration, then the implementing power, then the Ministry of Economy, then the Committee for European Integration, and then finally the European Commission in Brussels. We have connections with people on all these levels, so they know how serious and responsible we are, and that if there are problems we can fix them.

Our trip to Brussels was crazy, it broke all the rules. Because our proposal went step by step through the levels and was accepted, until in the European Commission someone didn't understand the application and said no. We heard about it from an acquaintance before it was official. It worried us so much that we warned the ministry that we're going and they told us not to, that it's unconventional behavior. But we had acquaintances in important positions. We drove all night to talk to them, show them evidence, and we persuaded them. It worked out. After just an hour or two, we got back in our car and drove back. We had barely returned the next morning, took a shower and went to work, when a fax came that they accepted our arguments.

The mayor emphasized that the methods he used are contrary to everything that the EU seeks to promote – he relied on direct personal connections rather than leaving the decision to objective processes and a vertical chain of communication. But he also had full confidence in the merit of the proposal, and was convinced that their failure to get funding was due to a misunderstanding. In addition, he knew that he could build on his reputation as a good money manager with a proven record of success on other EU-funded projects. He used a sports metaphor to justify his actions: "As long as the referee hasn't blown the whistle that the game is over, you have to play."

Other participants consider the rigid standards controlling EU funds a mechanism of exclusion. One school teacher said that she does not like the application process because it shows no trust in grantees nor does it provide them with any flexibility in realizing their goals. She pointed out that it is impossible to anticipate every detail and every expense. The director of a nonprofit agency noted how different her experience was with an American philanthropic organization:

I remember when we filled out our first proposal for the American donor. A woman came from New York to help us. There was a one-page budget for a request for about a million and a half dollars. It outlined in a clear enough manner what those funds were to be used for over the next year or two, and what kinds of inspection there would be. Those EU [applications] are very complicated … I must admit that there are so many procedures that I don't understand very well … It's a massive bureaucratic machine.

For these participants, EU oversight crosses the line into gatekeeping and hinders their ability to provide the services their region clearly needs.

An unintended consequence of exacting standards is that they may actually reproduce the very inequalities that EU structural funds set out to erase because the most impoverished communities lack the economic capital, and often the human capital, to even apply for subsidies. Participants, including those who have written proposals that were funded, identified a number of economic and structural challenges. Although agencies offer training sessions about the programs they administer, prospective applicants find it difficult to attend. Participants said these sessions are invaluable for learning how to fill out applications properly and how to address program priorities convincingly. However, it can be hard to find the money for all this training. Even more problematic than the attendance fee, training is usually offered in other towns and cities, which adds additional travel expenses. Moreover, sessions that take place during the week require leave from regular employment obligations, while weekend sessions mean giving up one's own free time. A principal explained that his school lacks money for their heating and electric bills; they certainly cannot afford the cost of training, especially if it lasts for more than one day. Teachers have found that they usually must cover at least some expenses themselves.

Other economic considerations make participation in EU-funded programs even more prohibitive. In most cases, project expenses must be paid for upfront, before the granting agency will provide refunds. Communities or organizations without ready sources of revenue can try to get a loan to cover those costs in the interim, but they generally only qualify for loans with high interest rates. An even greater financial challenge for many local applicants is acquiring the matching funds most programs require. The director of one NGO explained that because they lack an endowment of their own, they usually partner with local government agencies, but then government officials expect to have control over the project. Another participant said, "You have to have money to get money" – only applicants with the means to cover the matching funds are eligible for subsidies. He has been able to seek subsidies that required local matches as high as fifty per cent only because his district has its own resources from a hydroelectric plant and tourism. As competition for grant money has increased, he has sometimes preferred to submit to an agency with a higher match requirement because fewer districts apply, thus improving his chances.

The director of an NGO says that even a ten per cent match would be unattainable for farming villages and small local organizations.

Her foundation has instead offered small grants for such groups. She explained: "They know how to manage grants like we could give them, for up to $5,000. When grants went up to $15,000 or $20,000 [they said], 'Oh no, we prefer those smaller ones.' More was not necessary for them because they mobilized local volunteers, and just needed that boost for materials, to print something or to buy equipment. So it wouldn't have to come from their own pockets – which are, after all, empty."

EU integration has made it more difficult for this NGO to offer funding to their prior constituents. Specifically, the American foundation that was the organization's main supporter decided to phase out its backing, assuming that the EU would take care of the regional development needs of new member states. "We felt the expansion of the EU like a stick with two ends," the director explained. "It hit us pretty hard. Despite that, the foundation supported the expansion of the EU and promoted European values and European law." Nevertheless, because it was unlikely a new benefactor would be found to provide large blocks of money, the director started planning new kinds of projects that were compatible with the funding opportunities offered by the EU, such as a trade show featuring regional products, services and culture. While this remains true to the organization's mission of promoting the interests of the Carpathian Euroregion,[16] it provides less direct aid to the most vulnerable local communities.

To summarize, these examples show how EU funding opportunities socialize citizens to display initiative, flexibility and organization, all commonly associated with capitalism, while also encouraging social values such as multiculturalism and regionalism. The results can be seen throughout the Bieszczady region, in the form of agricultural, infrastructural and cultural revitalization projects. However, an unintended consequence has been to widen the gap between two categories of persons – the winners and losers in the transition from state socialism to European integration. Structural factors, including geographic location, profession and education, make it much more difficult for some to learn about funding opportunities, to find community partners, to obtain matching funds, and to meet the exacting standards of the application process and accounting requirements for projects. Furthermore, the failure to adopt the characteristics of personhood required by funding agencies effectively excludes many of the most impoverished from ever even trying.

Transnational Regional Community

Although "transnational regional community" sounds like an oxymoron, it is an apt description of the Bieszczady region for a number of reasons.

As Giddens (1991) has noted, reflexivity engendered by comparisons with an ever-expanding range of different groups often leads to the elaboration of the local. For residents of Bieszczady, membership in the transnational institution of the EU provides a context in which regional identities become more salient. Primarily, the EU becomes a basis for comparison – people strengthen their sense of who they are via contrasts with outside groups with whom they have more extensive contact. Further, within this international context, they find more reason to define themselves to outsiders; seeking to make their region appealing to tourists and investors, they search for what makes it distinctive. EU values of multiculturalism and diversity encourage residents to celebrate the cultural and historical roots of Bieszczady that lead not to the core of Polish society so much as to connections that extend beyond the political borders of the country. Cultural projects emphasize autochthonous groups who historically populated mountain villages in Poland, Ukraine and Slovakia.[17] Environmental projects focus on the ecosystem of the Carpathian Euroregion that includes these villages, as well as parts of Hungary and Romania. Yet another way in which regional communities extend beyond this particular locale is via memories of lost homelands, left behind when nation-states sought to engineer ethnic homogeneity during and after World War II.

The social actors interviewed for this study have been instrumental in shaping and disseminating information about Bieszczady's past and helping to preserve the distinctive character of its towns and villages against the backdrop of membership in the EU and increased tourism. The transnational context has served to strengthen regional ties, and international funding for cross-border projects has contributed to this process.[18] At the same time, most participants are positively oriented toward the EU. This is not simply a result of increased experience with EU institutions contributing to stronger identification with the EU, as Herrmann and Brewer (2004) suggest (see also Wodak 2004). I found that some of the individuals in the Bieszczady region who have the most contact with EU institutions remain Euroskeptics. Indeed, participants' affective bond with the EU is weak. They said EU membership has not really affected their lives. Participants' encounters with the EU bureaucracy have forced them to think and act in unfamiliar ways. Even when they see the benefits of this, it still demarcates for them the differences between the way they are used to getting things done locally, and the way in which the EU works.

In sum, the experiences of social entrepreneurs, public servants and volunteers help reveal the impact of EU membership on local identities in the Bieszczady region. By seeking EU funds and realizing regional development projects, these social actors become socialized by new standards that help to shape the relationship between locality and wider levels of affiliation.

They learn new ways of dealing with institutions that place a strong premium on organization, planning, accuracy and accountability. A common self-characterization among Poles is "Polak potrafi" (A Pole can do it). In the past, this referred to the ingenuity and resourcefulness that allowed Poles to get things done and make do when resources were in short supply and clear pathways to goals were seldom visible. These same personal traits continue to be useful for obtaining funds via EU-sponsored programs that clearly define institutional pathways to opportunities.

Halina: Organic Farmer

Halina lives with her husband and three children in a village deep in the mountains. They make a living as dairy farmers. They used to have a more diversified operation, but EU regulations prohibit contact between different kinds of livestock, and the required structural changes are too costly for a small farm such as theirs. I had not seen Halina since she was in high school, but I knew from her former classmates that she had moved to her husband's village. Without an address, I drove there one day and stopped at the village store to inquire about her, but before I got to the door, Halina drove up to pick up a few items. I recognized her right away – the same curly dark hair, sparkling eyes and easy smile. She told her story as follows:

> After I finished high school it was hard to find work here, so I traveled abroad a little to Germany. I worked in agriculture, harvesting lettuce, cucumbers, that kind of thing. I would go for two months a year and then return home. I did that until I got married and we began to work on the farm. And then, once we had children, there was no way we could go anywhere.
>
> This is a family farm. We live with my husband's parents. My parents have a farm also, and we work there, too. Mostly we grow hay for the animals there. It's not far from here and we have fields in both places. We have milk cows; we keep the milk in a cooler here until transporting it ourselves to a collection point. And then they take it to the milk processor.
>
> Everything is organic. We don't use any artificial fertilizers, first because they're expensive, and second because we're in these agricultural-environmental programs through the restructuring agency [ARiMR], and they have various requirements. To get money, you have to do everything organically. These are EU programs, managed by our own agencies, of course. It's not bad to get some money, you know? Because of course Poland, like all countries, must pay into the EU. Then, later the EU decides if it's for farmers or for various other things. If we had a normal, set price for milk, we wouldn't need those subsides, you know? They give us money, but the price of milk, of everything, stays very low.

My husband's father is already an old man; he doesn't really help much anymore. Mostly we do it ourselves. It's hard, and we can't even hire someone to help, because no one wants to work, or they've gone abroad. It keeps getting harder. It's hard with small children, too, because you always have to look out, with all the different equipment. There's no one to take care of the children; when they're on vacation you have to watch them.

My son goes to primary school. Also, for a year now we've had a preschool funded by the EU, and the girls go there until noon. It's through a program designed for villages, and eight children attend. It gives me a little time to get things done; after noon I have to somehow manage. I have to work and take care of them, you know? The preschool is only funded for a year, but maybe we can find another program to keep it going as long as possible. The children really love going because there is always something to play with there – toys, games; they sing, dance and have contact with other children. It's really great.

Are things getting better or worse? I think it depends where you work, who you are. For some it's better, and for others it's difficult; you know what kind of wages you get in some jobs, like sales clerk. Here in this region, pay is very low; but elsewhere there are people who live well, you know? If they have their own company, or they are involved in the market. But overall, there's nothing to complain about. It's better than communism, definitely. Because everything is, relatively speaking, available. Back then, there were no building materials. Now, the problem is money. Back then, there was money but nothing to buy. Now, people can travel, and build new homes. The standard of living is going up. Generally, there is freedom, not like it used to be. Back then, you had a job in some factory or state farm, and you didn't put much into it. Now there's no alternative; almost everything is private and you have to do your work.

I think things have improved for me. I can't say there have been big improvements, and there are so many expenses. We still have to finish our home and improve our barn. It would be good if we could live normally. Right now everything is under renovation, so it's a little hard for us. To meet new requirements we have to adapt the barn and the place where we collect and store the milk. The cows' stalls need to be redone so they are a specific size; the livestock have to have water at all times; the water has to be tested yearly. Where the milk is collected, there needs to be a system for washing the walls so everything will be perfectly clean. Those kinds of things. It's very expensive. And of course they come and inspect everything, and they don't tell you when they're coming.

There are subsidies you can try for that return 50 per cent of the cost of improvements, but they require so much – a lot of arranging, a lot of bureaucracy, a lot of walking from place to place, and quite frankly, the people who apply complain horribly about all the effort. I don't know if the people who work at those agencies create problems, but it's very difficult. Some farmers get refunds, but at the cost of their nerves. Also, it's a gamble; you can apply but they won't necessarily choose you. We're also trying. We got a loan and we're doing it on our own.

It's a lot of work for the two of us, here on the farm. But there are no options for going somewhere else to work. You know what this area is like. We have no workplaces, just some stores, some agritourism, hotels and that's it. It's hard to find work, and that's why people leave here.

We voted for EU integration because we looked at how things are in other Western countries, and we thought they live well. We thought our conditions might improve. It can't get any worse so it would definitely get better. And I think it has, in general.

I'll tell you one more thing: the EU has certain requirements they enforce, and our various governing institutions don't do it their own way, but rather have to accommodate those specific requirements, and that's good.

I think generally young people think there will be benefits. I think the EU will benefit, too, you know? Because Poland is still the kind of country where companies can come in, buy land, buy our companies and profit. Clearly Poland is a poorer country than, for example, Germany or France.

Although she lives in what could be called the eastern periphery of the EU, Halina has a multilayered knowledge of the EU, shaped by her own experiences. She witnessed German prosperity while working there seasonally, she has seen tourist hotels and workplaces built by foreign investors and subsidized by EU structural funds, and she has benefited from farm subsidies and a rural childcare program. She has also watched many of her friends and neighbors emigrate to jobs in other countries, and observed the houses some of them have built with the money they earned. Although she fits in some ways the stereotype of the social groups most negatively affected by market liberalization (she is a rural farmer with a secondary technical education), Halina supports EU integration and associates Poland's membership with greater promise for the future. When I visited her in 2011, I was once again struck by the whole family's cheerful orientation toward life. They barely make ends meet, but they are slowly renovating their house and barn. The new expansive kitchen has large windows, an electric range and an American-style island. In the new living room next to it, the furniture sits on the bare concrete subfloor. Halina's husband said that they are one of ten remaining farms in the village, but they have so far managed to adapt to the new regulations and the new markets within the EU.

Chapter 8

CONCLUSION:
COMING OF AGE IN EUROPE

As I was preparing for my sabbatical in 2005 after not visiting Poland for five years, I had a dream, a nightmare really, that I landed in Krakow only to find that Poland was no longer any different from the US. There were the same stores, the same advertisements and the same day-to-day preoccupations. The dream left me with an uneasy feeling until my actual arrival; I was quickly reassured by the checkerboard fields visible from the air, the drive into the city on narrow country roads and the visitors who came to see me as soon as they knew I had returned. What makes a place distinctive can be hard to identify, and even harder to put into words. Nevertheless, that specialness of place, particularly in a city like Krakow and a region like the Bieszczady Mountains, is undeniable; it is perceived through the senses, producing an aesthetic response. Every time I return to Poland, I see more of the trappings of modern development – shopping malls, big-box stores, traffic jams, suburban neighborhoods, Ikea renovations, iPads – but they exist in juxtaposition to places and people also shaped by Poland's particular historical trajectory. In other words, it is hard to talk about Europeanization (or Americanization, or globalization) without also taking note of the disjunctures and differences specific to Poland, and the powerful force of Polish culture and history. Throughout this book, I have shared a coming-of-age story that is situated within a particular time and place. I have traced two trajectories of change over a 20-year period – across the life course of participants from youth to adulthood, and in Poland from the fall of state socialism through EU integration. Ongoing contact with Poland reassures me that artifacts of place are resilient, and economic development and global integration need not destroy cultural distinctiveness.

The point of person-centered research is to listen to a diversity of voices, situated in the particular details of individual lives, and trace the constellations of debate about key cultural phenomena that emerge in participants' self-reflections. Participants are creative agents, reacting to top-down discourse and practices and making their own choices, either self-consciously or via their actions. In this book, I have focused on the psychological dimensions of identity, and have tried to explain what being and becoming European means for participants as they have grown up in a country undergoing democratization, market liberalization and supranational integration. I have considered the cognitive and emotional connections participants express toward categories of people and places, and the qualities of their loyalties to local, national and European scales, in order to better understand processes of European integration in a postcommunist context. These interfaces also provide insight into broader processes of globalization, interactions between local and global scales, and assumptions, needs, motivations and interests of ordinary people grasping for the opportunities promised by global capitalism (but which are not always within reach).

Life stories also reveal how certain collective narratives linger due to their ability to evoke emotions and social memories. These narratives remain a baseline from which individuals formulate opinions, even among those who reject their narrative arcs. I am reminded of the insights Roy D'Andrade derived from neuropsychological studies of the brain. Considering that "abstract cognitive systems" – highly conceptual processes of thought and reason – are the hardest to achieve and maintain, it is not surprising that more evocative, emotional, "fast" processing tends to condition responses to social phenomena, and takes over in traumatic situations (as occurred, for example, in initial responses to the fatal plane crash of President Kaczyński). I have shown that participants share common dilemmas, but not necessarily the same views on issues. I have distilled some common patterns: the shift in temporality toward a future orientation despite the continued visceral power of mythological narratives of the past; the tendency to view Europe as a wider scale of nested identities but to prioritize local and national allegiances; the sense that being European is fundamental to being Polish but that becoming European has been accelerated by EU membership; the hope that social advancement will be facilitated by opportunities for mobility and subsidies within the EU but concern about continued marginalization within those movements of people and capital. Person-centered ethnography is a valuable tool for interrogating the legitimacy the EU has gained via its promise of a better future within global capitalism. It also reveals the conditional nature of support, especially in relation to the ontological uncertainty many feel due to the privatization of risk and deepening economic inequality in some sectors.

A concept that has proven useful for describing geopolitical scales of identity and their relation to each other is that of nested identities. The Poles with whom I spoke said that attachment to region, nation and Europe are not in conflict, nor do they replace each other. This does not mean, however, that the various scales are considered equivalent. Most participants ascribe their strongest loyalty and attachment to the more immediate smaller scale, and loyalties weaken progressively at wider levels. As they describe it, local identity emerges out of the fact of having been born in a place (or of having chosen to live there), being familiar with and feeling at home, and being imbedded in a network of family and friends. Most participants from Bieszczady profess a stronger sense of attachment to region than to either nation or Europe. This is not simply a product of limited exposure to wider scales. Most have spent time working abroad or studying in a city outside the region, but have made the choice to return; others have settled elsewhere but still hold their native place close. The ease of travel and communication in the EU makes it easy to maintain intimate ties with people at home via regular communication and visits. Most Krakow residents express fondness for their city, but they tend to prioritize national loyalties. I have suggested this is because the history and culture of Krakow are so tightly intertwined with that of the nation.

The imagined community of the nation can harness the more situated emotional power emerging from intimate links to place and people, but it also tends to have an ideological component – specifically a connection to national mythology. Participants express competing sentiments toward the nation: pride on the one hand, and highly critical emotions on the other. Pride tends to be a quick, unreflexive response, taken as a matter of course and linked to past acts of heroism celebrated in the national mythology. Criticisms are equally scripted, though they tend to emerge from counterdiscourses attributing historic defeats to weaknesses of character such as drunkenness and political corruption. Life stories also reveal the way self-identity emerges from engagement with various temporal and spatial scales; by positioning themselves in time and space, participants reinscribe, revise and reinvent local heritage, national mythology and European identity.

I have also noted that in recent years Poles seem more willing to describe themselves as "happy," and they seem as surprised as anyone about this. The grayness and gloom long associated with Polishness has lifted, at least for a significant proportion of the nation, signaling a profound shift in collective dispositions and posing a challenge to fundamental elements of national mythology. It also reflects the relative success Poles have had materially and symbolically, both as individuals and as a nation, since rejecting state socialism and moving toward EU integration. However, "relative" is the operative term because what is at issue is not an absolute level of affluence and influence, but the degree of advancement compared to other countries on both sides of the East–West divide. Overwhelmingly, participants communicated the sense of possibility as EU citizens; their happiness seems to be linked to the hope that the future will be better than the past and that Poland is on the path to becoming more prominent in an imagined global hierarchy of nations. Of course, this growing optimism is not shared by everyone; whole segments of society feel increasingly disenfranchised, as reflected in the vocal and aggressive populism of some supporters of traditional national and religious values (Buzalka 2008; Kalb 2009).

There has also been a transformation of European identity in recent years. I have explored ways in which "Europe" has been gaining entitativity, to the extent that participants are increasingly likely to see it as something real in their lives. Still, it is envisioned as a fuzzy entity at best, with shifting boundaries and contents. Although there is some evidence of "in-group projection," in that some attribute Europe with qualities associated with the Polish nation, there is also an opposing trend toward "self-peripheralizing consciousness" wherein characteristics of outside groups are deemed more worthy than traits associated with Polishness.[1] In-group projection most often takes the form of claims that Poland can act as the moral compass for Europe, as for instance when some Poles argued for the inclusion of references to Christianity and Christian values in EU policy. These views have clear kinship with the Polish national mythology, and notions of Poland as the "Christ of Nations," bringing salvation to Europe. Self-peripheralization tends to be expressed via negative characterizations of Poles relative to other nationalities, as for instance when participants criticized their nation as lazy, corrupt, disorganized or intolerant, in contrast to hardworking, honest, orderly, tolerant Western Europeans.[2]

Nevertheless, the imagined "West" has lost some of its appeal as it competes with direct knowledge of life beyond Polish borders. Sometimes, this leads to renewed appreciation of everyday, familiar Polish practices. An example of this is the short-lived romance with American fast food, especially in Krakow. In the early 1990s, as milk bars (state-subsidized cafeterias that specialize in inexpensive traditional Polish fare) were closing, snack bars offering *hambergery* (the English word "hamburger" with the Polish plural ending added) were opening. By the late 1990s, however, new snack bars were featuring classic dishes such as *pierogi*, *gołąbki* and *barszcz*. With the restaurant Chłopskie Jadło (Peasant Food) leading the way, the market for more upscale eateries serving traditional fare has also blossomed. Though driven by consumer tastes, preservation of traditional cuisine has also had institutional support, as for example when McDonald's was prohibited from opening a branch on the central market square. When one eventually did open several blocks away, it had to conform to the historic architectural style of the Old City. McDonald's is very popular in Krakow, especially among youths and foreign visitors, but it has not replaced locales offering Polish food.

Even though European identity is not embraced in the same way as national or local identity, participants nevertheless tend to have positive associations with the idea of Europe. Europe is seen as closer to the center of an imagined hierarchy of nations, and as such, greater connection to Europe (via the EU) tends to be viewed as social advancement. The EU gains legitimacy as an instrument for obtaining a higher position within the global imaginary, both symbolically and materially. As some explained, Poland has just joined, so not enough time has passed for membership to have a big impact. In addition, participants tend to view EU membership in terms of what it can provide the nation and the region. However, as long as benefits are delivered, it is likely that positive perceptions will remain, and even grow. It is not clear that they will lead to the kinds of strong emotional bonds expressed toward locality and nation.

I further suggest that feelings of affiliation to Europe are for many an outgrowth of loyalty to nation. This may be seen in participants' assertions that of course they are European because Poland has always been a part of Europe; being European is in this way legitimated as a characteristic of being Polish. Correspondingly, being attached to their nation automatically means they feel some level of attachment to Europe, the broader geographic category in which their nation is located. This has implications for the shape the EU is likely to take in the future; there seems to be little popular support in Poland for a federalist system that replaces the national scale. However, support for the EU seems to be strengthened as long as it serves national political and economic interests. While the idea of Europe has primarily positive associations for participants, the long-term legitimacy of the EU seems dependent on the degree to which "Europe" and European integration can be wielded as an instrument of social advancement for Poles.

Another question I have tried to answer is why Poles have aspired to become members of the EU, whereas they fought to be freed of control by the Soviet Union. Structurally, both the EU and the Soviet Bloc required the resignation of some degree of national sovereignty to supranational levels of political economic organization. Judging from participants' comments, the simplest explanation is that membership in the EU is more likely to be viewed as chosen, while Soviet control tended to be regarded as imposed. Of course, some feel Poland was compelled by larger geopolitical circumstances to join the EU or risk being left behind, or worse still be vulnerable to attack from more powerful neighbors. But, crucially, EU membership is not seen as a product of strong-arm coercion; instead, accepting the invitation to join seemed to promise more benefits than losses. Furthermore, EU discourses of democracy, national autonomy, tolerance and human rights resonate better with the values Poles tend to ascribe to their nation than do state-socialist values of secularism and international collectivism. Even though participants sometimes point out discomfiting parallels between the European Union and the Soviet Union, European integration has legitimacy for the most part, while Soviet influence was at best tolerated.

The EU is sometimes accused of forcing rigid vertical lines of communication and control (common criticisms of Soviet-authorized state socialism) but this top-down structure is accepted because it has delivered on its promises (at least for now). By providing clear pathways to economic and social opportunities, and tools for adjusting to the privatization of risk, European integration has contributed to Poles' sense of security and stability. Participants are better able to project themselves into the future thanks to structures and policies that support four practices: pursuing higher education, obtaining mortgages, having children and planning for retirement. Additionally, opportunities for mobility and EU subsidies offer options outside and within Poland's borders. Some participants even express relief that a competent external structure keeps incompetent and corrupt Polish politicians in check. It is important to stress, however, that there has not been wholesale support for neoliberal reforms. Since the experiment in shock therapy in the early 1990s, there have been pendulum swings in political leadership between free market reformers and neosocialists, resulting in what some have called a "third way" between socialism and capitalism. Specifically, despite the rapid implementation of market liberalization, the privatization of state properties occurred at a more measured pace and more of a social safety net has been maintained. The nation-state stayed in control of the sequencing and pacing of reforms as Poland met the conditions for EU integration.

It is also worth emphasizing the distinction participants make between cultural and historic affiliation to "Europe" and the institutional authority of the "European Union." Despite the persistent distrust of state institutions in Poland, participants tend to express cautious support for the institutions of the EU. A number of my participants characterize the EU as impartial, less corrupt, more orderly and more competent than the Polish state, which is plagued by corruption and nepotism. Their words suggest that there is promise for the EU to gain legitimacy via the successful working of its institutions; as long as people feel their quality of life is improving, they have more opportunities, official structures run smoothly and Poland is treated as an equal partner, they are likely to extend their support to the EU. Simply put, this less emotional, more instrumental orientation toward the EU might actually provide a different avenue toward legitimacy than has functioned for regions and for nation-states. In 2005, participants often referred to the EU as "they" – the established member states; by 2011, they were more likely to consider Poland a full member, and to use the pronoun "we" in conversations about the EU. Through subsidies and direct investment, the EU came to be seen as more of a real entity in their lives, and one to which they belong.

Participants, most of whom were born between 1972 and 1976, belong to a bridge generation. They have childhood memories of state socialism, but they came of age during a period of fundamental institutional transformation and were young enough to adapt to the expectations placed on persons by global capitalism and European integration. This has positioned them well to feel a sense of forward momentum in their lives. However, life-story research also gives voice to a range of outlooks. I have described participants who break with typical generational patterns – who are skeptical about EU integration, who struggle to make ends meet, who see moral decay in processes of integration or who reject patriotism in favor of cosmopolitanism. Longitudinal person-centered research helps to make visible the range of commonalities and differences, and especially the constellations of debate, that constitute Polish culture.

The range of life stories and the balance of positions within constellations of debate would be different for those ten (or twenty) years older or younger. There would be different convergences between the personal life course and historical processes. For older generations, the process of market liberalization has generally been more challenging; it has been harder for many to learn new skills and adopt new ways of being that protect them from the privatization of risk. Younger generations have experienced a deeper break with the past, leading some to challenge traditional beliefs and practices, including church attendance, patriotism and heteronormativity, and leading others to embrace reactionary populism and religious orthodoxy. The net effect has been a fragmentation of Polish popular opinion and wider, sometimes contentious, constellations of debate. Participants noted that even their younger siblings grew up in a fundamentally different world than they did, with little knowledge of state socialism and no personal memory of material shortages or state oppression.

It is good to look back and take note of how much has changed in Poland, both socially and materially. For example, when I first moved to Lesko in 1992, few people initiated conversations with me, but I was watched everywhere I went. After all, I was the only American in town. Their eyes would follow me, but they would be just as likely to look away if I sought to engage with them directly. Going back today is a completely different experience. On the one hand, I can walk freely without drawing the attention of people who do not know me, and on the other I have acquaintances everywhere and we enjoy spending time together. In the early 1990s, few people had cars, which meant participants and I relied on slow, dirty buses to travel deeper into the mountains. Today, the same trips take one third to one quarter of the time by car. Whereas in the past visiting often required an overnight stay, now I can drop by for coffee. When I first went to Poland in 1986, I sent a telegram home from Krakow to let my parents know I had arrived safely. In the early 1990s, it was still necessary to order international phone calls

Figure 8.1. Lesko center, 1993. In the mid-1990s the bus stops were moved to a new station

Figure 8.2. Lesko center, 2011. New pavers and paint

and then wait until the operator established a connection. Phone numbers in Lesko were just four digits, and in nearby Ustrzyki Dolne they were only three digits; many mountain villages had no telephone service at all. Today, landline infrastructure has been bypassed by cellular service, and just about everyone has a cell phone.

The quality of social interactions has changed also. To summarize, in the past, everyone was busy (well, teenagers were not, though their parents definitely were) but they nevertheless made time for social interactions; I found that people were generally unsmiling and unwelcoming until I shifted from the category of "stranger" to that of "friend." Then, I became the recipient of *polska gościnność* (Polish hospitality); people opened their homes to me, sharing food, favors, conversation and very often laughter. Today, a different kind of busyness has taken over; gone are the days when someone was always home to greet a surprise visitor, and everyone would stop what they were doing to entertain them. It is now more common to call and make plans for a specific day and time. Agata, who lives on a farm and tries to maintain a more traditional outlook on hospitality, complained to me about this in 2005; she insisted visitors are always welcome and should just drop by.

2011 is a satisfying time to end this book because most participants were at a point in their lives when they had realized many of their aspirations and were confident about their prospects for the future. I would even venture to say most were happy. The country as a whole was prospering as well. Real estate values increased after EU accession but then stabilized. Mortgages became more readily available and interest rates declined, leading to a construction boom that has contributed to economic growth. Average salaries have increased by more than fifty per cent since 2004, and EU subsidies have contributed as much as one per cent to annual GDP growth. Of course, happy endings can be ephemeral; the Eurozone crisis has started to be felt in Poland and some participants have lost their jobs or left Poland to seek work abroad. For others, the prospect of returning to Poland is fading after many years of residence in another country.

Even though I have followed a group of people for twenty years, this book captures just a fragment of their lives, and their lives reveal a smaller fragment still of the changes Poland has undergone since 1989. Nevertheless, it tells a story about an extraordinary period – for participants as they have moved through the life course and for the country as it has restructured its political, economic and legal systems. As I have shown, forces and places associated with both EU integration and national and local identities have figured prominently in these dual trajectories.

Appendix

LIST OF PARTICIPANTS

Agata lives in Bieszczady with her parents, husband **Artur** and child. Taking advantage of new markets in the EU, she is a certified organic farmer and is building an inn for tourists.

Agnieszka balances employment as a librarian with motherhood and weekend classes to complete her university degree. She lives in Lesko with her husband and children.

Aneta has held a number of positions in the film and television industry. She has lived in her native Krakow, in Warsaw and in the US.

Ania is an artist who lives and works in her native Krakow. She has one child.

Artur is a native of Silesia who lives with his wife **Agata**'s family in Bieszczady.

Bartek is a teacher from Lesko who also loves hiking and works as a mountain tour guide. He and his wife have two children.

Basia was raised in Lesko, but moved to Warsaw after studying at one of the first private business schools in postcommunist Poland. She works for a multinational corporation, and loves to take business trips and vacations to other countries.

Beata left her native Bieszczady after high school to join her mother in the US. Eventually her husband **Janek** obtained a permanent visa and joined her. They have one child.

Bogdan is a Euroskeptic who works as a civil servant in a town near his native Bieszczady. He lives in an extended family household with his in-laws, wife and children.

Darek grew up in a tiny Bieszczady village but he and his wife live in a town where he works as a nurse. He also has a successful band that performs at folk festivals and weddings. Darek's sense of identity is profoundly shaped by the fact that his father is Ukrainian.

Dominik, a business owner, lives in Krakow with his wife **Ewelina** and their children.

Dorota lives in England with her husband and children. She worked in England during summers while attending university, but became a long-term resident after failing to find a job with a reasonable salary in her native Bieszczady.

Ewelina lives in her native Krakow with her husband and their children. She is a lawyer and her husband **Dominik** owns a private business. They attribute their financial success to their entrepreneurialism and work ethic, which have been rewarded in the neoliberal economy.

Grzesiek is a technical school graduate from Krakow with a computer repair shop. He loves to explore other countries and appreciates the greater ease of travel in recent years. He is married.

Halina lives with her children and her husband **Zygmunt** on his parents' farm in rural Bieszczady. They have managed the farm since his father retired, and they have made the necessary improvements to receive EU certification as organic producers.

Janek worked as a waiter in Bieszczady until he joined his wife **Beata** in the US. Because they have permanent residence, it is unlikely they will return to Poland except to visit family.

Joasia is a school librarian from a village in Bieszczady who has obtained EU funding for regional development and heritage projects at her school. She and her husband waited to have a child until he had returned from work abroad and they had mostly completed construction on their home.

Józef works at a regional government office in his native Bieszczady. He lives with his wife and children in a house he built near the homes of his brothers and parents.

Jurek is an architect from Krakow who specializes in designs inspired by traditional styles of the Górale (a subgroup from the Tatra Mountains). He lives with his wife and child.

Krzysiek is a Lesko native who supports himself with odd jobs and occasional trips abroad. He especially enjoyed managing a parking lot for a number of years.

Maciek is a nurse in Bieszczady. He lives with his aging parents in a village and travels on weekends to visit his wife and child in a nearby city.

Marcin has owned a series of small businesses in his native Bieszczady; he also performs most weekends with his band. He lived with his wife **Monika's** family until they could afford their own house. They have two children.

Marek is a computer programmer from Krakow who has lived in Prague since Poland and the Czech Republic entered the EU.

Marta left her village in Bieszczady right after high school and lived in Italy for many years until returning to Poland to have her children. She lives in a multigenerational household, and periodically returns to work abroad, leaving her children with her mother.

Marzena works for a bank in Warsaw. She and her husband moved to Warsaw for well-paying jobs in their professions, but she misses her native Krakow and visits her parents every other weekend. She has one child.

Michał has a law degree, but he manages real estate for large investors. He lives in his native Krakow.

Monika lives with her husband **Marcin** and their children in her native village in Bieszczady. She works at his various businesses.

Paulina went to Italy after technical school in search of work and adventure. She met and married an Italian man. She and her children try to visit family in Poland every other year.

Paweł is a sales manager and resident of Lesko. He is the divorced father of two children.

Piotr manages regional sales for an international company. He lives in Krakow with his partner and their two children.

Robert lives with his wife and children in Lesko. He works as a teacher during the school year, and earns money in Germany during the summer to build their house.

Stasiek had no trouble finding a job after studying computer science in Krakow. He lives in a city near his native Bieszczady with his wife and children. Now self-employed, he travels regularly to England for business.

Wala went to university in Krakow before returning to live in Lesko with her husband and children. She manages a store, which she took over when her mother retired.

Wiola lives in Bieszczady with her husband Tomek and their children. She is a civil servant at the local government offices not far from her home.

Wojtek grew up in a Bieszczady village, but he now lives in Krakow with his wife and children. He is a professor, and travels abroad occasionally for academic conferences or research.

Zbysiek returned to Lesko before finishing university. He runs his own computer-based business and spends as much time as he can outdoors exploring the Bieszczady Mountains.

Zosia lives in Bieszczady on the family farm with her extended family. Since her parents retired, she and her brother run the farm. Zosia has worked in retail in a town near her home, though she has also spent periods abroad, leaving her children in the care of her mother.

Zygmunt is a Bieszczady native who runs the family farm with his wife **Halina**. They have made improvements in conformity with EU regulations so they can qualify for EU farm subsidies and sell organic products to the European market.

NOTES

Chapter 1 Introduction: Being and Becoming European in Postcommunist Poland

1 Interviews were conducted in Polish. All translations are my own.

2 Following common practice in Poland, I use "postsocialist" and "postcommunist" interchangeably.

3 Other studies in this genre include *Coming of Age in New Jersey* (Moffatt 1989), *Coming of Age in Post-Soviet Russia* (Markowitz 2000) and even *Coming of Age in Second Life* (Boellstorff 2008).

4 This search was conducted in May 2012. Of the fifteen resources listed, only eight were research articles that engage with EU institutions, policies or identity. Also included were four book reviews, one film review, one grant proposal and one article that mentions the EU in its abstract, but actually focuses on broader global processes.

5 In Poland, a wide range of survey research is conducted by the Public Opinion Research Center (CBOS), Domoskop and the Central Statistical Office (GUS). The key source for statistical information about Europe as a whole is Eurostat; the chief researcher of public opinion for the European Commission is Eurobarometer.

6 Appadurai uses the term to describe the broader category of globalization.

7 See Friedman (2000) for an enthusiastic endorsement of this perspective. Borneman and Fowler (1997), Steger (2009) and Tsing (2000) all note the frequency with which this narrative is told.

8 Stiglitz defines globalization as "the closer integration of the countries and peoples of the world which has been brought about by the enormous reduction of costs of transportation and communication, and the breaking down of artificial barriers to the flows of goods, services, capital, knowledge, and (to a lesser degree) people across borders" (2002, 9). Why the flow of people is qualified as being "to a lesser degree" is ambiguous. He may have intended to emphasize that *artificial barriers* to the flow of people have been broken down to a lesser degree than barriers to other kinds of flows. This argument has been made in immigration studies, citing ongoing restrictions on labor markets that are inconsistent with neoliberal efforts to promote free trade and free markets. Nevertheless, the definition clearly singles out flows of people as a secondary aspect of globalization.

9 Gal and Irvine (1995) develop the idea of fractal distinctions with regard to linguistic and social dichotomies such as "public" and "private."

10 Let me review three other terms that mark key aspects of Anderson's definition. Besides being "imagined," nation is a particular kind of "community," based not on face-to-face relationships but nevertheless invoking the feelings of attachment that more intimate

relations do. We care about our nation much as we do about our religion or family; it becomes central to how we think of ourselves. This kind of attachment necessarily requires drawing lines between those who do and do not belong to the nation, making membership inherently "limited." And finally, nations differ from ethnic groups in that nations have the *expectation* of "sovereignty." Not all nations are represented by their own state, but they must want and expect to be politically autonomous.

11 The boundaries between disciplines can blur in studies of Europe, the EU and nationalism. Brubaker and his coauthors are sociologists, while Hobsbawm is a historian.

12 In his study of banal nationalism, Billig (a social psychologist) is even more dismissive. He calls the mind or bodies of individuals the "wrong place" to look for identity, arguing instead that attention be paid to "continual flagging" in the form of public symbols that are too familiar to individuals to register consciously (1995, 7–8).

13 He attributes this conceptualization to American social psychology, and in particular the work of Ralph Turner.

14 Linger (1994) makes a similar point about intersubjective communication; symbols function more like inkblots, he says, than like conduits of meaning. In other words, meanings do not get transferred whole from person to person but rather have to be interpreted by conscious individuals who sometimes rework the cultural material they receive.

15 D'Andrade (2008, 159) notes, "It is odd that as regular people social scientists are reasonably good at understanding the motivations of others, but as social scientists work so little with motivation." Keller (2007, 355) cites research in psychology that suggests the "capacity for mind reading" is a product of development, and the sense of "self" develops in tandem with the sense of "others." In other words, we learn to read our own mental states by the same processes we learn to read those of others. Keller also points out that the inability to do so is a characteristic of autism.

16 See Kahneman (2011) for an accessible account of fast and slow modes of thinking.

17 Most of these studies actually employ a combination of these approaches.

Chapter 2   "We Have Always Been in Europe": Deploying the Past to Shape the Present

1 In Polish secondary schools, students are assigned to tracks (*klasy*) with particular thematic profiles (*profily*); everyone in a track follows a set curriculum and takes the same classes together.

2 Ustrzyki Dolne is a neighboring town that competes with Lesko for the designation "Gateway to the Bieszczady Mountains." It has weaker historical ties to Poland, but twice the population of Lesko. By contrast, Lesko was the seat of the noble Kmity family, former residents of the town castle. Though Bartek's comments illustrate the way history was evoked to justify Lesko's bid for *powiat* status, these arguments ignore the fact that before World War II, the population of Lesko was divided among Jews, Poles and Rusyns (contemporary Ukrainians).

3 Towarzystwo Gimnastyczne "Sokół" was established in Lviv in 1866. Though its primary goal was to encourage physical fitness, it also defended the Polish nation's right for freedom during the Partitions of Poland, when the country was divided among the Russian, Austrian and Prussian Empires. The society continued to be active until

World War II. Sokół was not allowed to reorganize during state socialism, but was reactivated in 1989 (PTG "Sokół" 2012).

4 I base this historical overview on a number of sources, including Armour (2006), Davies (1984), Johnson (2002), Okey (1986) and Sanford (1999). See Galbraith (2011b) for a brief outline of Polish history, or Pogonowski (1988) for a historical atlas of Poland's shifting borders. I also draw from historical accounts told to me by participants, and by my mother who considers herself a Polish patriot even though she moved to the US in the 1940s.

5 Kościuszko fought in the American Revolution as well.

6 Wood does not dispute Krakow's significance as a historic and symbolic center, but rather shows convincingly how a different narrative, linked to the nineteenth-century growth of great cities, also dominated the political discourse and self-identity of Krakow residents. For example, a new emphasis on Krakow's development into a large metropolitan center is revealed in the inaugural speech of Mayor Juliusz Leo in 1904, who said, "The great past has passed, and the present is sad, but the future is ours if we work straightforwardly, sensibly, and enduringly for it" (Wood 2010, 109). These words would not have been out of place 100 years later as part of the discourse surrounding EU integration.

7 It is customary to refer to people in positions of authority by the titles "Pani" (Mrs/ Madam) or "Pan" (Mr/Sir).

8 Koczanowicz (2012) recounts the Smolensk disaster in similar terms, as a battle between political factions favoring tradition and those pushing modernization; his analysis even covers the same commemorations and public debates about who to blame for the disaster. His conclusion, however, is more pessimistic than mine; he emphasizes public disillusionment with the project of market liberalization and European integration, and the continued power of the national mythology to define popular opinion about contemporary events.

9 Wajda has long been associated with films promoting Polish national identity. *Man of Marble* (1977) and *Man of Iron* (1981) helped to document the disillusionment of workers with the socialist system, followed by the rise of the Solidarity trade union, through which workers sought to reform the system. His most recent film, *Walesa, Man of Hope* (2013), is a tribute to the Solidarity leader's accomplishments. Wajda has also directed film adaptations of nationalist literature such as Reymont's *The Promised Land* (1974) and Mickiewicz's *Pan Tadeusz* (1999), and films focused on other historically significant events such as *Kanał* (1954), which chronicles the Polish Home Army's escape via the sewers after their failed attempt to retake Warsaw from the Nazis in 1944.

10 In the actual elections in November, PO received 39 per cent of the vote while PiS received 30 per cent. These results suggest that PiS claimed a higher percentage of the votes of those who said they were undecided before the elections (Pankowski 2011).

11 I am reminded of religious retreats organized at schools by the Lesko clergy during the early 1990s. They culminated with a procession through town in which students, teachers and local leaders carried a large wooden cross while praying and singing religious songs. Years later, the crosses from several such processions still stand where they were erected at distinctive sites around town.

12 A recent survey shows that opinions of the way government handled the investigation into what happened at Smolensk continue to divide along party lines (Pankowski 2012). PiS supporters are the most critical, with 56 per cent reporting that "this government really failed to offer any possibility of a fair explanation of the tragedy," in contrast

to just 3 per cent of PO supporters who took such a position. Notably, this negative opinion of the government's handling of the investigation is held by 23 per cent of those surveyed. Also, over 60 per cent believe Russia has withheld information about the failures of the air traffic controllers and ground crew, and 25 per cent (including 60 per cent of PiS supporters) believe the accident was caused by an explosion.

Chapter 3   "Unbelievable! Poles Are Happy": Looking toward the Future

1 Quotes from 2011 are reconstructed from field notes; I did not record interviews that year.
2 I discuss the challenges of work–life balance and its influence on childbearing in Galbraith 2008.
3 A number of articles have explored how citizens in postcommunist countries characterized their lives as "not normal," and described a "normal life" in terms of ideal conditions such as economic security, material comfort, trustworthy politicians, mobility and a respected position among the world's countries (Fehérváry 2002; Galbraith 2003b; Greenberg 2011).
4 This may sound like a lot of money, but at the time, one dollar equaled about twelve thousand zloty. That means that unemployment compensation by this estimate equaled about sixty dollars. In 1995, the currency was revalued ten thousand to one; the new exchange rate was about two zloty to the dollar.
5 There were 112 institutions of higher education in 1990–91 and 456 in 2008–09 (European Commission 2010, 115).
6 This house actually has a fourth kitchen in the basement, which is used by Józef's parents to process farm produce. This is the oldest kitchen in the house, with a door leading directly out to the farmyard. It is not used for daily meals, but rather to process large batches of milk, sausages and the like.
7 Since 2011, Marcin has gotten out more on his bike. He regularly posts photos of his travels on Facebook.
8 See Stiglitz (2006) on the importance of sequencing and pacing of economic reforms in developing countries.

Chapter 4   "We're European because We're Polish": Local, National and European Identities

1 15 of the 23 I interviewed from Bieszczady said they prioritize their attachment to region over their attachment to the nation or to Europe. By contrast, 6 participants originally from Krakow prioritize their national attachment, while the other 3 claimed no priority.
2 Wala took over the business after her mother retired.
3 Now that her children are older, Marta has begun leaving them with relatives so she can work seasonally abroad again.
4 Two participants did not settle on a single answer. Zbysiek explained that depending on the situation he sometimes feels more Polish than European, and sometimes equally Polish and European. Answering this question was difficult for Darek because, he said, "My choice isn't here, is it? Because, even though I'm a Polish citizen, I have

a strong feeling for the place where my roots, my surname and my father are from. Essentially, I can say I have two nationalities." His complex Ukrainian-Polish history (discussed earlier in this chapter) makes it difficult for him to identify unambiguously as Polish.

Chapter 5   "EU Membership Gives Poland a Better Chance": Perspectives on European Integration

1 The European Economic Community (often just called the European Community) became the European Union after the Maastricht Treaty went into effect in 1993.
2 The Central and Eastern European countries slated for admission were Czech Republic, Estonia, Hungary, Latvia, Lithuania, Poland, Slovakia and Slovenia. Two other countries, Cyprus and Malta, were also set to be admitted at the same time.
3 We were speaking English when Aneta made these remarks.

Chapter 6   "Now We Can Travel without a Passport": Mobility in the European Union

1 The British Home Office is the government department that oversees immigration, as well as passports, drug policies, counterterrorism and the police.
2 In 2013, Dorota and her husband still lived in England together with their children, all of whom were born in England.
3 Bauman would not disagree with this. His intent is to outline a conceptual scheme, not identify categories that describe everyday experience. He notes that most social actors themselves have moments when they are unsure if they are tourists or vagabonds, and many fear that they could one day become vagabonds.
4 Nationals of any country that has fewer than ten thousand annual migrants to the US can apply for one of approximately fifty thousand green card visas made available by lottery each year. Because of the priority put on family reunification in US immigration policy, immediate relatives of citizens and legal permanent residents are also eligible for green cards.
5 For much of this period, as many as 70 per cent of applicants were denied US visas. By 2009, the visa refusal rate had decreased to 13.5 per cent (US Department of State 2014), but that was still too high for the visa requirement to be removed for Polish nationals. By contrast, in 2008 the visa requirement was dropped for citizens of most other new EU member states.
6 This ad can be viewed online: http://www.nytimes.com/2005/06/26/international/europe/26poland.html?pagewanted=all&_r=0 (accessed 18 March 2014).

Chapter 7   "This Region Is Our Priority": EU Subsidies and the Development of a Transnational Regional Community

1 "Gray" is usually associated with "ordinary." It also signals a lack of power to influence the public sphere. The state-socialist period is commonly characterized as gray – colorless, uninteresting and sad.

2 Started by Muhammad Yunis, the Grameen Bank offers microloans to rural poor Bangladeshis so they can begin small enterprises. This model has been adopted by aid agencies throughout the world.

3 Bornstein emphasizes the tireless commitment of social entrepreneurs who focus all their energy on realizing fundamental, sustainable solutions within communities.

4 The main targets for cohesion funds since 2007 are member states whose citizens earn less than ninety per cent of the EU average.

5 PHARE (Poland and Hungary Assistance for Reconstructing of their Economies, later known simply as Phare) first provided funds to Poland and Hungary in 1989 to help reform their economic systems, already with the idea of eventual EU integration; over the years, the program expanded to include other candidate countries in Central and Eastern Europe (Bokajło and Dziubka 2003, 211–14). SAPARD (Special Accession Program for Agriculture and Rural Development) operated in Poland from 1999 to 2006. Its goals were: to improve the competitiveness of Polish agriculture both nationally and internationally; to make sure that agriculture conformed to EU standards of hygiene and quality; and to promote development of infrastructure and nonagricultural economic resources in rural regions (Program SAPARD w Polsce; see also Bokajło and Dziubka 2003, 214–18). INTERREG is a Union-wide program that began in 1989 with the goal of encouraging cooperation across national and regional borders, both within the EU and between EU member and nonmember states. All of these programs advance broader EU goals to balance levels of economic development, which in turn is seen as an important component of "cohesion" within Europe.

6 See Pine (1995, 2007) on changes in Polish agricultural communities; studies of agricultural transformation after state socialism include Knudson (2012) on Lithuania, and Verdery (2003) on Romania.

7 Lamenting that things are *coraz gorzej* (worse and worse) was very common in the 1990s and remains a frequent communication genre among older generations. Few people in Zygmunt's generation still used the phrase in 2011. See Ries (1997, 83–125) for a fascinating discussion of laments in perestroika Russia.

8 ZPORR is a component of the European Regional Development Fund (ERDF).

9 A slideshow of ZPORR-funded projects in the Podkarpathian Voivodship can be found at: http://www.wrota.podkarpackie.pl/pl/zporr/s071113 (accessed 18 March 2014).

10 The EQUAL initiative, financed by the EU and EU member states during the 2000–2006 period, supported "innovative, transnational projects aimed at tackling discrimination and disadvantage in the labour market" (Welcome to Equal 2011).

11 This figure is based on the population of the following districts and communities: Powiat Bieszczadzki (22,262), Powiat Leski (26,643), Gmina Zagórz (12,658) and Gmina Komańcza (5,139), as reported by the Central Statistics Office (GUS 2006).

12 Ethnologists use the term *"Dolinianie"* to designate a prewar ethnic subgroup of valley-dwelling peasants who were more akin to ethnic Poles than to ethnic Ukrainians.

13 This seems to be changing, as revealed in national efforts like the new Museum of the History of Polish Jews in Warsaw, grassroots organizations dedicated to the preservation of Jewish heritage in Poland, and young citizens who feel an affinity to Jewish culture (see Lehrer 2013; Reszke 2013).

14 A description of the program can be found at http://www.ngo.pl/x/115742 (accessed 23 February 2014). With a budget of over forty-three million zloty, up to seventy-five thousand was given to about 480 schools.

15 Lampland (2009, 123) makes a similar point that Hungary employed scientific standards of work under state socialism to increase productivity, but by measuring and differentiating among "innate qualities and psychological states" of workers, standards also became the bases for justifying hierarchy and bolstering inequalities.

16 The Carpathian Euroregion, established in early 1993, was one of the first, and it encompasses the mountain range that spans Poland, Ukraine, Slovakia, Hungary and Romania. Euroregions are important conceptually because they challenge the hegemony of nation-state boundaries by grouping regions according to geographic criteria, thus contributing to the web that ties "Europe" together.

17 Falkowski and Pasznycki (1935) capture much of the history, customs and folklore of these groups in their ethnological study.

18 Chessa (2004) discusses similar processes along the German–Polish border.

Chapter 8   Conclusion: Coming of Age in Europe

1 See Mummendey and Waldzus (2004) on in-group projection, and Liechty (1995) on self-peripheralizing consciousness.

2 It is important to note that "European" is not always seen as a uniform category, and some nationalities were more strongly associated with the ideal European than were others.

REFERENCES

Adekoya, Remi. 2011. "Poland Is Still Coming to Terms with the Smolensk Air Disaster." *Guardian*. 2 August. Online: http://www.guardian.co.uk/commentisfree/2011/aug/02/poland-smolensk-air-disaster (accessed 8 August 2011).

Abélès, Marc. 2000. "Virtual Europe." In *An Anthropology of the European Union: Building, Imagining and Experiencing the New Europe*, edited by Irene Bellier and Thomas M. Wilson, 31–52. Oxford: Berg.

Anderson, Benedict. (1983) 1991. *Imagined Communities: Reflections on the Origin and Spread of Nationalism*. New York: Verso.

Anderson, Christopher J., and Karl C. Kaltenthaler. 1996. "The Dynamics of Public Opinion toward European Integration, 1973–93." *European Journal of International Relations* 2 (2): 175–99.

Anderson, James, Liam O'Dowd and Thomas M. Wilson, eds. 2003. *New Borders for a Changing Europe: Cross-Border Cooperation and Governance*. Portland: Frank Cass.

Antonsich, Marco. 2009. "National Identities in the Age of Globalism: The Case of Western Europe." *National Identities* 11 (3): 281–99.

Appadurai, Arjun. 2008. "Global Ethnoscapes: Notes and Queries for a Transnational Anthropology." In *The Anthropology of Globalization*, 2nd edition, edited by Jonathan Xavier Inda and Renato Rosaldo, 47–63. Malden, MA: Blackwell.

Armeanu, Oana I. 2010. "The Battle over Privileges and Pension Reform: Evidence from Legislative Roll Call Analysis in Poland." *Europe-Asia Studies* 62 (4): 571–95.

Armour, Ian D. 2006. *A History of Eastern Europe 1740–1918*. London: Hodder Arnold.

Asher, Andrew D. 2005. "A Paradise on the Oder? Ethnicity, Europeanization, and the EU Referendum in a Polish-German Border City." *City and Society* 17 (1): 127–52.

———. 2011. "A Divided City in a Common Market: EU Citizenship and Everyday Instrumentalities on the Polish-German Border." *Anthropological Journal of European Cultures* 20 (2): 43–67.

Bakhtin, Mikhail. 1981. *The Dialogic Imagination: Four Essays*. Austin: University of Texas Press.

Balcerowicz, Leszek. 1994. "Economic Transition in Central and Eastern Europe: Comparisons and Lessons." *Australian Economic Review* 27 (1): 47–59.

Barth, Fredrik. 1969. *Ethnic Groups and Boundaries: The Social Organization of Culture Difference*. Boston: Little, Brown.

Bauman, Zygmunt. 1998. *Globalization: The Human Condition*. New York: Columbia University Press.

BBC News. 2003. "Polish Press Basks in 'Yes' Vote." 9 June. Online: http://news.bbc.co.uk/go/pr/fr/-/2/hi/europe/2075100.stm (accessed 10 June 2003).

Beck, Ulrich. 1992. *Risk Society: Towards a New Modernity*. Translated by Mark Ritter. Thousand Oaks, CA: Sage.

Bellier, Irene. 2000. "The European Union, Identity Politics and the Logic of Interests' Representation." In *An Anthropology of the European Union: Building, Imagining and Experiencing the New Europe*, edited by Irene Bellier and Thomas M. Wilson, 53–73. Oxford: Berg.

Bellier, Irene, and Thomas M. Wilson, eds. 2000a. *An Anthropology of the European Union: Building, Imagining and Experiencing the New Europe*. Oxford: Berg.

_____. 2000b. "Building, Imagining and Experiencing Europe: Institutions and Identities in the European Union." In *An Anthropology of the European Union: Building, Imagining and Experiencing the New Europe*, edited by Irene Bellier and Thomas M. Wilson, 1–27. Oxford: Berg.

Berdahl, Daphne. 1999. *Where the World Ended: Re-unification and Identity in the German Borderland*. Berkeley: University of California Press.

Berend, Ivan T. 2009. *From the Soviet Bloc to the European Union: The Economic and Social Transformation of Central and Eastern Europe since 1973*. Cambridge: Cambridge University Press.

Biehl, Joao, Byron Good and Arthur Kleinman, eds. 2007. *Subjectivity: Ethnographic Investigations*. Berkeley: University of California Press.

Bijak, Jakub, and Isabela Koryś. 2009. "Poland." In *Statistics and Reality: Concepts and Measurements of Migration in Europe*, edited by Heinz Fassmann, Ursula Reeger and Wiebke Sievers, 195–215. Amsterdam: Amsterdam University Press.

Billig, Michael. 1995. *Banal Nationalism*. Thousand Oaks, CA: Sage.

Blazyca, George. 1999. "Polish Socioeconomic Development in the 1990s and Scenarios for EU Accession." *Europe-Asia Studies* 51 (5): 799–819.

Boellstorff, Tom. 2008. *Coming of Age in Second Life: An Anthropologist Explores the Virtually Human*. Princeton, NJ: Princeton University Press.

Bogucka, Teresa. 1993. "Okopani w Terazniejszości: Interview with Elżbieta Tarkowska." *Gazeta Wyborcza*, 4 April.

Bokajło, Wiesław and Kazimierz Dziubka, eds. 2003. *Unia Europejska: Leksykon Integracji*. Wrocław: Europa Wydawnictwo.

Borneman, John, and Nick Fowler. 1997. "Europeanization." *Annual Review of Anthropology* 26: 487–514.

Bornstein, David. 2004. *How to Change the World: Social Entrepreneurs and the Power of New Ideas*. Oxford: Oxford University Press.

Borovoy, Amy. 2005. *The Too-Good Wife: Alcohol, Dependency, and the Politics of Nurturance in Postwar Japan*. Berkeley: University of California Press.

Bourdieu, Pierre. 1977. *Outline of a Theory of Practice*. Cambridge: Cambridge University Press.

Brubaker, Rogers, Margit Feischmidt, Jon Fox and Liana Grancea. 2006. *Nationalist Politics and Everyday Ethnicity in a Transylvanian Town*. Princeton, NJ: Princeton University Press.

Bruter, Michael. 2005. *Citizens of Europe? The Emergence of a Mass European Identity*. New York: Palgrave Macmillan.

Bukowski, Jeanie, Simona Piattoni and Marc Smyri, eds. 2003. *Between Europeanization and Local Societies: The Space for Territorial Governance*. Lanham, MD: Rowman and Littlefield.

Buchowski, Michał. 2006. "The Specter of Orientalism in Europe: From Exotic Other to Stigmatized Brother." *Anthropological Quarterly* 79 (3): 463–82.

Buzalka, Juraj. 2007. *Nation and Religion: The Politics of Commemoration in South-East Poland*. Munster: Lit Verlag.

_____. 2008. "Europeanisation and Post-Peasant Populism in Eastern Europe." *Europe-Asia Studies* 60 (5): 757–71.

Cederman, Lars-Erik. 2001. "Nationalism and Bounded Integration: What It Would Take to Construct a European Demos." *European Journal of International Relations* 7 (2): 139–74.

Chessa, Cecilia. 2004. "State Subsidies, International Diffusion, and Transnational Civil Society: The Case of Frankfurt-Oder and Słubice." *East European Politics and Societies* 18 (1): 70–109.

Chlon-Dominczak, Agnieszka. 2009. "Retirement Behaviour in Poland and the Potential Impact of Pension System Changes." ENEPRI Research Report no. 61, January 2009. Online: http://www.ceps.eu/book/retirement-behaviour-poland-and-potential-impact-pension-system-changes (accessed 1 March 2012).

Cicero Consulting. 2012 "European Commission White Paper: An Agenda for Adequate, Safe and Sustainable Pensions." London/Washington: Cicero Financial Sector Communications. Online: http://www.cicero-group.com/wp-content/uploads/2012/02/Pensions-White-Paper-Special1.pdf (accessed 2 March 2012).

Citrin, Jack, and John Sides. 2004. "More than Nationals: How Identity Choice Matters in the New Europe." In *Transnational Identities: Becoming European in the EU*, edited by Richard K. Herrmann, Thomas Risse and Marilyn Brewer, 161–85. Lanham, MD: Rowman and Littlefield.

Cohen, Anthony P. 1994. *Self Consciousness: An Alternative Anthropology of Identity*. London: Routledge.

Cohen, Jeffrey H. 2004. *The Culture of Migration in Southern Mexico*. Austin: University of Texas Press.

Costano, Emanuele. 2004. European Identity: A Social-Psychological Perspective." In *Transnational Identities: Becoming European in the EU*, edited by Richard K. Herrmann, Thomas Risse and Marilyn Brewer, 40–58. Lanham, MD: Rowman and Littlefield.

Czarnocka, Ewa, Ewa Czechowicz, Wojciech Giermanowski and Jerzy Puchalski. 1992. "Bezrobocie Młodzieży." In *Raport o Młodzieży*, edited by Barbara Fatyga and Michał Szymańczak, 99–125. Warsaw: Interpress.

Dabrowski, Patrice M. 2004. *Commemorations and the Shaping of Modern Poland*. Bloomington: Indiana University Press.

D'Andrade, Roy. 2008. "General Theory." Unpublished manuscript, viewed 30 November 2008. Microsoft Word file.

Davies, Norman. 1984. *Heart of Europe: A Short History of Poland*. Oxford: Oxford University Press.

de Certeau, Michel. 1984. *The Practice of Everyday Life*. Translated by S. F. Rendall. Berkeley: University of California Press.

Demossier, Marion, ed. 2007. *The European Puzzle: The Political Structuring of Cultural Identities at a Time of Transition*. Oxford: Berghahn.

Desjarlais, Robert. 1997. *Shelter Blues: Sanity and Selfhood among the Homeless*. Philadelphia: University of Pennsylvania Press.

_____. 2003. *Sensory Biographies: Lives and Deaths among Nepal's Yolmo Buddhists*. Berkeley: University of California Press.

Drinkwater, Stephen, John Eade and Michael Garapich. 2009. "Poles Apart? EU Labor Enlargement and the Labor Market Outcomes of Immigrants in the UK." *International Migration* 47 (1): 161–90.

Dunn, Elizabeth. 2004. *Privatizing Poland: Baby Food, Big Business, and the Remaking of Labor*. Ithaca, NY: Cornell University Press.

_____. 2009. "Standards without Infrastructure." In *Standards and Their Stories: How Quantifying, Classifying, and Formalizing Practices Shape Everyday Life*, edited by Martha Lampland and Susan Leigh Star, 118–21. Ithaca, NY: Cornell University Press.

Eder, Klaus, and Bernhard Giesen, eds. 2001. *European Citizenship: National Legacies and Transnational Projects*. Oxford: Oxford University Press.

Eglitis, Daina S., and Laura Ardava. 2012. "The Politics of Memory: Remembering the Baltic Way 20 Years after 1989." *Europe-Asia Studies* 64 (6): 1033–59.

Elrick, Tim. 2008. "The Influence of Migration on Origin Communities: Insights from Polish Migration to the West." *Europe-Asia Studies* 60 (9): 1503–17.

Elrick, Tim, and Emilia Lewandowska. 2008. "Matching and Making Labor Demand and Supply: Agents in Polish Migrant Networks of Domestic Elderly Care in Germany and Italy." *Journal of Ethnic and Migration Studies* 34 (5): 717–34.

European Commission. 2010. *Organization of the Education System in Poland*. Warsaw: Eurydice.

_____. 2011. "Welcome to EQUAL." http://ec.europa.eu/employment_social/equal_consolidated/index.html (accessed 12 December 2012).

_____. 2012. "Interim Forecast." Report of the Directorate General for Economic and Financial Affairs, February. Online: http://ec.europa.eu/economy_finance/articles/eu_economic_situation/pdf/2012/2012-02-23-interim-forecast_en.pdf (accessed 4 March 2012).

Falkowski, Jan, and Bazyli Pasznycki. 1935. *Na Pograniczu Łemkowsko-Bojkowskim: Zarys Etnograficzny*. Lviv: Nakładem Towarzystwa Ludoznawczego.

Fastnacht, Adam. 1988. *Dzieje Leska do 1771 Roku*. Rzeszów: Krajowa Agencja Wydawnicza.

Fehérváry, Krisztina. 2002. "American Kitchens, Luxury Bathrooms, and the Search for a 'Normal' Life in Postsocialist Hungary." *Ethnos* 67 (3): 369–400.

Feldman, Gregory. 2005. "Culture, State, and Security in Europe: The Case of Citizenship and Integration Policy in Estonia." *American Ethnologist* 32 (4): 676–94.

Fihel, Agnieszka, and Paweł Kaczmarczyk. 2009. "Migration a Threat or a Choice? Recent Migration of Poles and Its Impact on the Polish Labor Market." In *Polish Migration to the UK in the "New" European Union: After 2004*, edited by Kathy Burrell, 23–48. Aldershot: Ashgate.

Fligstein, Neil. 2008. *Euroclash: The EU, European Identity, and the Future of Europe*. Oxford: Oxford University Press.

Follis, Karolina Szmagalska. 2008. "Repossession: Notes on Restoration and Redemption in Ukraine's Western Borderland." *Cultural Anthropology* 23 (2): 329–60.

Fox, Jon, and Cynthia Miller-Idriss. 2008. "Everyday Nationhood." *Ethnicities* 8 (4): 536–76.

Friedman, Thomas. 2000. *The Lexus and the Olive Tree*. New York: Anchor.

Gal, Susan, and Judith T. Irvine. 1995. "The Boundaries of Languages and Disciplines: How Ideologies Construct Difference." *Social Research* 62: 967–1001.

Galasińska, Aleksandra. 2009. "Small Stories Fight Back: Narratives of Polish Economic Migration on an Internet Forum." In *Discourse and Transformation in Central and Eastern Europe*, edited by Aleksandra Galasińska and Michał Krzyżanowski, 188–203. New York: Palgrave Macmillan.

_____. 2010. "Leavers and Stayers Discuss Returning Home: Internet Discourses on Migration in the Context of the Post-Communist Transformation." *Social Identities* 16 (3): 309–24.

Galasińska, Aleksandra, and Olga Kozłowska. 2009. "Discourses of a 'Normal Life' among Post-Accession Migrants from Poland to Britain." In *Polish Migration to the UK in the "New" European Union: After 2004*, edited by Kathy Burrell, 87–105. Aldershot: Ashgate.

Galbraith, Marysia H. 1997 "A Pole Can Die for the Fatherland but Can't Live for Her: Democratization and the Polish Heroic Ideal." *Anthropology of East Europe Review* 15 (2): 77–88.

———. 2000. "On the Road to Częstochowa: Rhetoric and Experience on a Polish Pilgrimage." *Anthropological Quarterly* 73 (2): 61–73.

———. 2003a. "Gifts and Favors: Social Networks and Reciprocal Exchange in Poland." *Ethnologia Europaea* 33 (1): 73–94.

———. 2003b. "'We Just Want to Live Normally': Intersecting Discourses of Public, Private, Poland, and the West." *Journal of the Society for the Anthropology of Europe* 3 (1): 2–13.

———. 2004. "Between East and West: Geographic Metaphors of Identity in Poland." *Ethos* 33 (1): 51–81.

———. 2008. "Choosing and Planning in a Climate of Insecurity: Balancing Professional Work and Family Life in Poland." *Journal of the Society for the Anthropology of Europe* 8 (2): 16–30.

———. 2011a. "'Poland Has Always Been in Europe': The EU as an Instrument for Personal and National Advancement." *Anthropological Journal of European Cultures* 20 (2): 21–42.

———. 2011b. "Poles." In *Ethnic Groups of Europe*, edited by Jeffrey Cole, 283–8. Santa Barbara, CA: ABC-CLIO Books.

Galbraith, Marysia, and Thomas M. Wilson. 2011. "Instrumental Europe: Practices of Daily Engagement with the European Union." *Anthropological Journal of European Cultures* 20 (2): 1–20.

Garapich, Michal P. 2008. "The Migration Industry and Civil Society: Polish Immigrants in the UK before and after EU Enlargement." *Journal of Ethnic and Migration Studies* 34 (5): 735–52.

Gazeta.pl. 2003. "Aleksander Kwaśniewski: Wracamy na Swoje Miejsce." 8 June. Online: http://wwwl.gazeta.pl/ue/1,42343,1520677.html (accessed 10 June 2003).

Geertz, Clifford. 1973. *The Interpretation of Cultures*. New York: Basic Books.

Gellner, Ernest. 1983. *Nations and Nationalism*. Ithaca, NY: Cornell University Press.

Giddens, Anthony. 1991. *Modernity and Self-Identity: Self and Society in the Late Modern Age*. Stanford: Stanford University Press.

Giesen, Bernhard, and Klaus Eder. 2001. "Introduction: European Citizenship: An Avenue for the Social Integration of Europe." In *European Citizenship between National Legacies and Postnational Projects*, edited by Klaus Eder and Bernhard Giesen, 1–13. Oxford: Oxford University Press.

Gille, Zsusza. 2010. "Is There a Global Postsocialist Condition?" *Global Society* 24 (1): 9–30.

Gliniecki, Judith. 2006. "Legal Eye: Women's Rights at Work." *Warsaw Business Journal*, 12 June. Online: http://www.wbj.pl/article-32513-legal-eye-womens-rights-at-work.html (accessed 23 June 2006).

Gomberg-Muñoz, Ruth. 2010. *Labor and Legality: An Ethnography of a Mexican Immigrant Network*. Oxford: Oxford University Press.

Gorton, Matthew, Carmen Hubbard and Lionel Hubbard. 2009. "The Folly of European Union Policy Transfer: Why the Common Agricultural Policy (CAP) Does Not Fit Central and Eastern Europe." *Regional Studies* 43 (10): 1305–17.

Greenberg, Jessica. 2011. "On the Road to Normal: Negotiating Agency and State Sovereignty in Postsocialist Serbia." *American Anthropologist* 113 (1): 88–100.

GUS (Główny Urząd Statystyczny). 2006. "Powierzchnia i Ludność w Przekroju Terytorialnym w. 2006 R." Online: http://www.stat.gov.pl/dane_spol-gosp/ludnosc/ powierz_teryt/2006/pow_lud_teryt_2006.pdf (accessed 10 February 2010).

_____. 2013. "Informacja o Rozmiarach i Kierunkach Emigracji z Polski w latach 2004–2012." Online: http://www.stat.gov.pl/cps/rde/xbcr/gus/L_Szacunek_emigracji_z_Polski_lata_2004-2012_XI_2012.pdf (accessed 18 October 2013).

Hadler, Markus, Kiyoteru Tsutsui and Lynn G. Chin. 2012. "Conflicting and Reinforcing Identities in Expanding Europe: Individual- and Country-Level Factors Shaping National and European Identities, 1995–2003." *Sociological Forum* 27 (2): 392–418.

Hallowell, A. Irving. 1955. *Culture and Experience*. Philadelphia: University of Pennsylvania Press.

Hann, Christopher. 1985. *A Village without Solidarity: Polish Peasants in Years of Crisis.* New Haven: Yale University Press.

_____.1998. "Postsocialist Nationalism: Rediscovering the Past in South East Poland." *Slavic Review* 57 (4): 840–63.

Hannerz, Ulf. 1996. *Transnational Connections: Culture, People, Places*. London: Routledge.

Hayden, Robert. 2007. "Moral Vision and Impaired Insight: The Imagining of Other Peoples' Communities in Bosnia." *Current Anthropology* 48 (1): 105–31.

Heinen, Jacqueline. 2002. "Ideology, Economics, and the Politics of Child Care in Poland before and after the Transition." In *Childcare Policy at the Crossroads: Gender and Welfare State Restructuring*, edited by Sonya Michel and Rianne Mahon, translated by Elizabeth Blount, 71–92. London: Routledge.

Heinen, Jacqueline, and Monika Wator. 2006. "Child Care in Poland before, during, and after the Transition: Still a Women's Business." *Social Politics: International Studies in Gender, State, and Society* 13 (2): 189–216.

Herb, Guntram H., and David H. Kaplan, eds. 1999. *Nested Identities: Nationalism, Territory, and Scale*. Lanham, MD: Rowman & Littlefield.

Herrmann, Richard K., and Marilyn Brewer. 2004. "Identities and Institutions: Becoming European in the EU." In *Transnational Identities: Becoming European in the EU*, edited by Richard K. Herrmann, Thomas Risse and Marilyn Brewer, 1–22. Lanham, MD: Rowman & Littlefield.

Herrmann, Richard K., Thomas Risse and Marilyn Brewer, eds. 2004. *Transnational Identities: Becoming European in the EU*. Lanham, MD: Rowman & Littlefield.

Hipsz, Natalia. 2011. "Siedem Lat Obecności Polski w Unii Europejskiej." Center for Public Opinion Research report. BS/52/2011.

PTG "Sokół." 2012. "Historia PTG 'Sokół.'" Online: http://www.sokol.pl/index.php?option=com_content&task=view&id=130&Itemid=152 (accessed 14 June 2012).

Hobsbawm, Eric J. 1990. *Nations and Nationalism since 1790: Programme, Myth, Reality.* Cambridge: Cambridge University Press.

Hobsbawm, Eric. (1983) 1992. "Introduction: Inventing Traditions." *The Invention of Tradition*, edited by Eric Hobsbawm and Terrence Ranger, 1–14. Cambridge: Cambridge University Press.

Hooghe, Liesbet, and Gary Marks. 2001. *Multi-Level Governance and European Integration*. Lanham, MD: Rowman & Littlefield.

_____. 2004. "Does Identity or Economic Rationality Drive Public Opinion on European Integration?" *Political Science and Politics* 37 (3): 415–20.

Horolets, Anna. 2006. *Obrazy Europy w Polskim Dykursie Publicznym*. Krakow: Universitas.

Iglicka, Krystyna. 2000. "Mechanisms of Migration from Poland before and during the Transformation Period." *Journal of Ethnic and Migration Studies* 20 (1): 61–73.

_____. 2001. *Poland's Post-War Dynamic of Migration*. Aldershot: Ashgate.

Ilieva, Polya. 2010. "Bulgaria at the Cross-Roads of Post-Socialism and EU Membership: Generational Dimensions to European Integration." *Journal of the Society for the Anthropology of Europe* 10 (2): 18–28.

Irwin-Zarecka, Iwona. 1994. *Frames of Remembrance: The Dynamics of Collective Memory.* London: Transaction.

Jasińska-Kania, Aleksandra, and Mirosława Marody. 2004. "European Integration and Polish National Identity." In *Poles among Europeans*, edited by Aleksandra Jasińska-Kania and Mirosława Marody, 229–37. Warsaw: Wydawnictwo Naukowe Scholar.

Johnson, Lonnie R. 2002. *Central Europe: Enemies, Neighbors, Friends.* Oxford: Oxford University Press.

Kahneman, Daniel. 2011. *Thinking, Fast and Slow.* New York: Farrar, Straus & Giroux.

Kalb, Don. 2009. "Conversations with a Polish Populist: Tracing Hidden Histories of Globalization, Class, and Dispossession in Postsocialism (and Beyond)." *American Ethnologist* 36 (2): 207–23.

Kaufman, Michael T. 1989. *Mad Dreams, Saving Graces: Poland; A Nation in Conspiracy.* New York: Random House.

Keller, Evelyn Fox. 2007. "Whole Bodies, Whole Persons? Cultural Studies, Psychoanalysis, Biology." In *Subjectivity: Ethnographic Investigations*, edited by Joao Biehl, Byron Good and Arthur Kleinman, 352–61. Berkeley: University of California Press.

Kideckel, David. A. 2008. *Getting by in Postsocialist Romania: Labor, the Body, and Working-Class Culture.* Bloomington: Indiana University Press.

Klumbyte, Neringa. 2010. "The Soviet Sausage Renaissance." *American Anthropologist* 112 (1): 22–37.

Knudsen, Ida Harboe. 2012. *New Lithuania in Old Hands: Effects and Outcomes of EUropeanization in Rural Lithuania.* London: Anthem Press.

Kockel, Ulrich. 2007. "Heritage vs. Tradition: Cultural Resources for a New Europe?" In *The European Puzzle: The Political Structuring of Cultural Identities at a Time of Transition*, edited by Marion Demossier, 85–101. Oxford: Berghahn.

Koczanowicz, Leszek. 2008. *Politics of Time: Dynamics of Identity in Post-Communist Poland.* Oxford: Berghahn.

———. 2012. "The Politics of Catastrophe: Poland's Presidential Crash and the Ideology of Post-Postcommunism." *East European Politics and Societies and Cultures* 26 (4): 811–28.

Kolarska-Bobińska, Lena. 2001. *Polacy wobec Wielkiej Zmiany: Integracja z Unią Europejską.* Warsaw: Institute of Public Affairs.

Kubik, Jan. 1994. *The Power of Symbols against the Symbols of Power.* University Park: Pennsylvania State Press.

Kublik, Agnieszka, and Piotr Pacewicz. 2003. "Niedziela Wygrała z Sobota." Gazeta.pl, 9 June. Online: http://www.gazeta.pl/ue/1,42343,1522688.html (accessed 11 June 2003).

Kutkowska, Barbara. 2003. "Wspólna Polityka Rolna Unii Europejskiej." In *Unia Europejska: Leksykon Integracji*, edited by Wiesław Bokajło and Kazimierz Dziubka, 518–21. Wrocław: Wydawnictwo Europa.

Lampland, Martha. 2009. "Classifying Laborers: Instinct, Property, and the Psychology of Productivity in Hungary (1920–1956)." In *Standards and Their Stories: How Quantifying, Classifying, and Formalizing Practices Shape Everyday Life*, edited by Martha Lampland and Susan Leigh Star, 123–42. Ithaca, NY: Cornell University Press.

Lampland, Martha, and Susan Leigh Star, eds. 2009. *Standards and Their Stories: How Quantifying, Classifying, and Formalizing Practices Shape Everyday Life.* Ithaca, NY: Cornell University Press.

Ledeneva, Alena V. 1998. *Russia's Economy of Favours:* Blat, *Networking, and Informal Exchange.* Cambridge: Cambridge University Press.

_____. 2006. *How Russia Really Works: The Informal Practices that Shaped Post-Socialist Politics and Business.* Ithaca, NY: Cornell University Press.

Lehmann, Rosa. 2009. "Social(ist) Engineering: Taming the Devils of the Polish Bieszczady." *Communist and Post-Communist Studies* 42: 423–44.

Lehrer, Erica T. 2013. *Jewish Poland Revisited: Heritage Tourism in Unquiet Places.* Bloomington: Indiana University Press.

Lester, Rebecca. 2005. *Jesus in Our Wombs: Embodying Modernity in a Mexican Convent.* Berkeley: University of California Press.

Leven, Bozena. 2011. "Avoiding Crisis Contagion: Poland's Case." *Communist and Post-Communist Studies* 44: 183–7.

Levy, Robert. 1973. *Tahitians: Mind and Experience in the Society Islands.* Chicago: University of Chicago Press.

Liechty, Mark. 1995. "Media, Markets and Modernization: Youth Identities and the Experience of Modernity in Kathmandu, Nepal." In *Youth Cultures: A Cross-Cultural Perspective,* edited by Vered Amit-Talai and Helena Wulff, 166–201. London: Routledge.

Linger, Daniel T. 1994. "Has Culture Theory Lost Its Minds?" *Ethos* 22 (3): 284–315.

_____. 2001. *No One Home: Brazilian Selves Remade in Japan.* Stanford: Stanford University Press.

_____. 2010. "What Is It Like to Be Someone Else?" *Ethos* 38 (2): 205–29.

MacDonald, Maryon. 1996. "'Unity in Diversity:' Some Tensions in the Construction of Europe." *Social Anthropology* 4 (1): 47–60.

Mach Zdzisław, ed. 1998. *Integracja Europejska w Oczach Polaków.* Krakow: Foundation "International Center for Development of Democracy."

Mach, Zdzisław, and Dariusz Niedźwiedzki, eds. 2002. *Polska Lokalna wobec Integracji Europejskiej.* Krakow: Jagiellonian University.

Malinowski, Bronisław. (1922) 1961. *Argonauts of the Western Pacific.* New York: E. P. Dutton.

Markowitz, Fran. 2000. *Coming of Age in Post-Soviet Russia.* Chicago: University of Illinois Press.

McLaren, Lauren. M. 2006. *Identity, Interests and Attitudes to European Integration.* New York: Palgrave Macmillan.

McManus-Czubińska, Clare, William L. Miller, Radosław Markowski and Jacek Wasilewski. 2003. "Understanding Dual Identities in Poland." *Political Studies* 51 (1): 121–43.

Mead, Margaret. (1928) 1961. *Coming of Age in Samoa.* New York: Morrow.

Meinhof, Ulrike H., ed. 2002. *Living (with) Borders: Identity Discourses on East–West Borders in Europe.* Aldershot: Ashgate.

_____. 2004. "Europe Viewed from Below: Agents, Victims, and the Threat of the Other." In *Transnational Identities: Becoming European in the EU,* edited by Richard K. Herrmann, Thomas Risse and Marilyn Brewer, 214–44. Lanham, MD: Rowman & Littlefield.

Moffatt, Michael. 1989. *Coming of Age in New Jersey: College and American Culture.* New Brunswick: Rutgers University Press.

Mucha, Janusz, ed. 1999. *Społeczeństwo Polskie w Perspektywie Członkostwa w Unii Europejskiej.* Warsaw: IFiS PAN Publishers.

Mummendey, Amelie, and Sven Waldzus. 2004. "National Differences and European Plurality: Discrimination or Tolerance between European Countries." In *Transnational Identities: Becoming European in the EU,* edited by Richard K. Herrmann, Thomas Risse and Marilyn Brewer, 59–72. Lanham, MD: Rowman & Littlefield.

Nagengast, Carole. 1991. *Reluctant Socialists, Rural Entrepreneurs: Class, Culture, and the Polish State*. Boulder: Westview Press.

Niżyńska, Joanna. 2010. "The Politics of Mourning and the Crisis of Poland's Symbolic Language after April 10." *East European Politics and Societies* 24 (4): 467–79.

OECD. 2011. *Education at a Glance 2011: OECD Indicators*. Paris: OECD. Online: http://dx.doi.org/10.1787/eag-2011-en (accessed 1 March 2012).

Offermann, Frank, Hiltrud Nieberg and Katrin Zander. 2009. "Dependency of Organic Farms on Direct Payments in Selected EU Member States: Today and Tomorrow." *Food Policy* 34: 273–9.

Okey, Robin. 1986. *Eastern Europe 1740–1985: Feudalism to Communism*. 2nd edition. Minneapolis: University of Minnesota Press.

Ossowski, Stanisław. 1967. *Dzieła: Z Zagadnień Psychologii Społecznej*, vol. 3. Warsaw: Państwowe Wydawnictwo Naukowe.

Pajo, Erind. 2008. *International Migration, Social Demotion, and Imagined Advancement: An Ethnography of Socioglobal Mobility*. New York: Springer.

Pankowski, Krzysztof. 2011. *Preferencje Partyne Miesiąc po Wyborach*. Center for Public Opinion Research report BS/142/2011.

———. 2012. *Katastrofa pod Smoleńskiem- Kto Wierzy w Teorię Zamachu*. Center for Public Opinion Research report BS/85/2012.

Pederson, Thomas. 2008. *When Culture Becomes Politics: European Identity in Perspective*. Aarhus: Aarhus University Press.

Pine, Frances. 1993. "'The Cows and Pigs Are His, the Eggs Are Mine': Women's Domestic Economy and Entrepreneurial Activity in Rural Poland." In *Postsocialism: Ideals, Ideologies, and Local Practices in Eurasia*, edited by Chris M. Hann. 227–42. London: Routledge.

———. 1995. "Kinship, Work, and the State in Post-Socialist Rural Poland." *Cambridge Anthropology* 18 (2): 47–58.

———. 1996. "Naming the House and Naming the Land: Kinship and Social Groups in the Polish Highlands." *Journal of the Royal Anthropological Institute* 2: 443–59.

———. 1998. "Dealing with Fragmentation: The Consequences of Privatisation for Rural Women in Central and Southern Poland." *Surviving Post-Socialism: Local Strategies and Regional Responses in Post-Socialist Eastern Europe and the Former Soviet Union*, edited by Sue Bridger and Frances Pine, 106–23. London: Routledge.

———. 2007. "Dangerous Modernities? Innovative Technologies and the Unsettling of Agriculture in Rural Poland." *Critique of Anthropology* 27 (2): 183–201.

Pogonowski, Iwo C. 1988. *Poland: A Historical Atlas*, revised edition. New York: Dorset Press.

Program SAPARD w Polsce. Online: http://www.sapard.ant.pl/osapard.html (accessed 22 March 2013).

Pudlak, Monika. 2003. "Europejski Fundusz Społeczny." In *Unia Europejska: Leksykon Integracji*, edited by Wiesław Bokajło and Kazimierz Dziubka, 447–49. Wrocław: Wydawnictwo Europa.

Reczyńska, Anna. 1996. *For Bread and a Better Future: Emigration from Poland to Canada 1918–1939*. North York: Multicultural History Society of Ontario.

Reszke, Katka. 2013. *Return of the Jew: Identity Narratives of the Third Post-Holocaust Generation of Jews in Poland*. Boston: Academic Studies Press.

Ries, Nancy. 1997. *Russian Talk: Culture and Conversation during Perestroika*. Ithaca, NY: Cornell University Press.

Risse, Thomas. 2004. "European Institutions and Identity Change: What Have We Learned?" In *Transnational Identities: Becoming European in the EU*, edited by Richard K.

Herrmann, Thomas Risse and Marilyn Brewer, 247–71. Lanham, MD: Rowman & Littlefield.

Robyn, Richard. 2005. *The Changing Face of European Identity: A Seven-Nation Study of (Supra) National Attachments.* London: Routledge.

Rodriguez, Magdalena. 2010. "Migration and a Quest for 'Normalcy': Polish Migrant Mothers and the Capitalization of Meritocratic Opportunities in the UK." *Social Identities* 16 (3): 339–58.

Roguska, Beata. 2000. *Opinie o Integracji Polski z Unią Europejską.* Center for Public Opinion Research report. BS/137/2000.

———. 2002. *Poparcie dla Integracji Polski z Unią Europejską.* Center for Public Opinion Research report. BS/86/2002.

———. 2004a. *Opinie o Integracji w Przedzień Rozszerzenia Unii Europejskiej.* Center for Public Opinion Research report BS/75/2004.

———. 2004b. *Opinie o Skutkach Członkostwa Polski w Unii Europejskiej.* Center for Public Opinion Research report BS/196/2004.

———. 2005. "Polska Droga do Unii Europejskiej." In *Polska, Europa, Świat: Opinia Publiczna w Okresie Integracji*, edited by Krzysztof Zagórski and Michał Strzeszewski, 16–57. Warsaw: Scholar Academic Publishers.

Rothschild, Joseph, and Nancy Wingfield. 2008. *Return to Diversity: A Political History of East Central Europe Since World War II*, 4th edition. Oxford: Oxford University Press.

Ruane, Joseph. 1994. "Nationalism and European Community Integration: The Republic of Ireland." In *The Anthropology of Europe: Identities and Boundaries in Conflict*, edited by Victoria A. Goddard, Josep R. Llobera and Cris Shore, 125–41. Oxford: Berg.

Ruiz-Jimenez, Antonia. M., Jarosław. J. Górniak, Ancika Kosic, Paszkal Kiss and Maren Kandulla. 2004. *European and National Identities in EU's Old and New Member States: Ethnic, Civic, Instrumental and Symbolic Components.* European Integration Online Papers 8 (11). ECSA Austria. Online: http://eiop.or.at/eiop/texte/200e4-011a.htm (accessed 18 March 2013).

Ryan, Louise, Rosemary Sales, Mary Tilki and Bernardetta Siara. 2009. "Family Strategies and Transnational Migration: Recent Polish Migrants in London." *Journal of Ethnic and Migration Studies* 35 (1): 61–77.

Sachs, Jeffrey. 1993. *Poland's Jump into the Market Economy.* Cambridge, MA: MIT Press.

Said, Edward W. 1979. *Orientalism.* New York: Random House.

Sampson, Steven. 1985–86. "The Informal Sector in Eastern Europe." *Telos* 66: 44–66.

Schimmelfennig, Frank, and Ulrich Sedelmeier, eds. 2005. *Europeanization of Central and Eastern Europe.* Ithaca, NY: Cornell University Press.

Schneider, Deborah C. 2006. *Being Góral: Identity Politics and Globalization in Postsocialist Poland.* Albany: State University of New York Press.

Schwartz, Theodore. 1978. "Where Is the Culture? Personality as the Distributive Locus of Culture." In *The Making of Psychological Anthropology*, edited by George D. Spindler, 419–41. Berkeley: University of California Press.

Sciolino, Elaine. 2005. "Unlikely Hero in Europe's Spat: The 'Polish Plumber.'" *New York Times*, 26 June. Online: http://www.nytimes.com/2005/06/26/international/europe/26poland.html?pagewanted=all&_r=0 (accessed 18 March 2014).

Shore, Cris. 1995. "Usurpers or Pioneers? EC Bureaucrats and the Question of European Consciousness." In *Questions of Consciousness*, edited by Anthony P. Cohen and Nigel Rappaport, 217–36. London: Routledge.

Shore, Cris, and Annabel Black. 1994. "'Citizens' Europe and the Construction of European Identity." In *The Anthropology of Europe: Identities and Boundaries in Conflict*, edited by Victoria A. Goddard, Josep R. Llobera and Cris Shore, 125–41. Oxford: Berg.

Siapera, Eugenia. 2004. "EU Correspondents in Brussels: Between Europe and the Nation-State." In *Transnational Identities: Becoming European in the EU*, edited by Richard K. Herrmann, Thomas Risse and Marilyn Brewer, 129–57. Lanham, MD: Rowman & Littlefield.

Siedlecka, Ewa. 2011. "Jarosław Kaczyński Nie Musi do Psychiatry." *Gazeta Wyborcza*, 13 August.

Słomski, Wojciech. 2001. "Społeczności Lokalne w Polsce w Perspektywie Integracji z Unią Europejską." In *Społeczności Lokalne w Perspektywie Integracji ze Strukturami Europejskimi*, edited by Danuta Walczak-Duraj, 23–34. Płock: Wydawnictwo Naukowe Novum.

Smith, Robert C. 2006. *Mexican New York: Transnational Lives of New Immigrants*. Berkeley: University of California Press.

Stacul, Jaro. 2006. "Claiming a 'European Ethos' at the Margins of the Italian Nation-State." In *Crossing European Boundaries: Beyond Conventional Geographical Categories*, edited by Jaro Stacul, Christina Moutsou and Helen Kopnina, 210–27. Oxford: Berghahn.

Stacul, Jaro, Christina Moutsou and Helen Kopnina. 2006. "Crossing European Boundaries: Beyond Conventional Geographical Categories." In *Crossing European Boundaries: Beyond Conventional Geographical Categories*, edited by Jaro Stacul, Christina Moutsou and Helen Kopnina, 1–19. Oxford: Berghahn.

Stankiewicz, Andrzej, and Piotr Śmiłowicz. 2011. "Trzecia Prawda o Smoleńsku." *Newsweek Polska*. 24 July.

Star, Susan Leigh, and Martha Lampland. 2009. "Reckoning with Standards." In *Standards and Their Stories: How Quantifying, Classifying, and Formalizing Practices Shape Everyday Life*, edited by Martha Lampland and Susan Leigh Star, 3–24. Ithaca, NY: Cornell University Press.

Steger, Manfred. 2009. *Globalization: A Very Short Introduction*, 2nd edition. Oxford: Oxford University Press.

Stiglitz, Joseph. 2002. *Globalization and Its Discontents*. New York: W. W. Norton.

————. 2006. *Making Globalization Work*. New York: W. W. Norton.

Strojwas, M. 2010. "The Polish Banking System: Hit by the Crisis or Merely by a Cool Breeze?" *ECFIN Country Focus* 7 (2).

Taylor, Mary N. 2009. "Intangible Heritage Governance, Cultural Diversity, Ethno-nationalism." *Focaal: European Journal of Anthropology* 55: 41–58.

Thomas, William, and Florian Znaniecki. 1984. *The Polish Peasant in Europe and America*, edited and abridged by Eli Zaretsky. Chicago: University of Chicago Press.

Triandafyllidou Anna, and Ankica Kosic. 2006. "Polish and Albanian Workers in Italy: Between Legality and Undocumented Status." In *Illegal Migration in Europe: Beyond Control?*, edited by Franck Düvell, 106–36. New York: Palgrave Macmillan.

Tsing, Anna. 2000. "The Global Situation." *Cultural Anthropology* 15 (3): 327–60.

US Department of State. 2014. "Adjusted Refusal Rate: B-Visas Only by Nationality; Fiscal Year 2009." Online: http://travel.state.gov/content/dam/visas/Statistics/Non-Immigrant-Statistics/RefusalRates/FY09.pdf (accessed 18 March 2014).

Uścińska, Gertruda. 2010. "Kierunki Rozwiązań w Zakresie Wieku Emerytalnego." In *Gospodarka i Czynniki Demograficzne a System Emerytalny*, edited by Aleksandra Wiktorów and Bohdan Wyżnikiewicz, 64–71. Warsaw: Instytut Badań nad Gospodarką Rynkową.

Vachudova, Milada Anna. 2005. *Europe Undivided: Democracy, Leverage, and Integration after Communism.* Oxford: Oxford University Press.

van Riemsdijk, Micheline. 2010. "Variegated Privileges of Whiteness: Lived Experiences of Polish Nurses in Norway." *Social and Cultural Geography* 11 (2): 117–37.

Verdery, Katherine. 1996. *What Was Socialism and What Comes Next?* Princeton: Princeton University Press.

————. 2002. "Whither Postsocialism?" In *Postsocialism: Ideals, Ideologies and Practices in Eurasia,* edited by Chris M. Hann, 15–28. London: Routledge.

————. 2003. *The Vanishing Hectare: Property and Value in Postsocialist Transylvania.* Ithaca, NY: Cornell University Press.

Wagstaff, Peter. 2007. "Remapping Regionalism." In *The European Puzzle: The Political Structuring of Cultural Identities at a Time of Transition,* edited by Marion Demossier, 161–82. Oxford: Berghahn.

Wedel, Janine R. 1986. *The Private Poland.* New York: Facts on File.

————, ed. 1992 *The Unplanned Society.* New York: Columbia University Press.

West, Barbara. 2001. *The Danger Is Everywhere! The Insecurity of Transition in Postsocialist Hungary.* Prospect Heights, IL: Waveland Press.

White, Anne. 2009. "Family Migration from Small-Town Poland: A Livelihood Strategy Approach." In *Polish Migration to the UK in the "New" European Union: After 2004,* edited by Kathy Burrell, 66–85. Aldershot: Ashgate.

————. 2010. "Young People and Migration from Contemporary Poland." *Journal of Youth Studies* 13 (5): 565–80.

White, Anne, and Louise Ryan. 2008. "Polish 'Temporary' Migration: The Formation and Significance of Social Networks." *Europe–Asia Studies* 60 (9): 1467–1502.

Wiktorów, Aleksandra. 2007. "Pension Reform in Poland." *Geneva Papers on Risk and Insurance: Issues and Practice* 32 (4): 483–93.

Wilson, Thomas. 1996. "Sovereignty, Identity, and Borders: Political Anthropology and European Integration." In *Borders, Nations, and States: Frontiers of Sovereignty in the New Europe,* edited by Liam O'Dowd and Thomas Wilson, 199–219. Aldershot: Avebury.

————. 2000a. "Agendas in Conflict: Nation, State and Europe in the Northern Ireland Borderlands." In *An Anthropology of the European Union: Building, Imagining and Experiencing the New Europe,* edited by Irene Bellier and Thomas M. Wilson, 137–58. Oxford: Berg.

————. 2000b. "The Obstacles to European Union Regional Policy in the Northern Ireland Borderlands." *Human Organization* 59 (1): 1–10.

Wilson, Thomas M., and Hastings Donnan, eds. 1998. *Border Identities: Nation and State at International Frontiers.* Cambridge: Cambridge University Press.

Wintle, Michael J., ed. 1996. *Culture and Identity in Europe.* Aldershot: Avebury.

Wodak, Ruth. 2004. "National and Transnational Identities: European and Other Identities Constructed in Interviews with EU Officials." In *Transnational Identities: Becoming European in the EU,* edited by Richard K. Herrmann, Thomas Risse and Marilyn Brewer, 97–128. Lanham, MD: Rowman & Littlefield.

Wolf, Eric. 1982. *Europe and the People without History.* Berkeley: University of California Press.

Wood, Nathaniel. 2010. *Becoming Metropolitan: Urban Selfhood and the Making of Modern Cracow.* DeKalb: Northern Illinois University Press.

Zabusky, Stacia. 2000. "Boundaries at Work: Discourses and Practices of Belonging in the European Space Agency." In *An Anthropology of the European Union: Building, Imagining and Experiencing the New Europe,* edited by Irene Bellier and Thomas M. Wilson, 179–200. Oxford: Berg.

Żakowski, Jacek. 2011. "Chce Nam Się Żyć." Interview with Janusz Czapiński. *Polityka* 29 (13–19 July): 18–20.

Zielonka, Jan. 2006. *Europe as Empire: The Nature of the Enlarged European Union.* Oxford: Oxford University Press.

Zubricki, Jerzy. 1988. *Soldiers and Peasants: The Sociology of Polish Migration: A Lecture.* Edited by Keith Sword. London: Orbis.

Zubrzycki, Genevieve. 2006. *The Crosses of Auschwitz: Nationalism and Religion in Post-Communist Poland.* Chicago: University of Chicago Press.

———. 2011. "History and the National Sensorium: Making Sense of Polish Mythology." *Qualitative Sociology* 34: 21–57.

Życie Warszawy. 1994. "Zbyt Wysokie Bezrobocie, Zbyt Niskie Płace." 15 February.

INDEX

www.ingramcontent.com/pod-product-compliance
Lightning Source LLC
Chambersburg PA
CBHW030836300326
41935CB00036B/175